Walter L. Gerash

MURDERS IN THE BANK VAULT

The Father's Day Massacre

and the Trial of James King

By Phil Goodstein
as told by Walter L. Gerash

DENVER
NEW SOCIAL PUBLICATIONS
1997

*To the people of America who serve on
juries and those who struggle against the
state to see that justice is done.*

Cover design by Jan McConnell.

*Murders in the Bank Vault:
The Father's Day Massacre and the Trial of James King.*

© 1998 by Phil Goodstein and Walter L. Gerash.
New Social Publications.
Box 18026; Denver, Colorado 80218.
(303)333-1095.

Printed in Denver, Colorado.
First Edition: January 1998.

Library of Congress Number: 97-91982.
ISBN: 0-9622169-6-8.

Contents

It is all well enough to say that a man is presumed innocent until he is proven guilty, but those who seriously make the statement know nothing about psychology. As a matter of fact, most persons who are accused are presumed guilty, and if a jury finds them not guilty it is thought a miscarriage of justice.

—Clarence Darrow

If there is no struggle, there is no progress. Those who profess to favor freedom, and yet deprecate agitation, are men who want crops without plowing up the ground. They want rain without thunder or lightning. They want the ocean without the awful roar of its many waters.

This struggle may be a moral one or it may be a physical one. Or it may be both moral and physical, but it must be a struggle. Power concedes nothing without a demand. It never did and it never will.

—Frederick Douglass

Prologue

"No chess player sleeps well," observed H. G. Wells. At least I couldn't sleep that night in October 1981. I was in the middle of a crucial high-profile federal trial. Kiko Martinez, lawyer and outspoken political activist, stood accused of sending a letter bomb to an opponent of Chicano liberation. As I pondered my next moves, the phone suddenly rang, loud and piercing. It was my brother Jerry from Los Angeles. He was calling with the worst possible news: our father, Benjamin, had died. I needed immediately to come out for the funeral.

Judge Frank G. Theis, who had been especially appointed by the Chief Justice of the United States, Warren Burger, to preside at the trial, agreed to let me go. The next thing I knew, my two sons, Douglass and Daniel, were sitting next to me on the plane, flying to that dark destination.

Relatives welcomed us at my mother Leah's condo in Santa Monica. I didn't hear a word. Leaden feet carried me directly to my father's chess table at the far end of the living room, by the sliding doors that led to the flower-bedecked balcony. The chess pieces were on the board.

Suddenly, the awful realization that he was gone forever seized me. I uttered an anguished cry. Tears welled in my eyes. The chess table was the alter next to which Ben and I sat, communing silently, hour upon hour. Dad was a chess fanatic, and he passed his love of

I ponder my next move over the chess board.

this ancient game to me. My paternal chess partner, my father, was gone.

Chess had been my respite and escape from the storms of my personal and professional struggles. It was soon to become an ever greater passion and dedication than before. Whenever I play, I can almost feel the comforting presence and mirthful grin of my father, Benjamin Gerash, standing behind me as I contemplate the myriad possibilities and challenges the game presents.

Douglass gave a eulogy by reading a poem that brother Jerry had written the night before. Then, before anyone could blink, it was off to the airport, back to Denver, back to the trial.

A decade later, the scene was repeated. Once more the phone jangled in the middle of the night. Once more the chess board loomed.

1

A Bloody Bank Heist

They finally found the fourth body. On their second sweep, the police entered the dusty, litter-filled incinerator room in the sub-basement of the giant United Bank Tower. Shoeprints led to a corpse lying in a pool of drying blood. The victim had been shot four times in the back of the head and twice in the back. He was the last of the murdered men found on Sunday, June 16, 1991, Father's Day. The deaths were linked with the robbery of nearly $200,000 from Denver's largest bank. The media labeled the slaughter the Father's Day Massacre, reporting it at great length as Colorado's "bloodiest bank heist."

At 9:14 that morning, a man identifying himself as United Bank vice president Bob Bardwell called the main guard station in the basement of the bank. He was at a street-level security access phone next to the freight elevator in the bank garage near the northeast corner of East 17th Avenue and Lincoln Street.

This was not unusual. The freight entrance was the preferred place from which weekend employees who had forgotten their pass cards called for admission. Guard William R. McCullom Jr. responded, going up in the elevator up to let Bardwell in.

1

As McCullom opened the door, a disguised gunman burst into the elevator. Overpowering the unarmed guard, the intruder forced McCullom to take the elevator to the depths of the building. They got off on the lowest floor, a subbasement known as the lower concourse. Near an unused incinerator bin in a dingy, locked, storage room, the gunman smashed McCullom's skull before finishing him off with a volley of shots.

The killer grabbed McCullom's electronic pass card and keys. Showing a good knowledge of the labyrinth of the subbasement, the intruder proceeded to staircase C. An alarm sounded at 9:20 when he opened the door. Ignoring it, the intruder walked up the stairs to the main bank concourse level.

Two stories underground, the concourse was where money was processed. Couriers from armored cars delivered weekend deposits to a cash vault there on early Sunday mornings. A driver had to pass through two secured gates before getting out of his truck, loading the money into a cart, and taking it to a receiving room next to the vault. Security cameras recorded everything.

The intruder proceeded down the hallway. He passed through the office of Risk and Bank Security before entering the monitor control room close to the vault. The killer had to open two locked doors, using both a cipher code and McCullom's access card, to get into this nerve center of the bank.

Variously known as the guard shack, security center, monitor room, or control room, it was where guards checked in at the beginning of a shift, picking up a set of keys and a radio. None of the keys were marked—the guards had to know which keys fit which locks. At least one guard was always supposed to be on duty in the monitor control room, observing the images on the surveillance cameras throughout the bank and monitoring alarms. The computer recorded that the door to the room opened at 9:24.

Meanwhile, another guard, Todd A. Wilson, 21, who was legally blind in one eye and who had trouble reading anything but large print, had been dispatched to investigate the cause of the alarm on the subbasement door. This was only his sixth day as a bank guard. He had taken the post after having worked elsewhere in the bank for about a year. Despite his vision problems, Wilson was a hardy, six-foot-tall, outdoor-type who handled himself well at the bank.

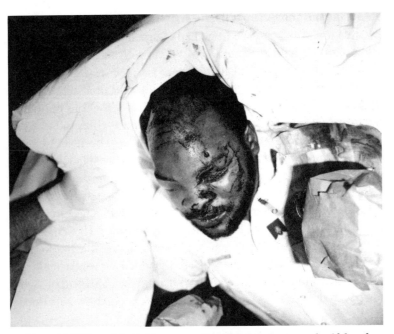

Guard William McCullom was found lying in a pool of blood.

Two guards remained in the control room, Phillip L. Mankoff, 41, and Scott McCarthy, 21. Mankoff had been on the job with McCullom since midnight. The two guards had been joined by Wilson and McCarthy at 6:00 AM. This McCarthy's first day at work. As a close friend of Wilson, he was eager to join his buddy at the bank. McCarthy was dressed in street clothes since he had yet to acquire a guard's uniform. Mankoff was assigned the task of training him and showing him through the maze of bank corridors.

While Wilson was investigating the alarm to staircase C, the intruder burst into the control room and surprised Mankoff and McCarthy. At gunpoint, he forced them into the battery room, next to the guard shack. After he ordered them to get on their knees with their backs to him, he executed Mankoff in cold blood, shooting him once in the back of the head and twice in the back. McCarthy, hearing the bullets, whirled around, seeking to resist. As he threw his hand in front of his face, the gunman shot him in the arm, wrist, and front of the head. McCarthy was left in a pool of blood atop Mankoff's back.

Just about this time, Wilson came back into the control room. Unable to locate staircase C, he had returned to check a map. The gunman systematically murdered Wilson with six shots, including a bullet to the back of the guard's head.

Throughout the bloody morning, the intruder fired at least 17 or 18 shots: 17 bullets were found in the bodies of the four murdered guards; one bullet was taken from a doorknob. Since no powder burns were found on the victims, they must have been shot from a distance greater than 18 inches. Bullet fragments splattered about and damaged a computer keyboard in the monitor room.

The intruder tried to seize all evidence which might have recorded the slaughter, especially videotapes which he removed from the numerous VCRs in the control room. The killer also apparently tried to get to the power source of the table holding the television screens to turn them off, but he failed. Several panels and a door that should have been locked behind the console table were discovered open. So was a safe which contained backup floppy disks.

The killer also shot the doorknob to a locked supervisor's office, a room which could have contained the tape of a surveillance camera which watched the security headquarters. The intruder was unable to penetrate the office, but that did not matter. The surveillance camera was pointed away from the control panel toward a storage room. The VCR for it was in the monitor room and the tape was taken from that machine.

The murderer also kicked several times at the window and door to a room where the bank had once stored ammunition and guns for the guards. He left shoeprints from the edge of his foot on the Plexiglas window about four feet from the ground. Other shoeprints were found where the intruder broke drywall near the door. The evidence showed they were violent, desperate kicks. Could they have been left by someone trained in the martial arts? But the kicks were to no avail. Plywood under the drywall prevented the killer from getting inside.

The killer made off with ten videotapes, a two-way radio, numerous sets of keys, and three pages from the log book. The last would have indicated why McCullom had first left the control room. One videotape and many sets of keys were left in place in the guard

Left to right are Phillip Mankoff, William McCullom, Scott McCarthy, and Todd Wilson, the four guards murdered at the United Bank on Father's Day, 1991.

shack. With this heavy load, the gunman continued down the hall to a main bank vault where employees were counting weekend receipts. Computerized records showed the door to the vault opened at 9:48 AM.

The Cash Vault

Deliveries of cash to the bank were usually completed by 8:30 AM on Sundays when about $1 million was counted. A six-member crew was on duty in the vault. The tellers were informally dressed for a summer's day. A radio was playing in the background when suddenly the employees realized that something was wrong.

Vault manager David Barranco, tall and debonair, was standing near the main money-counting station talking with tellers Maria Christian and David Twist. Two people always worked together in that cage. It was where big deposits were processed and was designed so that the two workers would ensure the honesty of each other. Large bills frequently passed through the station.

All of a sudden, out of the corner of his eye, Twist saw an unauthorized person in the vault. He mentioned this to Christian and Barranco. They followed the intruder. After they had only taken a few steps, the man whirled around, pulling out a big black-barreled revolver. He pointed it at them as he cocked the hammer. One witness remembered the gun had a "silver pin."

"Back up! Get on the floor, on your stomach! Cover your eyes with your hands! Don't look at me!" the robber ordered in a calm,

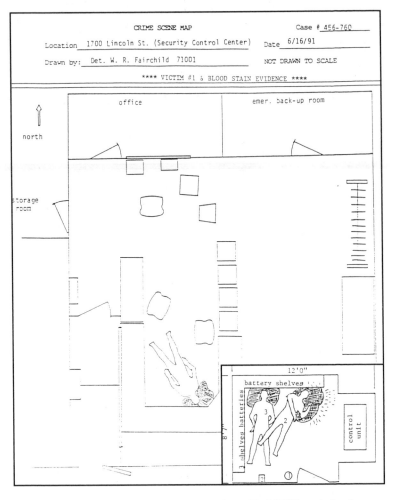

CRIME SCENE MAP   Case # 456-760

Location 1700 Lincoln St. (Security Control Center)   Date 6/16/91

Drawn by: Det. W. R. Fairchild 71001   NOT DRAWN TO SCALE

**** VICTIM #1 & BLOOD STAIN EVIDENCE ****

A sketch of the monitor room shows where Todd Wilson's body was found, near the central console. At the bottom left is the door the police removed from its hinges to gain entry after the crime. At the top left is the storage room where the intruder kicked the wall and the supervisor's office where he shot the doorknob. At the upper right, is the battery room. A detail of it, insert at the lower right, shows Scott McCarthy (2) was found atop Phillip Mankoff (3).

steady, deep, stern voice. He waved the gun at them, firmly gripping it in his right hand. Warning the employees not to set off any alarms, the gunman noticed a couple of other tellers, Chong Choe and Kenetha Whisler. He told them to join Barranco, Christian, and Twist facedown on the floor. The sixth employee, Nina McGinty, saw the gunman, ducked down, and hid behind a wastebasket under the counter of teller station nine. There was no cash in her cage where she had been counting food stamps.

Once the employees were lying on the floor, the gunman demanded: "Who is the cashier?" At first nobody said anything—there was no cashier. After a fateful pause, Barranco identified himself as the vault manager. The intruder ordered Barranco to get up and take the "bag around the corner." When the vault manager hesitated, the robber told him in an emphatic voice to "hurry up, get the bag!"

About 15 feet away, in a corridor between two of the cubicles, Barranco found an empty, double-handled, black, doctor-like satchel. This was not the area from which he had seen the man come. Had the bag been placed there earlier? Was an accomplice lurking? But the head teller did not have time to ponder these points. At gunpoint, the robber instructed Barranco to take him around the various teller stations that were open that morning. At each of them, he commanded the manager to take cash and place it in the bag.

"No loose money, no bait money, no ones or fives. I want straps of twenties, fifties, and hundreds," the gunman informed him. Strapped money refers to packages of a hundred bills of the same denomination, which have been counted and bound with paper wrappers. There was no bait money, i.e., marked bills, in the vault. The gunman seemed satisfied that Barranco had put enough money into the bag because he did not request that it be filled to the top. As the intruder made his getaway with a bundle that must have weighed at least 30 pounds, there was still nearly $2 million in cash easily within reach in the vault. Mysteriously, the robber had made no effort to get money from two safes in the vault that were packed with cash. A police video of the crime scene taped shortly after the robbery showed a considerable amount of loose money lying around the vault.

While Barranco was filling the satchel, the gunman ordered the other employees to crawl on their hands and knees into the "little room" adjacent to the vault. Technically known as the "mantrap," it is a small security chamber/hallway, about five feet by six feet, with two doors. Open one door and the other automatically locks. An electronic pass card or key is necessary to get in or out. The same card must be used on both doors. This procedure is designed to catch somebody improperly in the chamber. The top half of the mantrap is enclosed by glass where a guard can easily look in and see if someone is lurking there.

As the employees crawled into the mantrap, the handle to the door broke off. The robber saw this, demanding to know where the handle was. Maria Christian showed him, and he seemed convinced that the handle had broken accidentally and nobody had tripped an alarm. Once Barranco had put enough money in the bag, the gunman ordered him to join the others in the mantrap. Warning everyone to remain on the floor below the glass partition, the intruder once more prowled around the vault. His last words as he made his getaway were: "Get down on the floor! Don't get up for any reason." One witness recalled him saying: "Don't open your eyes or I'll kill you."

Computer records showed that the robber had only spent eight minutes in the vault, making his exit at 9:56 AM. The police thought that he took elevator number three to level seven of the parking garage since they found the limited-access elevator locked on that level at around 9:00 PM. The floor was reserved for bank officials and a guard's key or pass card was needed to access that part of the bank. The invader had vanished without a trace.

Escape from the Mantrap

Inside the mantrap, the five benumbed employees exchanged whispered prayers and reassurances. After about 20 minutes, they decided it was safe to get up and seek help. They pounded on the windows and sought to see if the other teller, Nina McGinty, was around and could open the mantrap door for them. There was no response to their call. Nor was there an emergency buzzer in the mantrap where the employees could ring for assistance. They hoped that a guard would make an appearance since guards were supposed to continually patrol the area. Nobody came.

As they pondered what to do, Kenetha Whisler noticed a metal spoon laying on a doorsill. Perhaps, in violation of bank rules, someone had used the mantrap as a lunch spot. The bank was most concerned about workers removing anything from the employee cafeteria. Signs filled the eating area, stating that no one was to

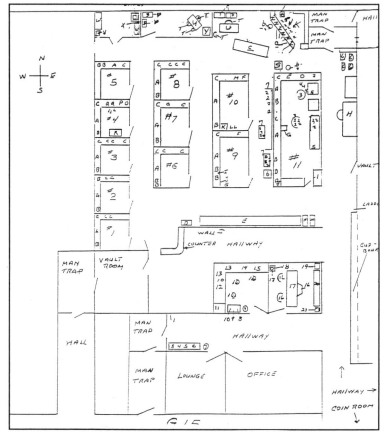

Police drawing of the main money vault. Tellers David Twist and Maria Christian were working in station eleven at the time of the robbery. Vault manger David Barranco was standing outside it, near booths nine and ten. Chong Choe was in booth ten, Nina McGinty was in booth nine, and Kenetha Whisler was in booth four.

remove utensils from it. Or had the spoon been placed there as part of the preparations for the robbery? Regardless of its origins, the spoon's presence was vital. Using it, in approximately 20 minutes, Whisler was able spring open the lock of the door to the room where couriers from armored cars delivered money to the vault.

The employees forced open a second door from the money receiving room and made their way down a hallway to a parking garage through an emergency stairwell. Their movements were traced by computer records which showed that the stairwell door opened at 10:44 and closed at 10:46 AM. From the parking lot, the vault employees ran outside and crossed the street, going into the main atrium of the bank. There they approached private guards who were employed by the company managing the bank complex, not by the United Bank. The tellers excitedly gasped out what had happened. After the security personnel had called in the robbery, the guards noted that they had been seeking information from the vault and control room for the past 40 minutes.

About this time, Nina McGinty, who had been crouching under her desk in terrified silence, courageously got up and dialed 911. She frantically told the dispatcher that she had been robbed and was all alone in the vault. At 10:55, a simulcast, a call on all five police radio frequencies, went out for officers to go to the bank.

Among the first officers to arrive was Richard Tartar. He had previously worked part-time as a United Bank guard. Initially, he and other police officers thought that this was a false alarm. Who would rob a bank on a Sunday? But when no guard answered their buzzing at a security door, the police began to think something was amiss. Their frustration grew when bank employees leading them to the vault became disoriented and momentarily lost.

In the vault, McGinty heard the police ringing for admission and pounding on the windows. She wanted to let them in, but she had no key to open the door. That forced the police to find a different means of entry. When they finally got to McGinty, she was hysterical and crying.

The police also had severe problems gaining access to the control room. They could not open a steel door leading to it. Sometime

*The United Bank Tower, often called the "cash register building,"
is the structure in the center with the curving roof that dominates the
Denver skyline.*

before the robbery, a key had apparently broken off in the door and
the lock had never been properly repaired. Security access cards
designed to open the door did not work. After futilely attempting
to open the door for ten minutes, the police took more drastic action.
They pulled off the door's hinges and used a pry bar to get inside.
The door would not open because the door at the other end of this
mantrap had been propped open by a partially filled can of Mountain Dew.

Once inside the control room, the police came face-to-face with
the terrible reality of the bank job, discovering the bodies of Wilson,
McCarthy, and Mankoff. When the officers tried to radio this
information to the dispatcher, they found that their radios did not
work and had to find a telephone to call in the news of the robbery
and murders. The Metro SWAT team was summoned and officers
with automatic weapons stood outside the bank, guarding it from
the curious.

The police systematically searched each of the building's 52 main floors. Though an alarm light on the central console in the control room showed that the subbasement door had been opened during the course of the crime, only near the end of their search did the police go to that level. There, about 5:45 PM, they discovered Bill McCullom's body.

The police found the dead guard by accident. Members of the SWAT team were on a second sweep of the lower concourse where they had previously failed to locate the missing bank employee. Looking closer this time, they discovered McCullom in the unmarked storage room. He was lying in a pool of blood atop his bank radio.

It was understandable that the police had initially missed McCullom. He was in a dirty, secluded, generally neglected area, 70 feet from the elevator. The light switch was in an unusual place in the room, not by the door, but on an adjacent wall far to the left of the

A teller booth in the vault shows a good deal of loose cash lying around immediately after the robbery.

entrance. Until they found the switch, the police lacked proper illumination to spot the body.

Unaccounted for since the robbery, the 33-year-old, six-foot-tall, 190-pound McCullom had been the prime suspect. During the course of the day, the authorities had sought to locate him. Nobody was at his home, leading the police to get a warrant to break into his apartment at 1439 Moline Street. They found nothing amiss.

McCullom had grown up in Denver and Texas. Generally an "A" and "B" student, he had accumulated considerable debts while in college. At the time of his death, he owed $15,744.99 in student loans that were 88 days delinquent. To pay them off, McCullom had taken the part-time job as a weekend bank guard on September 11, 1990. It was in addition to his regular job at an insurance company. He had been as responsible a debtor as a student. Now he was dead.

The Tellers' Descriptions

From the outset, bank officials and the police agreed that this had to be an inside job. The robber showed far too much knowledge of the specifics of the bank security system for him to have been a rank outsider. Originally, the authorities believed that more than one person was involved as they talked about the "suspects."

More than 30 police officers, plus approximately 40 FBI agents, were assigned to the case. They seemed to have a great lead: the descriptions of the intruder given by the six robbed employees. But these portraits of the gunman quickly proved problematic.

Interviews with the tellers brought wide-ranging descriptions of the robber. All agreed he wore a hat. One said it was black, another said brown, and a third said it was gray. It might have been plaid or tweed, and did or did not have a feather in it. The headwear was variously described as a derby, fedora, or cowboy hat.

The intruder had on mirrored or dark brown sunglasses. They had either metal or plastic frames. One employee believed they were flip-up sunglasses.

Accounts had the killer standing anywhere from about five-foot, five-inches to six-foot, two-inches or taller. He was said to weigh between 170 and 250 pounds. The culprit wore a sports jacket, dark pants, and black maintenance shoes with thick rubber soles. One identified him as having on a brightly striped red, blue, and yellow necktie. His clothes were rather baggy, almost Salvation Army-type wear according to one witness. Two others, though, insisted that he was extremely well dressed and looked like a businessman.

Some of the eyewitnesses recalled the robber had a shiny, salt-and-pepper mustache. Vault manager David Barranco, however, was not sure that it was a real mustache. There appeared to be something on it that looked like glue and the mustache seemed to be a quarter inch off the robber's nose and on the verge on falling off. Kenetha Whisler similarly thought that the mustache was a fake. Reports also noted that the robber had long, narrow sideburns.

The witnesses observed that the perpetrator wore a small adhesive strip on his left cheek. According to one witness, it was a regular rectangular bandage that was about two by three inches; another said it was a square patch; a third insisted it was a miniature Band-Aid comparable to that a man would use who had cut himself while shaving. None of the witnesses mentioned any moles, scars, acne, or other facial blemishes.

The Photographic Parade

At first, the authorities did not think much would be accomplished by composing a sketch of the suspect. Since the intruder wore a very good disguise and the tellers' descriptions varied widely, they feared that such a drawing would only highlight the gunman's disguise. Instead, they hoped that the vault employees might be able to pinpoint a suspect by looking at photos of past and present bank personnel.

On June 20, FBI Special Agent John Kirk showed five of the tellers 50 photographs of current and former bank guards and employees. The pictures, one to a page, were in two big three-ring notebooks: a blue one, with 35 photos of past guards, and a red one, with 15 current guards. One after another, the witnesses were called into a bank conference room to meet with Agent Kirk. He told them to take their time in looking at these pictures. Among the photos were those of women guards, i.e., persons who did not have any relevance to the gunman described by the robbed tellers. While the witnesses pinpointed five different men—one current and four previous guards—who looked somewhat like the robber, they could

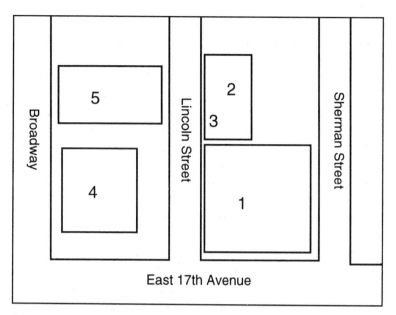

Map of the United Bank complex. The United Bank Tower, 1, is the so-called cash register building. Next to it, 2, is the parking garage and where armored cars made their deliveries. The freight elevator used by the intruder is 3. The Mile High Center is 4. The bank proper is 5. The guard shack and money-counting vault were located two stories under Lincoln Street, between the bank, the parking garage, and the bank tower. North is up.

not identify any one man. Later, on June 25, Nina McGinty, who had been hospitalized by the trauma of the robbery, also failed to finger any of the suspects.

On June 28, after the eyewitnesses were repeatedly unable to pinpoint a suspect in the photo lineups, the FBI sent visual information specialist George P. Nobel to Denver. He had worked his entire 31-year career in the FBI lab. His technique was to get all of his information directly from the eyewitnesses, preferring to know nothing about the previous descriptions of the suspect before he talked to them.

Nobel first interviewed vault manager David Barranco. During the course of their discussion, Nobel showed the witness pictures of various shapes of eyes, ears, noses, chins, and other identifying traits. He asked Barranco for specifics about which ones looked most like those of the robber.

Over three-plus hours, piece by piece, Nobel committed Barranco's memory to paper. He then called in Maria Christian and Kenetha Whisler. They discussed the initial sketch. The two women only suggested minor changes in the hat. Nobel next visited Chong Choe and Nina McGinty at their homes. McGinty agreed that the sketch was a "remarkable likeness" of the robber. Neither she nor Choe could suggest any changes.

Finally, Nobel took the sketch to David Twist. This victim urged the artist to make the cheeks fuller. More than that, he suggested that Nobel add a tie to the sketch—so far nobody had told Nobel that the gunman had on a tie despite their previous statements to the police. Nobel modified the portrait, again showing it to Barranco who agreed with the changes. On July 1, the artist submitted the composite drawing to the FBI. The authorities, in turn, tried to see if one of the faces from the photo books fit the sketch.

Other Leads

By the time the picture was completed, numerous other leads had been investigated. As is usual when there is a sensational crime, the authorities immediately checked escape routes, including the bus station and the airport. At the latter, four different rental car agents noted that they had been approached on the early afternoon of Father's Day by a man claiming he had plenty of cash on him. He had wanted to reserve a rental car in Los Angeles for cash without a credit card. All had turned him down. Their accounts of this man were somewhat similar to the bank employees' descriptions of the robber: he was about six-foot-one, had a kind of graying hair, a thick mustache, and some sort of scar on his left cheek. He said he had anywhere from $10,000 to $100,000 in cash which he was carrying in a double-handled black doctor's bag. Meanwhile, the search went on.

The bank was nebulous about how much money was stolen. N. Berne Hart, the chairman of United Banks of Colorado, the holding company owning the bank, first stated that only a "nominal amount

The composite drawing of the suspect.

of money" had been taken. Others claimed that more than $100,000 had been stolen. Rumors floated that the job could be an elaborate case of embezzlement or money laundering made to look like a robbery. Perhaps the robber's real goal was not money, but secret bank records. Some speculated that more than $2 million had disappeared. Eventually, the police and bank disclosed that a total of $197,080 was missing. Despite this, a few people believed more had been taken—the bank had determined how much was missing based on the records of deposits it had received that morning. Possibly, not all of the deposits had been recorded at the time of the robbery.

The financial institution, FBI, and police all agreed that whoever committed this mass murder must have had some past or present

connection with the United Bank. All former and current guards
and others knowledgeable about the bank's security system were
systematically investigated. Though the eyewitnesses had failed to
identify any of the guards in the photo books, the police continued
to believe that a past or present guard was responsible for the
slaughter.

The Physical Evidence

There were no spent cartridges or ejected shells at the crime
scenes. Based on the slugs removed from the bodies of the dead
guards, the police determined that a revolver had been the murder
weapon. Many of the bullets and bullet fragments were so badly
obliterated it was impossible to tell what kind of gun had fired them.
Hoping to learn more, the police ordered detailed lab tests, both in
Denver and at the FBI lab in Washington.

*A bullet fragment damaged the keyboard of the computer in the
monitor room.*

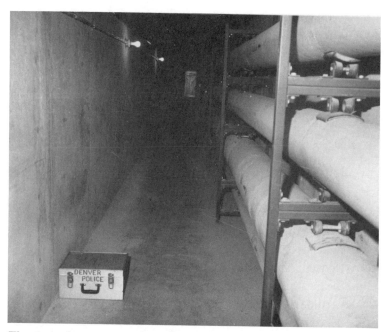

The intruder apparently passed through a pipe tunnel in the subbasement of the United Bank.

"Many different firearms could have fired these bullets," was the initial conclusion of police firearms expert Detective Frank Kerber. An examination of the bullets showed that they were of a different make than the ammunition which had been previously issued to the bank's guards. Three different types of bullets were found in the bodies of the deceased. Among them were semi-jacketed, hollowpoint projectiles, technically known as +Ps, which had been standard issue of the Denver Police Department during the 1980s.

Based on their examination of the markings and grooves on the +Ps, the authorities determined that the bullets used to murder the guards were most likely discharged from a .357 or .38 Colt revolver. Among the weapons listed as possibly having been employed by the killer were "the .38 spl. Colt Cobra, Detective Special, Police Positive, and .357 Python." Possibly more than one gun had been used.

Also of importance were the shoeprints which the robber had left behind. The room where McCullom was slain was dusty and showed two very distinctive, different sets of prints. Shoeprints were also found on pieces of cardboard and computer paper in the domestic water room in the subbasement next to the room where McCullom's body was discovered. These prints matched those where the gunman had kicked the wall of the storage room next to the supervisor's office. The police were also able to lift shoeprints from the window which the intruder had kicked. Hoping to identify the prints, the authorities removed them and systematically checked the shoes and boots of all of the guards and police officers who had responded to the call. None matched, adding weight to the belief that they were those of the gunman.

Though the robber had made off with the log sheet, by tracing the impressions under the missing pages, the police were able to determine that the last writing in the book was by Mankoff. It noted that McCullom had been dispatched to let a "Bardwell" into the bank. Nothing identified the man as a vice president, but the authorities were quickly able to establish Bob Bardwell's role at the bank. The vice president denied he had gone to the bank that day. Others supported Bardwell's alibi that he had been in the mountains with his family when the crime was committed.

An investigation of the United Bank's computerized security records showed some strange things had happened shortly before the robbery. At 5:04 AM, an alarm had gone off in a records tunnel. It was a heat sensor alarm which indicated that someone was lurking there. A guard had immediately turned off the alarm. For some reason, no report was filed about the alarm. It was only reset at 9:33, right when the crime was in progress. A disposable coffee cup, partially crushed Seven-Up can, and cigarette butts were found by the police in the tunnel during their initial sweep of the bank after the murders. Rather than examining them, the police left this evidence where they found it.

Sometime between 6:00 and 7:00 on Father's Day morning, a motorist had seen a big man in his 40s, with silver-flecked hair, wearing a hat with a yellow feather in it, driving an old car very erratically near the bank. Next, a couple of employees, reporting for

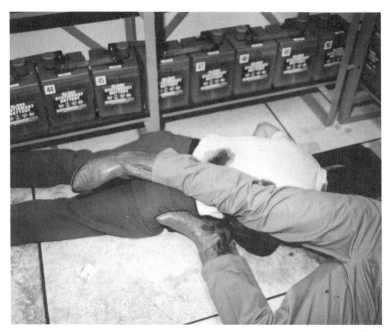

Scott McCarthy was found lying atop Phillip Mankoff in the battery room.

work at around 7:00 AM, discovered that the secured parking gate to the garage was improperly in the up position. It was still in the up position as late as 11:00 AM.

Around 8:30 AM, vault employees noted a guard walking through the vault with a non-uniformed man. The two were checking the doors near a mantrap and jiggling the lock to the main door of the vault. For a while, it seemed as if the guard and his companion were locked in the mantrap. This was highly unusual. Weekend guards were not supposed to be in the vault when the money was counted.

The uniformed guard was described as a clean-shaven, short, Hispanic man, unlike Mankoff who had a beard and mustache. Eyewitness descriptions of the civilian with him so differed that it was impossible to tell if he was McCarthy. One person said he was quite tall and in a business suit. Another stated he was wearing a Hawaiian-style shirt. McCarthy had on cowboy boots and a short-sleeved shirt at the time he was murdered.

Short of a better explanation, the bank concluded that Mankoff and McCarthy had been in the vault. Mankoff's access card had been used to enter the vault at 7:54. McCarthy had tried to use his card to exit from a vault mantrap at 7:59. But he had placed his card in the reader out of sequence—it had no record that he had entered the mantrap so it would not allow him to get out. Hence the door did not open. The authorities, though, made nothing of this mysterious sequence as they intensified their search for a suspect.

2

The Search
for a Suspect

In the wake of the massacre, many bank employees were asked to take lie detector tests. The police and FBI also interrogated former employees. The authorities requested that people who had been near the financial institution at the time of the robbery contact them with any information they might have. A week after the crimes, on Sunday morning, June 23, 1991, the police stopped more than 300 people who happened to be close to the United Bank and questioned them, hoping that they might have seen something the previous week.

Numerous leads turned up. One witness, for example, related that he almost hit the robber. He stated that, as he was driving north on Lincoln Street by the bank at about 10:15 AM on Father's Day, a man carrying a black, expandable briefcase suddenly darted into the street. The suspect was wearing a black uniform with an American flag on the left shoulder. Though the media prominently reported this, it did not result in an arrest. Proving to be of no account, the witness vanished from the case.

The bank posted a $100,000-reward for information leading to a conviction for the murders and robbery. But nothing turned up to provide any specific clues to implicate a suspect. Rumors spread that the police and FBI were at each other's throats. The media screamed for action.

After a week of furious efforts, the authorities focused on a former bank employee, 51-year-old Paul Tillman Yocum, who had worked as a guard between August 1985 and August 1990. About a year before the Father's Day Massacre, Yocum had been arrested when he was accused of making off with $29,600 from a secured room behind the automated tellers at the United Bank on Saturday, May 26, 1990, at 8:31 AM during Memorial Day weekend. (Guards were responsible for servicing the automated teller machines.) The thief had managed to turn off the lights to prevent the surveillance cameras from filming him.

Yocum had been the last guard in the automated teller room before the theft. An eyewitness reported seeing a man who was about five-foot-ten, 180 pounds, and had salt-and-pepper hair, making a getaway from the automated teller room, i.e., a man roughly comparable to that described by the eyewitnesses in the Father's Day Massacre.

Shortly after the theft from the automated teller, Yocum was charged with the crime. He was about six-feet tall and weighed around 175 pounds, approximately fitting the physical description of the thief. First Yocum swore complete innocence, followed by a partial confession. He quickly retracted the admission and again insisted he was innocent. The eyewitness identification of him was extremely nebulous and the prosecution did not have much of a case. After deliberating for 90 minutes, a federal jury found Yocum not guilty on August 29, 1990. He resigned from the bank two days later, bitterly denouncing those who had accused him of the felony.

There seemed to be a connection between the theft from the automated teller and the Father's Day Massacre. Yocum appeared the natural link. He was a gung-ho military enthusiast and often wore fatigues. His apartment at 1200 Pearl Street was only ten blocks from the bank.

The police initially suspected that Paul Yocum had robbed the United Bank.

An activist in a neighborhood watch program reported having observed Yocum, dressed in a sports coat and black pants with thick rubber-soled black shoes, carrying a dark satchel near the bank on the morning of June 16.   One of the held-up tellers, Kenetha Whisler, recalled seeing a beat-up old car, that looked a lot like Yocum's 1974 Mustang, parked in the United Bank garage in the months immediately before the robbery. The automobile had been shown on television and Yocum was interviewed on camera when he appeared to be a prime suspect in the Father's Day Massacre.

Dark personal impressions of Yocum came from his colleagues. Bank security supervisor James A. Prado called Yocum "weird and a hard-ass."   While Yocum was afraid physically to confront anyone, Prado observed, the former guard was fully capable of shooting people. He was precisely the kind of man who was might murder the guards in cold blood.   Risk and Security Manager Thomas A. Tatalaski Sr., who hired and fired all guards, was sure Yocum had committed the crimes.

What made Yocum even more of a suspect were the events of June 24. By that time the authorities were vigorously investigating him. Shortly before noon, FBI agents visited Yocum at his apartment. They discussed the crime with him and asked him if he owned any weapons. In his slow monotone, he admitted that he did, including a shotgun, a .45 Colt semi-automatic pistol, and a .357 Smith & Wesson revolver. He had carried the last weapon while working as a United Bank guard. At the request of the authorities, he showed them some of the firearms he kept in a closet which was secured by a pair of handcuffs. Yocum denied that he had any hard feelings against the United Bank.

After talking with the slack-jawed Yocum for quite a while, the FBI agents left at about 2:10 PM. They came back an hour later, accompanied by the police, including homicide Detective Jonathan W. Priest, the lead investigator in the case. Yocum invited them in, asking them to wait a bit since he was on the phone with his attorney. The lawyer instructed him not to permit the police to search the apartment without a warrant or allow the authorities to take anything from the apartment without a warrant. Despite this sound advice, Yocum permitted the officers to search his living quarters.

The authorities found a considerable cache of weapons, including two 12-gauge shotguns, a Ruger mini 14 rifle, and bullets for a

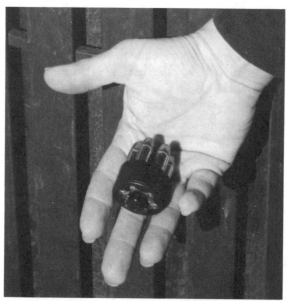

Photo by Phil Goodstein

A speed loader for a .38 revolver in the hand of Denver Police Captain Miriam S. L. Reed.

.357 or .38 revolver. The .45 Colt semi-automatic was hidden behind a heating vent. There were also two police-type batons, a Colorado State Patrol badge, thumbcuffs and handcuffs, an assortment of disarmed grenades, and a police scanner.

Yocum also had numerous speed loaders—small devices that are about an inch-and-a-half long which are used to quickly reload a revolver. Authorities suspected that the killer had used two speed loaders since he fired off 18 shots within a brief period while committing the murders. Yocum's speed loaders were designed to work on a .357 or .38 Smith & Wesson, but not on a Colt revolver.

During the search, Yocum again called his attorney. He now listened to his lawyer's advice that the police not be permitted to take anything from the search and that Yocum should order them to leave. By this time, Detective Priest had placed a good deal of incriminating materials in an empty blue United Bank gym bag which he had found in the apartment. He wanted to take and examine this evidence, but left it at Yocum's request. After the police exited the apartment at about 4:15, they staked out the place. On the basis of their initial observations, they obtained a warrant to search the apartment again.

While the police were applying for the warrant, Yocum talked to his attorney about what he should do with the sports bag. The former guard put the container, filled with ammunition and speed loaders, into a green duffel bag. He stepped outside his apartment with the satchel at 8:30 that night.

The police immediately "challenged" him. At least that was the term used by Lieutenant David Abrams of the Metro SWAT team who stopped Yocum at gunpoint. The SWAT team was necessary, according to the authorities, because they feared booby traps and figured the search was a high-risk operation.

Lieutenant Abrams patted Yocum down for weapons. The suspect did not have any guns on him. Detectives were called as five officers conducted the court-sanctioned search of the apartment. Though no bombs or booby traps were found, they uncovered a virtual arsenal in his apartment.

Yocum informed the police that his lawyer "told me to get rid of it," referring to the incriminating evidence in the bag. Eleven speed loaders and 26 boxes of ammunition were in the bag—all materials previously placed there by Detective Priest. Among the bullets were semi-jacketed hollow points for a .357 and a .38 revolver. At first glance, they seemed very similar to the bullets found at the crime scene. On further investigation, it was determined that none of the projectiles matched those found at the United Bank.

None of the revolvers discovered at Yocum's apartment would fire the bullets. Not all of the weapons registered to Yocum were on the premises. Other guns, not registered to the former bank guard, were found at his living quarters. The pair of boots Yocum was wearing appeared to have a sole pattern comparable to the shoeprints found in the subbasement of the United Bank. Despite intensive efforts, no match was made. The police also searched Yocum's car.

An incriminating diary was found. In it Yocum vowed his revenge against the bank for its false accusations against him about the theft from the automated teller. The journal consisted of a notebook marked "Confidential need to know only." Yocum noted on the bottom of the first page that entries "will be blunt and brutal. Sensitive psyches are advised not to read this. If you are hurt emotionally, keep your eyes off." The diary continued: "To you nasty people: This caveat—the deepest secrets are not revealed here. You will never know. I trust no one either implicitly or explicitly." Believing the diary would only be discovered after his death, and thinking that the police would read it, he mocked them: "Your investigative abilities at best are guesswork and luck. To your detriment you are too late with too little."

Yocum boasted of his quest for revenge. "I have a character flaw—I don't forget who screwed me. I have another flaw in my character—patience. I am patient to a fault. I will get even. I have the patience to do it. I may wait 50 years, but I will get even eventually."

At great length, Yocum discussed the charge that he had stolen the money from the automated teller. The accusation had "ruined my life." The security supervisors at the United Bank were "assholes." He would "never recommend them as employers to anyone." The bank's Risk and Security Manager, the "lying" Tom Tatalaski, "can go to hell. The Lord will have his way. He belongs

in the federal pen raking rocks with a 16-pound hammer, not me."
He was equally demeaning in his description of Alvin K. Lutz, a
bank vice president in charge of security. "There are two things
wrong here—Tatalaski and Lutz." He wrote that his prosecution
was an embarrassment to their careers.

The suspect also lamented how he had to borrow $10,000 from
his father, Edwin L. Yocum, for his legal defense. The loan and
bank robbery charges had destroyed his relationship with his father,
a man whom he had always considered his best friend. Edwin
Yocum, a highly respected resident of Flagler, Colorado, had
worked for more than 50 years at the First National Bank of Flagler.
People in that town of less than 800 citizens, 120 miles from Denver,
on the eastern Colorado plains, described Paul Yocum as the
spitting image of his father. Edwin Yocum died on January 8, 1991,
a few months after his son's acquittal.

The former United Bank guard moaned that his father would
never forget that he had been tried on the theft charge. While he had
immediately sent his father $1,000 out of the $2,073 in back pay he
had received from the bank after his acquittal, Yocum was sure that
his father "will continue to complain about it [the $10,000 debt]
until the first shovelful of dirt is placed on his grave." Amateur

Photo by Phil Goodstein

Paul Yocum lived in the Skylark at 1200 Pearl Street.

psychologists argued that in killing the bank guards on Father's Day, Yocum might have been murdering his father.

With his protruding ears, a broad forehead, and a slightly receding hairline, the bespectacled Yocum, looked little like the man in the composite drawing. But something was strange about the man. Associates reported he gave them goose bumps.

Perhaps, Yocum had never recovered from a tragedy that had haunted his youth. His diary reflected this, notably how his seven-year-old younger sister, Jean, was one of 19 people killed by debris from a plane crash at an air show the Yocum family attended during the Flagler Harvest Festival on September 15, 1951. Paul Yocum was then struck in the head by a wing of the airplane. Could he be getting his warped revenge by killing the guards?

Yocum still frequently visited his mother in Flagler. He had gone to see her on June 23, a week after the bank robbery. The former guard noted that he was taking a risk every time he drove there because of his poor health. He had suffered epileptic seizures since the time of his arrest. The middle-aged, pudgy-faced man was also plagued by severe heart problems.

The diary contained a lot of personal reflections. The former bank guard noted he was a virgin and would remain one until his death. He also showed his prejudices when he described the United Bank as being "like any Jew outfit. The pay is low and they expect you to bust your ass to earn what little you get." Yocum likewise smeared a black employee of the United Bank as an "old jig."

The suspect bemoaned his nightmares of being falsely accused. He told how and why he sought revenge against the United Bank and the heads of the security department. "My accusers will be judged by a higher authority, and may he have mercy on you. I will not," he concluded.

A search of his mother's home in Flagler turned up more weapons belonging to Yocum. There were also massive amounts of ammunition, speed loaders, holsters, empty shells, and primer boxes. The police further discovered money wrappers from the United Bank. Ashes from a fire set by Yocum in a rusty, corrugated iron barrel in the backyard of his mother's house revealed papers with some sort of United Bank connection. One burnt letter clearly contained the word "guard" on it, but little else could be deciphered.

The freight elevator which was used by the man who had identified himself to the guards as bank vice president Bob Bardwell.

The trash was filled with gun advertisements and notices of weapons which Yocum had hauled to Flagler from Denver. The authorities even searched the Yocum family plot in the Flagler cemetery. Nothing of substance was found there. Still, the police continued to attempt to uncover anything they could against Yocum, getting a further warrant to search the garage of his mother's house in Flagler.

Another former guard told the FBI that Yocum had previously discussed owning a Colt Cobra revolver—a weapon which could have been used in the murders. Risk and Security Manager Tatalaski believed that the composite drawing of the robber looked a lot like Yocum, but the ears did not match. Neil D. Tubbs, a security guard staff coordinator who had overseen Yocum, similarly thought that Yocum might be involved. So did other guards who had worked with Yocum.

Nor did Yocum have a strong alibi for his activities on the morning of Father's Day. He explained that, due to his health problems, he took the bus almost everywhere. At the time of the murders, he claimed to have been in his apartment, making copies of Dave Brubeck tapes. He later went out, stopping at a local bookstore. But the police and FBI could not confirm this. The suspect, in turn, had a good record of paying his rent in the apartment which he had occupied since 1978. Yocum did not own any sunglasses since the lenses of his glasses were photo sensitive, military style.

In spite of the immense storehouse of weapons and other incriminating materials discovered at Yocum's apartment and his mother's house, the authorities failed to uncover any physical evidence directly linking Yocum to the robbery. Similarly, when the eyewitnesses were shown a six-man photo lineup including Yocum, they were unable to identify him as the robber. Even so, it was still possible that he might have been either the killer or a collaborator of the bank robber. The police and FBI continued to delve into his doings on Father's Day even after the eyewitnesses had cleared him. The police knew, in light of the excellent disguise the robber had been wearing, that the eyewitness identifications were not necessarily reliable. When Yocum was asked whom he thought could have committed the crime, he specifically mentioned a retired Denver police sergeant who had worked part-time at the bank for about a year, James W. King.

Mike McKown

For the time being, the police left this last hint alone. Rather, they focused their attention on Michael Kenneth "Mike" McKown, another former guard who had left the bank under less than friendly circumstances. His name had immediately popped up on Father's Day as a possible suspect. When the authorities sought to check the fingerprints of past and present guards compared to those found on the Mountain Dew can, they discovered that McKown's fingerprint file had disappeared from the bank's records.

Even more suggestive was that, after quitting as a bank guard, McKown had worked as a courier for Wells Fargo, delivering money to the United Bank. The suspect was reported to have discussed how easy it was to rob the bank. Already on the evening of Father's Day, a television station had received an anonymous call identifying McKown as the perpetrator. The FBI immediately took action.

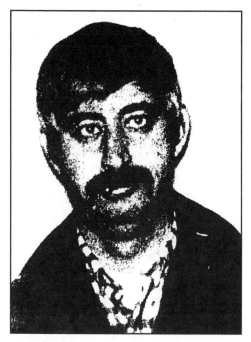

*Mike McKown was immediately suspected
of having staged the bank heist.*

McKown, who pronounced his name McGown and was sometimes called "Mac," was located in suburban Seattle, living with his
sister. Phone records showed that he had been engaged in a long-
distance call at the time of the murders. Interviews with members
of his family confirmed that he had been at his sister's home on
Father's Day morning. Still, the FBI grilled McKown on June 17.
The witnesses were shown a six-man photo lineup featuring
McKown. Some stated he looked a lot like the gunman.

After the composite drawing of the robber was made, bank
security supervisor Tatalaski again identified McKown as a likely
suspect. When asked who they thought could have committed the
crime, former and current guards specifically mentioned McKown.
One described McKown as a "psycho" and told how McKown was
always talking about how to set booby traps and rob the bank. But
sleeping in Seattle meant that McKown could not have committed
the crime. The authorities discovered that McKown's friend and

former partner at the United Bank was retired police sergeant James W. King.

Harry Glass

Once more, the police ignored this tip; instead, they looked at Harry William Glass. A print of Glass's little left finger was found on the can of Mountain Dew. A very nervous Glass had shown up quite late for his afternoon shift at the bank on Father's Day. More foreboding was that the 25-year-old Glass was supposed to have worked the shift during which the murders occurred. At the last minute, he had been told to report for the afternoon shift since Scott McCarthy had just been taken on for the morning job.

A fellow guard, Richard L. Rosenberg, reported that he and the six-foot-tall Glass had discussed in great detail how someone could rob the bank on a Sunday morning. But Rosenberg also admitted that all of the guards had talked about how easy it was to rob the

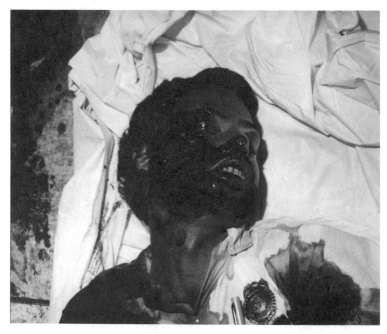

Slain guard Phillip Mankoff had ties to Michael J. Kazmier, a rogue FBI agent.

bank. It was "common knowledge" that an intruder would not have much difficulty gaining access to the concourse level.

When Glass was questioned about his fingerprint on the pop can and other subjects, he became quite angry and resigned his job as a guard the next day. Rumors floated that he had previously been out drinking with one of the slain guards, William McCullom, the night before the murders.

Glass claimed he was upset by the murder of his fellows, men whom he considered his friends. He quit the bank because the killings showed how shoddy its security system was. Once more, the authorities did not have enough evidence to arrest him.

Many other people were initially named as suspects. Douglas Bagley, for example, had been fired as a guard for propping open a mantrap door with a pop can—the same method of operation used by the killer. Former guard Kenneth A. Iverson had a thick mustache and long blond hair. A well-educated man with a degree in economics, he had continually clashed with management over his hours and pay. Iverson had quit the bank a few months before the Father's Day Massacre in disgust with the working conditions. No evidence, however, linked him or Bagley to the crimes.

Rumors also floated about murdered guard Phillip Mankoff. He had worked at the bank since March 12, 1991. Not only had he filed for bankruptcy before taking the bank job, but he had had dealings with Michael J. Kazmier. An FBI agent, Kazmier was something of a role model for swashbuckling officers who freely engage in illegal tactics on many television police shows. Over the years, Kazmier, a consummate actor, had openly encouraged people to commit crimes. Once they had done so, he claimed credit for their arrests. He was dismissed from the FBI in 1985 after he was picked up for shoplifting. These connections sparked allegations that Kazmier had ties to drug dealers. But there was nothing to tie him or Mankoff to the robbery and murders.

Guards and former guards alike agreed that many people had the know-how to pull the robbery. An outsider might have heard about the flaws in the bank's security system from a disgruntled, but otherwise innocent employee. The notion that an outsider and insider had collaborated on the job was also very tenable. So was the idea that the insider was one of the dead guards.

Meanwhile, the authorities were stymied. Having failed to find the murder weapon, loot, sunglasses, clothes, or hat, by Tuesday, July 2, the police were lamenting that they did not have any strong suspects in the case. They continued to insist that the robber was in his 40s, about six-foot-one, and 180 pounds. Still a front-page story, the pressure grew hotter, the trail grew colder, and police efforts grew desperate.

3

The Chess Connection

A decade after my father's death—about the same time the police were claiming they had no strong suspects in the Father's Day Massacre—the phone rang again. I was in my office on Monday, July 1, 1991, when my secretary, Annette Calvert, called out. "A James King, Walter. He says he has to speak to you immediately. He says he used to play chess with you."

James King. I couldn't quite place the name. At the most, I vaguely recalled him as a fellow member of the Denver Chess Club, but he had dropped out some years ago. Wasn't he a cop?

"Walter, this is Jim King. We used to play at the Denver Chess Club at the Capitol Hill Community Center at Cheesman Park," he told me. "You might remember me as a cop. I retired from the Denver Police Department a while back. A year or so ago, I worked as a security guard at the United Bank. The FBI has been questioning me about that robbery and the murders on Father's Day. So has a reporter from the *Rocky Mountain News*."

Then it came to me. King had won a chess game from me in the late 1970s or early 1980s. I was paired against him in a timed tournament game. Misunderstanding the starting time, I had arrived at the chess club an hour after the game began. King had punched his chess clock at the appropriate starting time. He refused to cancel his considerable time advantage. I cursed myself for being late, and was chagrined by King's fastidiousness toward the rules. Why do they start these things before I arrive, I wondered? Anyway, it was going to be rough because our chess ratings were about the same.

"After I retired as a cop," King explained, "I worked weekends for about a year as a United Bank security guard. I applied on July 13, 1989, started on July 20, 1989, and quit on August 12, 1989. I remember these dates because John Ensslin of the *Rocky Mountain News* came out and talked to me."

John Ensslin was an aggressive investigative reporter for the *News*. By systematically going through the files of registered guards with the city, shortly after the slaughter he had discovered King's former employment at the bank. The journalist went out to King's house and interviewed him on June 23. The retired police sergeant was dressed in a T-shirt and shorts. King told the reporter that he was surprised that a journalist was the first person to ask him about the case.

"Don't worry. They'll get around to you," Ensslin answered King. The former guard, Ensslin noted, was stunned when he learned of the robbery and murders. He felt great sorrow about what had happened. If anybody was at fault, it was the United Bank. It had rotten security. Adding a curse, King told the reporter that it was criminal that the bank had disarmed the guards. Finally, he stated that he could not imagine who had committed the crimes.

King also told me two FBI agents had approached him the next day, June 24, asking his whereabouts on the fateful June 16. I wasn't sure what he said to the FBI, but he informed me he had been near the bank on Father's Day morning. "I was looking for a game at the chess club, but I couldn't find it. Is the club still at its longtime home at the Capitol Hill Community Center?"

"It moved about three years ago, Jim," I said. He was clearly disturbed—he had no alibi since apparently no one saw him at the community center. That, plus his previous employment at the bank and the visits by the reporter and the FBI, led him to fear he could be implicated in the murders.

I have a wood carving on my desk in my office that faces my clients. It declares in big, carved letters: "DON'T WORRY!" The unstated words are: "THAT'S WHAT YOU PAY ME FOR!" It seems to work.

Since King wasn't in my office where he could see the sign, I simply told him to calm down, and again get involved with chess.

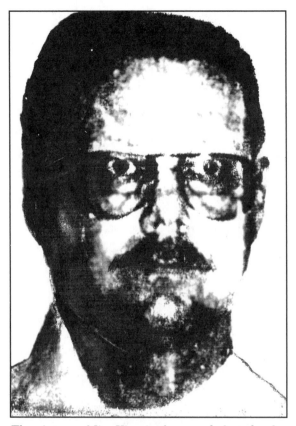

The picture of Jim King in the guard photo books. As with virtually all the pictures shown to the eyewitnesses, it was of poor quality. None of the bank vault employees pinpointed King as the robber when they first saw the picture on June 20.

The club's weekly session occurred the next evening, July 2, when a four-week tournament was to start. It gathered at VFW Post No. 501 at West Colfax Avenue and Wolff Street. Ironically, by lot, I was assigned to play King. Suddenly, memories of my games with my father flashed back to me.

Typical of my and my father's involvement in chess were our activities when we visited the Soviet Union with my son Douglass in 1975. Besides seeing the usual sights and going to my father's hometown of Shimshlea in Moldova, we tested our mettle playing chess in parks, beaches, and at clubs against locals in Armenia, Georgia, the Ukraine, and the Crimea, as well as in Russia proper.

After my father died, I established the Benjamin Gerash Memorial Tournament at the Denver Chess Club. I had been a member of the club since 1958. Over the years, I actively participated in it, served as its president, and helped underwrite tournaments and exhibitions by visiting grandmasters. Fellow chess players sometimes contacted me for legal advice.

I was born in the Bronx Maternity Hospital on November 24, 1926. My father, born in 1895, had run away to the United Sates in 1912 when he was 17. Having read the Russian classics and books about the United States, he was enthralled by the image of free America. As a Jew living under the reactionary tsarist empire, he had suffered from anti-Semitism and had witnessed a number of pogroms (government-sponsored attacks against Jews).

In New York, my father discovered the dark side of the American dream, the harsh by-products of industrial capitalism: the slums, disease, and ignorance. His hunger for justice drew him to the oratory of Leon Trotsky, Rosa Luxemburg, Emma Goldman, Eugene Debs, Norman Thomas, and Scott Nearing. As a worker in the New York garment industry, he emerged as a shop steward and trade unionist. At the start, he lived in Philadelphia, working at the Baldwin Motorworks, while he attended night school.

During the depression, he was in and out of work. He refused to stay at home during the day when he was unemployed; instead, he would leave the apartment as usual in the morning and spend his time at the 42nd Street New York Public Library. In the process, he picked up an excellent command of English and became familiar with many of the English and American classics.

The family of my mother, Leah, was from the area north of Odessa in the Ukraine. Her family was also heavily impacted by the upheavals in the Russian Empire in the early 20th century. Five of my mother's maternal uncles had already come to the United States before the 1917 revolution. They were financially successful here. After the Bolshevik Revolution, when famine, compounded by counterrevolution, swept the Ukraine, they sent for my mother's family in 1921-22. It took approximately a year for the family to get from the Ukraine to Antwerp, Belgium. They sailed on the

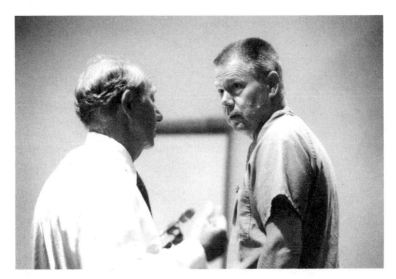

Little did I expect that a casual chess connection was to lead me into one of my most controversial cases when I defended Jim King who was accused of staging the Father's Day Massacre.

Aquitania to the new world. My mother was about 17 when she arrived in the United States. Shortly thereafter, she met and married my father.

Before graduating from James Monroe High School in the Bronx, at age 17, I enlisted in the Army, serving from May 1944 until August 1946. After my discharge, I joined my family in Los Angeles where it had moved during World War II. I earned a bachelor's degree from the University of California at Los Angeles (UCLA) in 1949. The University of Chicago awarded me a master's degree in history in 1951.

I could not use my degree. During the Korean War, college enrollments dropped and professors were no longer in demand. Having been a student activist during the peak of McCarthyism, I was not wanted. In face of this, I worked as a labor organizer in industry in Los Angles. Amidst the repression of the McCarthy era, I was having a hard time in that post. I held many jobs, including stints as a machinist, auto worker, truck driver, and as a steel worker.

As I moved from job to job, lamenting my lost career, my wife saw a sound, if not a simple, solution: "You love to argue and you're good at it. Be a professional arguer. Be a lawyer." I enrolled at the UCLA Law School in 1953. I transferred to the University of Denver Law School in the summer of 1955. I was admitted to the bar on Wednesday, September 5, 1956. Within a few years, I established a successful local practice, mostly in criminal defense, personal injury litigation, and civil rights cases.

My cases have garnered much publicity. During the 1960s, 1970s, and 1980s, I took, pro bono, politically charged cases when I defended people who were struggling for peace, protesting the Vietnam War, fighting against racial discrimination, seeking to end environmental devastation, and asserting their First Amendment rights of free speech, discussion, and dissent. My clients included members of the Black Panther Party, the Chicano Crusade for Justice, and the Students for a Democratic Society. During my career, I would estimate I have given $3-4 million in free legal services to those working to bring about a more democratic society.

It was as a chess player, not as a lawyer, that I had met King when he was on active duty as a police officer in the late 1970s or early 1980s. Chess players are everyday people. King exemplified this. It did not matter to me whether he was a police officer or clerk or sports star or convict. I knew he would give me a challenging, hard-fought game. There was nothing spectacular about his play. He did not go in for wild sacrifices, unusual openings, or bizarre combinations. He just played a good, steady game, carefully protecting his pieces, working to control the center of the board, and slowly attacking his opponent. Fortunately, I was able to get the better of him that evening at the chess club—maybe he had more on his mind.

I had not seen King in nearly ten years. At the club on Tuesday, July 2, I introduced him to the group's new president. As a sign that he was resolved to get active again in the club, he gave the president a check for $26 for his annual dues in the Colorado State Chess Association and the United States Chess Federation. Little did I know that, at the same time I was playing King in chess, the police were watching the hall where the chess club was meeting. When Jim left the building, the police followed him to his home, calling off their surveillance at around midnight.

With my mind on chess, I gave no thought to the robbery and murders that evening. When I learned about the crime, it had struck close to home. My law office had once been in the Mile High Center

Photo by Phil Goodstein

The United Bank Tower is sometimes called the "cash register" or "mailbox" building because of the distinctive shape of its roof. The Mile High Center, where I had my law office from 1958 until 1979, is the structure on the left.

at East 17th Avenue and Broadway. That structure, an early work of I. M. Pei, is one of the three buildings that make up the United Bank complex. I had been there from the time I opened my own practice in September 1958 until July 1979, when I moved into the distinctive old downtown house that serves as my current law office. Out of one side of my Victorian office window I can see the United Bank; out of the other is the Denver City & County Building which houses the city's courts and where I try most of my cases.

At the time of the Father's Day Massacre, my older son, Douglass, an award-winning video producer, was dating the woman he was to marry who was a trust officer at the United Bank. My younger son,

Daniel, a public defender for eight years, is a partner with me in my law firm of Gerash, Miranda, and Gerash.

My account had been at the bank for many years and I knew the financial institution well. I sometimes called it by its old name, the Denver-U.S. National Bank. Recognizing my reputation in the community, shortly before the robbery, the bank had featured me along with a number of other visible Denver characters in a series of advertisements. John Alonzo, a highly acclaimed Hollywood cameraman, had shot 15 takes of a scene where I was not identified, but only shown for a few seconds as I talked on the phone in my office during the commercial. The bank quickly pulled my visage from the ad when it learned I would be involved as a lawyer in defending the man accused of staging the Father's Day Massacre.

By the time of the robbery, the United Bank Tower was the city's most distinctive modern highrise. The skyscraper was often called the "cash register" or "mailbox" building because, with its semi-circular roof, it somewhat resembled those items. Since the edifice had been completed in 1983, employees had reported hearing strange noises in the tower and feeling gusts of wind. On occasion, snow avalanched off the roof of the structure.

Photo by Phil Goodstein

My law office, at 1439 Court Place, is located in the only house still standing in the Denver central business district.

I later learned of a strange coincidence about the location of the bank building at the northeast corner of East 17th Avenue and Lincoln Street where the crime had been committed. A little more than a century earlier, on March 29, 1889, David Moffat was the city's leading financier. The president of what was Denver's largest and most powerful bank, the First National Bank of Denver, Moffat was robbed at gunpoint at his bank when $21,000 was stolen. Newspapers had immediately christened it the bank robbery of the century. Authorities never solved the crime which was rumored to have been pulled by a member of the Butch Cassidy gang. In the wake of the robbery, the shaken bank executive returned to his mansion at the northeast corner of East 17th Avenue and Lincoln Street, the exact location where the Father's Day Massacre occurred. Events at the bank were about to lead me into one of my most controversial cases.

A Chess Player and Police Officer

James William "Jim" King was born James W. Ette in San Francisco on July 10, 1936. His mother, Doris Louise, divorced his father, a sailor off at sea, when King was about three years old. After the divorce, the boy went to live with his mother's parents. Shortly thereafter Doris married Harold Scott King, a member of the Navy who subsequently worked in the United States Civil Service. After the marriage, Jim and his younger brother, Tom, moved in with their mother, stepfather, and new half sister, Myra. Jim's mother was a native of Delta, Colorado, on the state's western slope. Myra later settled there.

King's family moved frequently to and from California as his father's assignments dictated. He spent a while in Guam and Hawaii. Consequently, Jim frequently transferred to different schools, attending a dozen academies before receiving his diploma from Castlemont High School in Oakland in 1954. He excelled in mechanical drawing and was an officer in the junior Reserve Officer Training Corps.

Upon graduating, King entered the Army. He served from August 4, 1954, until July 25, 1957. During that time, he received training as a military policeman and was a security guard at a top secret nuclear service installation in Siegelsbach, Germany. After mustering out of the Army with an honorable discharge, Jim attended Long Beach City College in California before transferring to the University of Colorado at Boulder in 1959. His father then worked at Rocky Flats, a war plant northwest of Denver which produced triggers for nuclear bombs.

The five-foot, eleven-inch-tall, 175-pound King briefly served as a cadet with the Los Angeles Police Department in September 1958. After driving a cab in Boulder, working as an insurance investigator in Denver, and seeking a job in the United States Civil Service, he applied to the Denver Police Department on April 27, 1961. He graduated first in a police academy class of 37 in September-November 1961.

King joined the force at a time when the department was embroiled in scandal. During the fall of 1961, many members of the Denver Police Department were arrested for staging numerous burglaries over the past few years. Eventually, more than 50 officers were implicated in these disgraceful activities. The rookie class was instilled with how abhorrent crooked police officers were and the absolute necessity of ethical practices by Denver's finest.

During his police career, King had served as a patrolman, a three-wheel motorcycle officer, in the parking control division, a dispatcher in the radio room, in the ID bureau, and at the airport detail. Promoted to sergeant on January 1, 1975, he retired on September 17, 1986, after 25 years on the force.

By the time of the Father's Day Massacre, King had three grown sons by his wife of 29 years, Carolyn Ann, whom he called Carol. A Denver native, born on July 24, 1943, she had met King in 1961 and married him in April 1962. Since 1987, she had worked part-time at branches of Weight Watchers as a receptionist and weigher.

The Kings' sons were delightfully different. The oldest, James Jr., born in March 1963, was a computer enthusiast. The middle son, Greg, followed in April 1964. A military veteran like his father, he worked as a tattoo artist. The youngest, David, born in October 1966, was an automobile buff who lived with his parents. A number of older cars he owned were usually sitting in the driveway of his parents' house. He frequently worked on them in the garage of his father's modest suburban home.

Since his youth, Jim King had been an avid chess player, serving as the president of his high school chess club. In retirement, King

Jim King in 1961 when he applied for the police department.

read a great deal, liked to put together model boats, bridges, airplanes, and railroads, and spent a good deal of time puttering around his yard. Virtually from the time he had joined the police department, he had worn his ash blond hair in a flattop cut.

While on active duty, King sometimes moonlighted. One job, which he held for about a year, was as a guard at the Bank of Denver (a separate, independent institution that should not be confused with the United Bank of Denver). In this capacity, on April 2, 1973, he successfully foiled an armed robbery. Both the Denver Police Department and the FBI commended him for his quick thinking in subduing the robber without having to fire a shot.

When he was assigned to the communications bureau of the police department, King supplemented his income for approximately 12 months as a traffic announcer on KLZ-FM, where he informed listeners of traffic problems based on information which had been reported to the police. He subsequently held the post of security guard for a couple of years in the late 1970s at the old Beth Israel Hospital at West 16th Avenue and Lowell Boulevard, a facility that included a senior citizens' home. He had not worked off duty during the last six years of his police career.

As a police officer, King had the reputation for quiet professionalism. He relied on his badge and ability to resolve disputes, not brute force, to enforce the law. If anything, he was seen as something of a misfit who was not one of the boys. His assignment to the airport was evidence of this fact. Well into the 1980s, police officers at Stapleton Airport were considered to be the outcasts of the department.

By the time King retired from the police department, he had a bad back from his years on the force stemming from an accident at police headquarters in September 1971. While he pondered claiming a medical disability, he figured it was not worth the effort. He kept 18 rounds of police-issued ammunition for his .38 Colt Trooper revolver upon leaving the force.

He carried the pistol during his police career. King bought it about the time he was appointed to the force, on September 18, 1961, for $61.93. After years of regularly firing it on the test range, the revolver was beaten up and he had occasionally had it repaired. Shortly after taking the job at the United Bank, he submitted the gun to a police department inspection on September 29, 1989. The examination showed that the revolver had a timing problem which King had fixed on October 10, 1989. Like other officers who carried revolvers, King also had two speed loaders. With the bullets in the pistol, this added up to the 18 rounds of ammunition he kept upon his retirement. As a former police officer in good standing, King was granted a permit to carry a concealed weapon.

After retiring from the police department, King worked part-time as a draftsman for the city's leading cartographer, Pierson Graphics, from November 1986 until July 1989. There he put the names of streets on maps. He quit that job because he was having trouble with his eyes and needed powerful lenses to see the fine print. The company was owned by Frank Pierson whose brother, Tony, was a police officer who had served under King at the airport. Tony Pierson was responsible for King getting the job at his brother's company.

King next took the job at the United Bank. The retired sergeant had seen a bank advertisement for help and had sent in a query letter. The income from the job, he hoped, would allow him extra spending

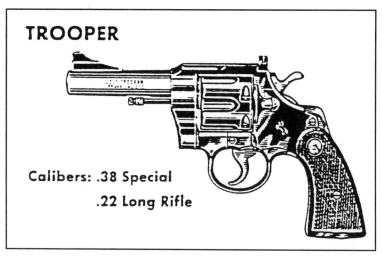

TROOPER

Calibers: .38 Special
.22 Long Rifle

Jim King carried a .38 Colt Trooper during his career as a police officer. A gun comparable to it could have been the murder weapon.

money to dine out with his wife. The bank was most eager to have him. It called him for an interview the same day it had received his letter. He had been trained by guard supervisor Jim Prado and a fellow guard, Mike McKown.

The FBI had been slow in questioning King about the bank robbery. He did not appear as a likely suspect. His name had not popped up in the list of the 15 initial suspects. Not until eight days after the Father's Day Massacre did the FBI call on King on June 24.

By this time, the FBI had teamed up with the Denver Police Department in investigating the bank robbery. Usually, a police detective was paired with an FBI agent for interviews of past and present bank employees. For some reason, two rookie agents who had recently graduated from the FBI academy, John P. Gedney and Kevin S. Knierim, were assigned to work together. They went out to see King shortly after noon on June 24. No one was at home. They left and called again about an hour later by which time King had returned to his house. He invited the two G-men in to talk about the robbery.

Agents Gedney and Knierim informed him that they were talking to all past and present guards. King said he had been shocked by the murders. He freely shared with the FBI his belief that the United Bank had a very poor security system. Virtually all the other guards agreed on this point, as did other employees. In the wake of the robbery and murders, people working at the bank were so worried about the inadequate security that they sent an angry letter to the media complaining about the bank's policies.

King told the rookie agents that the control keys to the elevator that the killer probably used were not reliable. One time, he had accidentally inserted the wrong key into the elevator, which worked. Already during the investigation, shortly after June 16, the police had learned from guard Dennis Foust that the freight elevator could be accessed via a screwdriver head.

Like other guards, King sometimes used the freight elevator to reach the concourse level. His supervisors at the bank had not been interested when he had informed them about the wrong key working on the elevator. King noted that guards were poorly treated at the bank. He was not at all happy about rumors he had heard that a new owner planned to disarm the bank guards—he left the bank about the time Norwest Banks of Minneapolis bought United Banks of Colorado. King further speculated that the robbery was an inside job. He suspected that Paul Yocum had committed it.

During the interview, which lasted about a half-hour, King criticized the FBI and the head of the detective squad of the Denver Police Department, Captain Jerry Kennedy. The feds interpreted this to mean that King "showed animosity toward the FBI, the bank, and detective division chief Kennedy." Such an outlook, the authorities claimed, made King a suspicious character. Actually, it was not only typical of the divisions within the Denver Police Department, but another of the strange coincidences of the case.

Since the 1960s, Captain Kennedy had been a visible member of the department, heading the vice and narcotics bureau. Over the years, he had recruited a loyal corps of supporters who were known as Kennedy's boys. Others in the department, including King, did not like Kennedy. During his last years on the police department, King had served under Kennedy when the latter was the captain of the airport command. Meanwhile, Kennedy had met Elvis Presley during one of the latter's performances in Denver. Elvis and Kennedy became friends.

During the 1960s and 1970s, Kennedy and other police officers accompanied Elvis around town and served as his bodyguards when the music star vacationed in Colorado. The payoff came in January

Elvis Presley is flanked by Denver Police Captain Jerry Kennedy on the left and Police Chief Art Dill on the right. Jim King served under Captain Kennedy at Stapleton Airport. Chief Dill issued King a commendation for stopping a bank robbery. Elvis bought Kennedy a Lincoln Continental at Kumpf Lincoln-Mercury at West Ninth Avenue and Broadway, a space later occupied by Pierson Graphics where King worked upon retiring from the police department.

1976, when Elvis bought Kennedy and four others Cadillacs or Lincoln Continentals. Some of the sedans, including Kennedy's Lincoln Mark IV, were purchased at Kumpf Lincoln-Mercury at West Ninth Avenue and Broadway. After Kumpf Lincoln-Mercury moved out of that location, part of it became the headquarters of Pierson Graphics where Jim King had worked after retiring from the police department.

Following media accounts of the Father's Day Massacre, King realized that the authorities were getting desperate. He started to reflect on the fact that he did not have a good alibi for his whereabouts at the time of the murders. On July 1, he called me, telling me of his worries. To help a fellow chess player in need, I agreed I would give him, pro bono, some basic legal advice: if you are a suspect, do not talk to the authorities outside of the presence of your attorney—this advice came a bit too late. Similarly, in view of their notorious unreliability, do not take a lie detector test.

King had not only freely spoken to the authorities, but also to a reporter from the *Rocky Mountain News*. He also wanted to take a lie detector test. I discouraged him from doing either. All too many people think that, if they are innocent, they have nothing to fear by freely speaking with the authorities. Unfortunately, detectives are masters of making suspicious events appear to be well-calculated criminal premeditation.

Polygraph machines are more likely to measure how nervous an individual is than the accuracy of his statements. Psychopathic liars have no trouble beating such machines while honest individuals frequently have problems with them. In light of all this, and how the criminal defense attorney serves as something of the minister for those suspected of crimes, it is vital that he be at a person's side from the beginning of an investigation.

Before we played chess on Tuesday evening, the FBI and police had again called on King at 11:00 AM that day. Upon my advice, he stated that he would not talk to the authorities without the presence of a lawyer. He also, at my advice, declined to take a lie detector test. As a former police officer who wanted to help the authorities, he explained to the police and FBI, he might willingly take a polygraph examination later, but he was right now so nervous he knew the results would be of dubious worth. Only after FBI Special Agent Alfonso Villegas and Denver Police Detective Calvin Hemphill assured him that he was *not* a suspect did King talk to them.

First off, the police asked King how he knew me. They quoted him as saying "he's a close friend of mine and I played chess with him. I don't think he is going to bill me for this." King continued on that "the polygraph scares me and I'm nervous as it is. I just don't trust it."

The retired police sergeant explained his duties as a bank guard and how he had taken immense pride in his professionalism. To ensure that he would be able to protect the bank to the best of his ability, he sought to learn the layout of the numerous corridors under the bank that connected the three buildings of the United Bank complex. He volunteered for security runs that took him to the different nooks and crannies of the bank. He always carried his .38

Jim and Carol King in 1985.

Colt Trooper while on duty in a Sam Browne belt with two speed loaders.

(A Sam Browne belt refers to a belt specially designed to hold a firearm. It sometimes has a strap passing over the shoulder. King's did not. The belt, King's leather holster, and the speed loaders had been issued to him by the Denver Police Department. He had not been asked to return them when he retired from the force.)

The bank did not have a standard policy on whether its guards should be armed. Most of the full-time guards who worked during the week were armed. The bank provided them with .38 Smith & Wesson revolvers. Guards also had the option of carrying their own gun if the weapon had been approved by the Denver Police Department and they had shown their proficiency in firing the pistol.

To qualify to carry his .38 Colt revolver as a bank guard, King had to fire it at test range. Since retiring from the police department, he and his youngest son David had periodically fired the gun at a shooting gallery. He then used range or bank ammunition, not the 18 semi-jacketed, hollow-point Remington +P bullets he had kept from his retirement from the police department. Reports showed that he had practiced with the revolver at the shooting range in the basement of the local Federal Reserve Bank on June 20, 1990.

After Norwest Banks took control of the United Bank in the spring of 1991, all guards were ordered disarmed on April 19, 1991. The financial institution claimed that armed guards were not a good public relations measure and that their having guns only increased the likelihood of violence. All guards who had been armed were ordered to surrender their weapons. By the time this policy was instituted, King had left the bank.

One reason that King had taken the bank job was to learn about how private security systems work. He hoped to become a writer in his retirement, planning to put together a manual on police procedures. With his military and police careers behind him, he wanted a first-hand look at the workings of a bank security system for his research. By June 1991, he already had completed 361 double-spaced pages of what he tentatively called *The Police Officers Guide*. Chapters included "Community Relations and Crime Prevention," "Mechanics of Arrest," "Disturbance Calls," and "Mentally Disturbed Persons and Medical Emergency Calls." So far, King had only finished seven chapters of what he hoped would be a 28-chapter tome. He began it in 1986 and was slowly completing the work at about a chapter a year. He had been writing the book on his personal computer since 1990. King was also dabbling in an action-adventure science fiction novel besides drafting the outline for an autobiography which he tentatively gave the hauntingly retrospective title *A Life! What For?*

King was not happy at the United Bank. Wages were low and benefits were few. He worked two 12-hour shifts each weekend, but was only paid for 11 hours a shift—the other hour was for lunch and breaks even if he was required to work during this time. Sometimes the guard posts were understaffed and guards were expected to give the bank extra labor with no compensation. There was an extremely high turnover among the 12 weekday and five weekend guards who were usually employed at the bank. Guards were constantly coming and going.

The retired police sergeant also bemoaned what he noted were inadequate security measures at the bank. Guards frequently went up from the basement control room to let in bank officers, secretaries, and even part-time workers who had little or no identification. The surveillance cameras were rarely cleaned and the images on the monitors were out of focus and often so fuzzy as to be of no value. A letter of reprimand was in King's file because he had not immediately allowed members of a moving crew into secured areas of the bank on February 17, 1990, when he had been unable to confirm that they were to be allowed into the bank because his two-way radio did not work. Bank officers and maintenance workers freely prowled through supposedly restricted sections during weekends. Pass cards did not always work. As a matter of trust and convenience, guards buzzed weekend employees into secured parts of the bank.

About a year before the robbery, a United Bank internal audit noted that there were severe lapses in the security system. The key system was rife with incomplete records of the distribution of master keys and their retrieval. Not all the doors were alarmed and often unauthorized persons were allowed in sensitive areas. The audit, however, concluded, that it would be "cost prohibitive" to fix these shortcomings.

Other problems with the bank's security system were exposed in the wake of the robbery. Three of the four murdered guards had been illegally hired by the bank. According to city ordinances, all security guards must first pass police checks and be licensed by the city. Only McCullom had completed this procedure. Shortly after the Father's Day Massacre, the head of security retired from the United Bank and the chief of the shift during which the robbery had occurred was discharged. Generally, however, the United Bank sought to atone for its weak security system by vehemently blaming the guards for the institution's thoroughly inept management.

Not only had the police followed King home from where I had played chess with him on July 2, but they had continued to follow him the next day. On July 3, Detective Doug Hildebrandt called him in the morning, discussing the case again. Later that day, Detective Hildebrandt visited King with Lieutenant Tom Haney. They went to the retired sergeant's modest house on a dead-end street in the Pleasant View section of Golden. Once more, King openly spoke to them as they extensively grilled him about his knowledge of the crime. The same day, teams of FBI agents and police detectives interviewed King's wife and youngest son at their workplaces. This set the stage for the fireworks at King's house, 665 Juniper Street in suburban Jefferson County, on the eve of the Fourth of July.

4

Fireworks

At about 10:00 on Wednesday night, July 3, exploding, bursting stars lit up the western sky—a fireworks display was in progress at the Jefferson County Fairgrounds, a block south of Jim King's house. Many had come to the area for the show. They were joined by residents who were standing outside, watching the sparkling sky. Among them was King's youngest son, David. Suddenly, more than 30 police vehicles, including those of the Denver Police Department, the FBI, and the Jefferson County Sheriff's Department, swooped down on the house in which King was viewing the television news. Both Denver Police Chief Ari Zavaras and FBI Special Agent in Charge Bob Pence were on the scene.

In a T-shirt and khaki pants, King was ordered out on the porch where he was handcuffed to a table. Armed with a search warrant, the authorities spent the next four and a half hours going through the house, garage, cars King owned, and his attic, roof, and yard, seeking incriminating evidence. His wife, Carol, who had been awakened by the invasion, came out in her nightgown. She was allowed to put on a thin robe. The police instructed her to sit silently on the front porch, separated by the table from her husband. All this was in the full view of all her neighbors.

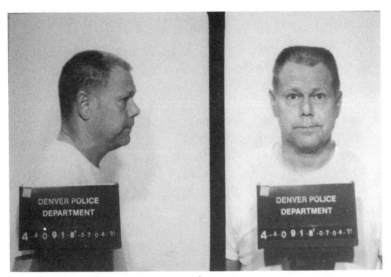

Jim King's mug shots.

Carol was scared and shaking. For some time, the police refused King's three separate requests to take a blanket from the house and give it to Carol, who was shivering on the porch. Other than protesting the mistreatment of his wife, King quietly bore his arrest.

During their search, the police came across a box secured with a combination lock. They were sure that that was where King had kept his .38 Colt Trooper. He readily provided them with the lock's combination when they requested it. When the police opened the box, it was empty.

Just after midnight, the police took King to jail. At 2:30 AM, the authorities completed their search. Immediately thereafter, Carol King called my office. My answering service awakened me, telling me the news. Climbing out of bed, I set out for the Denver City Jail to visit my client. He was extremely nervous and depressed. Just what he feared might happen, had happened.

After listening to his account, closely questioning him about it, I believed him—it is the responsibility of a defense attorney to believe his client. I felt that King was not guilty. Taking the case, a rush of combative energy surged through my body. I would be locked in a mortal legal struggle with the state and federal government, fighting forces of overwhelming power.

The Search

During their search of King's house, the police found a bloody tissue in the trash and a blue-green Weight Watchers gym bag in the garage. They were sure it was the bag the robber had used. Some of the shoes looked like they might match the shoeprints at the murder scene. Not only were three pairs of King's shoes seized, so were all the shoes of his son David.

The police, however, failed to discover any loot or the murder weapon. Nor did they find a pair of sunglasses, a hat, or clothes that matched those reported to have been worn by the robber. The bloody tissue in the trash turned out to be the result of David King cutting his elbow the previous weekend. Scabs were visible on his elbow from his injury. The gym bag did not come close to matching the satchel described by the eyewitnesses.

Still, the police probed further. They made a lot, for example, of the fact that not only my phone number, but also those of a couple of other attorneys were found scribbled on a piece of paper in King's wallet. Why would an innocent man be so concerned about getting a lawyer?

Even more ominous for the authorities was the currency. Two-hundred and ninety-five dollars in cash was found in King's wallet. Another $500 in twenty-dollar bills was discovered in a nightstand near King's bed.

There were two reasons for the money. One was that King had been forced into bankruptcy in 1987 due to abuse of his credit cards and a bad experience in real estate. Since then, he had tried to pay for most of his purchases with cash to avoid any new credit card debt. The other was that he and his wife had booked a flight on June 11 for July 8 to go to Las Vegas via Phoenix where King's mother lived in a trailer camp in Mesa, Arizona. The couple usually visited her before going elsewhere for a vacation. Las Vegas was a favored stop which they had visited approximately ten times. Jim liked the shows, but was not a gambler. Carol enjoyed playing the slot machines. The cash was to pay for their expenses on the trip. They were scheduled to return to Denver on July 14.

The police were skeptical about the cash. It might be money taken from the United Bank. The FBI dusted the bills for finger-prints of vault manager David Barranco who had placed the money in the robber's satchel. All such tests were negative and the authorities could find no link between the money in King's home and the currency stolen from the United Bank.

The Faulty Identification Process

Though the evidence against King did not implicate him in the crimes, upon apprehending King, the police announced that he was the man responsible for the Father's Day Massacre. When asked for specifics, the authorities admitted that they did not have any bombshell, but all the little bits of evidence pointed to King. He was a former employee of the bank and had been heard to state that he thought that the bank had an atrocious security system. King also looked like the man described by the robbed tellers.

Since the robber had been in disguise, police artist Paige Lida was assigned the task of touching up the photo of King which the eyewitnesses had previously seen so the picture would look like the man in the disguise. Lida cropped the photo of King which the FBI had shown to the eyewitnesses on June 20. The artist cut off the forehead to simulate a face that was partially obscured by a hat. By doing so, the authorities seemingly hoped this doctored photo would change the results of the original showings. At the initial lineups of pictures of former and current guards, only one victim had mentioned that King looked somewhat like the perpetrator. Four had claimed that photo number eight, that of John Perpetua, looked a good deal like the robber.

On July 3, the authorities sought to test this modified photo on the employees. They were only able to locate eyewitness David Twist. He was asked to pick out King's picture from a six-man photo lineup. The 25-year-old bank employee noted that it, photo number two, looked a good deal like the gunman. The police used this identification in their affidavits requesting the search and arrest warrants from Denver County Court Judge Aileen Ortiz-White. She signed them. Then, with King in custody, the authorities were eager to have the eyewitnesses identify him as the robber. This called for another lineup—a live one.

The district attorney's office was immediately concerned that the media might taint the lineup. By the time the police could assemble the eyewitnesses, the tellers would have already learned of the arrest through the media and might have seen King's picture prior to the lineup. In a televised press conference on the morning of July 4, Chief Deputy District Attorney Craig Silverman begged the media not to publish or broadcast King's picture prior to the lineup. He feared that this would pollute the lineup whereby the tellers might pick King out because they had seen his picture as the suspect. Despite this, the same day a television interview of King's oldest son, Jim Jr., was widely broadcast in the city. He naturally looked somewhat like his father. Unable to resist a dubious scoop, a different channel briefly showed an image of King.

Members of the police department worked to arrange a live lineup on July 4. In addition to King, a number of detectives were slated to be included. Then, somebody issued an order to cancel this lineup. The authorities, rather, insisted that they would only conduct a photo lineup, using the cropped, modified picture which had been identified by David Twist on July 3.

I immediately objected to this procedure. Photo lineups are only to be used when the suspect is not available. When the police have a suspect in custody, the appropriate procedure is to have a live lineup. That way witnesses can see the size, body, posture, and gait of the suspect.

The authorities argued that the photo lineup was necessary due to another coincidence that cast suspicion on King—his mustache. Over the years, King had worn a well-trimmed mustache. About ten days after the United Bank robbery, he shaved it off *after* he had first talked with the FBI. Around the same time, the mustacheless retired police sergeant discovered that he had lost his driver's license. He had the license replaced on June 28, 1991.

This, according to the authorities, was further proof of King's guilt. They insisted that King actually got his license replaced because he was seeking to alter his appearance. The new license showed a mustacheless photo of the retired police officer.

When working to arrange the live lineup, the police had been fully cognizant of the problems the missing mustache posed. Some of the men selected for the lineup had mustaches, others did not. I agreed that King would wear a false mustache, if needed and properly secured, during the lineup. But now the hierarchy was paying no attention to this sensible measure as it used the issue of

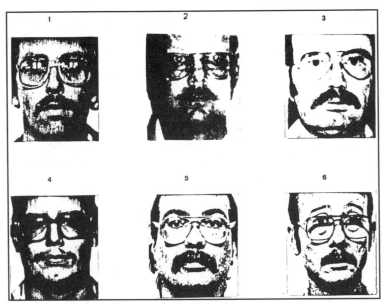

The six-person photo lineup shown to the robbed tellers.

the mustache to deny King a live lineup. The authorities argued that King's appearance without the mustache so changed his looks that a live lineup would not be the appropriate procedure.

This was a blatant effort to slant the evidence and lineup against my client. The eyewitnesses had claimed they "would never forget" the face of the robber, mustache or no mustache. But instead of giving the eyewitnesses a fair chance to identify King from a group of other men, the authorities arranged for them to view the six-photo lineup. In addition, the police refused my request to be present at the lineup. I wanted to be there to make sure the authorities said or did nothing which would indicate that they hoped the eyewitnesses would identify suspect number two as King's retouched photo was listed in the lineup.

From the start, I thought the previous showing of King's picture to the eyewitnesses tainted the photo lineup. The robbery victims had already seen King's face in the first batch of pictures on June 20. They had never viewed any of the five other persons in the photo lineup. Nor were any of the other five pictures those of past and present United Bank guards. On the contrary, they were mug shots of Denver, Adams County, Colorado, and Sparks, Nevada, prisoners. King's picture was highlighted, clearly standing out from the other five suspects. No effort was made to videotape the photo lineup so the authorities could prove that it had been conducted fairly.

On the basis of previously having seen King's photo and being shown the cropped photo of King, three of the employees now definitely identified King as the robber. Two others stated there was a strong similarity between King and the robber. The sixth eyewitness, Chong Choe, was unable to identify any of the six photos as that of the gunman. All five tellers who identified King, however, had previously failed to finger him when their memories were freshest right after the robbery when they were first shown his photo. Now, the eyewitnesses seemed sure. King was the man!

Trial by Media

On this basis, King was instantly pilloried by the police and district attorney's office, with the full cooperation of the media. Even before the tainted photo lineup, the media reported that the police are "really, really sure they have the right man." They are "pretty satisfied" and "pretty convinced" that King did it. At a joint press conference on the morning of July 4, Police Chief Zavaras, FBI Special Agent in Charge Pence, and Chief Deputy District Attorney Silverman publicly stated that King was doubtlessly guilty. Zavaras and Pence both boasted that the arrest was due to hard, detailed, minute, step-by-step police work. All the evidence, they noted, pointed to King as the killer.

Following an arrest in a sensational case, the media seek information from those who know the suspect. In King's case, the reports were that he was a quiet, honest, generous man who had been a good, efficient, responsible police officer during his 25 years on the force. "He's so mellow," one neighbor reported. "They have the wrong man," stated another. A fellow guard noted: "He was a great guy. He checked out the building well and got along with everyone. [He was] very friendly and professional." Something, therefore, was needed to denigrate King's character, leading the police, intentionally or recklessly, to create a story about his "brothers."

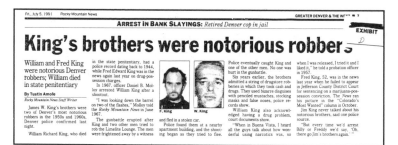

Fri., July 5, 1991   Rocky Mountain News   GREATER DENVER & THE WEST ■ 7

ARREST IN BANK SLAYINGS: *Retired Denver cop in jail*

EXHIBIT D

King's brothers were notorious robbers

William and Fred King were notorious Denver robbers; William died in state penitentiary

By Tustin Amole
Rocky Mountain News Staff Writer

James W. King's brothers were two of Denver's most notorious robbers in the 1950s and 1960s, Denver police confirmed last night.

William Richard King, who died

in the state penitentiary, had a police record dating back to 1944, while Fred Edward King was in the news again last year on drug-possession charges.

In 1967, officer Daniel B. Molloy arrested William King after a shootout.

"I was looking down the barrel on two of the flashes," Molloy told the *Rocky Mountain News* in June 1967.

The gunbattle erupted after King and two other men tried to rob the Limelite Lounge. The men were frightened away by a witness

and fled in a stolen car.

Police found them at a nearby apartment building, and the shooting began as they tried to flee.

Police eventually caught King and one of the other men. No one was hurt in the gunbattle.

Six years earlier, the brothers admitted a string of drugstore robberies in which they took cash and drugs. They used bizarre disguises with penciled mustaches, stocking masks and false noses, police records show.

William King also acknowledged having a drug problem, court documents show.

"When in Buena Vista, I heard all the guys talk about how wonderful using narcotics was, so

when I was released, I tried it and I liked it," he told a probation officer in 1957.

Fred King, 52, was in the news last year when he failed to appear in Jefferson County District Court for sentencing on a marijuana-possession conviction. The *News* ran his picture in the "Colorado's Most Wanted" column in October.

Jim King never talked about his notorious brothers, said one police source.

"But every time we'd arrest Billy or Freddy we'd say, 'Oh, there go Jim's brothers again.'"

The police fabricated the story that King had two "brothers" who were notorious robbers. I filed a copy of this article as Exhibit D during a July 8, 1991, court hearing when I protested the slanted media coverage designed to bias the community against my client.

According to the July 5, 1991, *Rocky Mountain News*—the same issue that reported King's arrest—King had two brothers who were notorious robbers. Since the 1950s, William Richard King and Frank Edward King had repeatedly staged armed robberies. William King, who had a police record dating from 1944, had died in the Colorado State Penitentiary in the 1980s, while the police had recently been after Frank King for the illegal possession of marijuana. Everybody knew that they were the brothers of Denver Police Sergeant James William King according to Police Chief Zavaras.

The story was a total fabrication. The next day, when I challenged Chief Zavaras on it, he admitted that he had no evidence to substantiate his claims and that it was up to the newspaper to double-check the piece. The *News*, in turn, insisted it naturally believed what the police told it about King. The paper was forced to retract the story. Its correction, with no banner headline, ran in a much less conspicuous part of the paper.

Another smear against King regarded his pistol. He had visibly worn the weapon while serving as a guard as bank regulations had permitted him to do. However, since the bank had changed its policy about nine months *after* King had retired from the bank, King was reported to have broken bank rules since he had carried the revolver when he was a guard.

The media readily reported and even created rumors about King. He was said to have been the mysterious man seeking to rent a car at Stapleton Airport on Father's Day a couple of hours after the murders. Likewise, though the composite sketch of the robber, which the FBI had completed on July 1, was not released to the media until September, television reports in the wake of King's arrest asserted that members of the Denver Police Department, who had seen the sketch, noted that it looked just like a certain retired police sergeant.

Once more, there was little credence to the media accounts. Typical of the views of rank-and-file police officers about King were the comments Kenneth Mulvey made to one of my investigators. A retired policeman, Mulvey had attended the police academy with King and had served on the force with him. He noted that King had a very mild temperament. "He was not quite milquetoast, but as close as you can get." King did not smoke or drink and swore very little compared to his fellow officers. The retired sergeant was "very soft spoken, introverted, and always pleasant."

Mulvey's opinion was comparable to others who knew King on the department. If anything, King's mild disposition had made him the object of scorn among his fellow officers. A primary reason that King had failed his oral examination in his effort to be promoted to lieutenant was that he was not a forceful enough character and did not have the hard-boiled attitude the police wanted from a ranking

Photo by Phil Goodstein

Jim King's house at 665 Juniper Street.

official. He was the kind of man who would go out of his way to avoid an argument or needless confrontation.

During my investigation, I came across a rumor that, during King's early years on the force, his partner had been involved in a barroom brawl. Rather than intervening, King had locked himself in his patrol car, placing a call for help. He did not, however, get out of the car to assist his fellow officer. There was no foundation to this story. Still, the fact that this allegation circulated showed that King was anything but a crazed, violent, out-of-control police officer.

Meanwhile, though more and more rumors were reported about King, the physical evidence against him proved non-existent. The authorities, for example, had made a great deal about the shoeprints found at the scene of the crime. The marks were made by a $9\frac{1}{2}$-sized shoe, the same size that King wore—or so the police claimed. King actually wore size $10\frac{1}{2}$ and usually bought size 11 shoes. The police were so eager to link the shoeprints to King that they took the size 8 shoes of his son David when they searched the Kings' house. David's shoes more closely approximated the prints found at the United Bank than did his father's shoes.

The police found a dirty pair of shoes during their search of King's house that seemed to match the prints at the scene of the crime. When the shoes were sent to the FBI lab in Washington, the tests proved negative compared to the shoeprints found at the murder scenes. King's shoes were quite worn and the central ridges on the bottom of the shoe were non-existent. The shoeprints at the murder scene showed a crisp set of marks. Nor were King's shoes the same size as the prints found at the United Bank.

The evidence showed that the shoeprints at the crime scene had been made by a pair of Stacy Adams shoes, either model 46019 black or model 46020 burgundy. The authorities found that only one store in Denver, Toth's Specialty Footwear at 705 16th Street, sold them. They examined the store's records of who had purchased pairs of these shoes which might match the prints at the scene of the crime. One familiar name was Harry Glass, the guard whose fingerprint had been found on the can of Mountain Dew. But Glass had bought a brown pair of model 00016, size 12 shoes. J. E. "Buddy" King had also bought a pair of Stacy Adams shoes, but he had no relation to Jim King.

Jim King was a cautious, conservative man. He strapped a fire extinguisher to the floor of the front seat of his Ford Fiesta.

Despite a second five-hour search of King's house on July 8, during which the authorities dug up the backyard after sweeping it with a metal detector, the police were unable to produce any loot or murder weapon from King. This time they seized King's personal computer for more clues.

Meanwhile, lacking any physical evidence, the authorities loudly broadcast the fact that King had refused to take a polygraph test. The implication was that this indicated guilt as if lie detectors are fool-proof means of detecting all criminal statements and activities. They also started talking about King's service revolver.

Since the ballistic evidence showed that the bullets which killed the guards had been fired from a .357 or .38 Colt revolver, King, who had carried a .38 Colt Trooper during his career on the police department, was once more seen as a likely suspect. In addition to the Colt, King also owned a 12-gauge 93 Winchester shotgun, a bolt-action .22 caliber Winchester rifle, and a five-shot .22 North American Arms revolver. King kept the last in a nightstand drawer by his bed. In November 1989, he had sent it back to the manufacturer as part of a recall to get its cylinder replaced.

King did not have his police revolver. He claimed that its cylinder had cracked and it was not worth getting the old, beat-up weapon repaired. Because the gun was damaged, it was not safe. As a cautious man, King had disposed of it. Typical of his prudent temperament, he had a fire extinguisher strapped to the floor of the front seat of his 1978 Ford Fiesta. He never sped, and had the reputation of being a conservative man. The retired sergeant did not want to have a defective gun in his possession because it might explode when fired.

The disappearance of the gun, however, seemed incredulous to the authorities and their echoes in the media. Some gun amateurs claimed that cylinders do not crack on Colt Troopers. Nor did Carol King back up her husband's initial statement that he had dismantled and disposed of his gun because she thought it was unsafe to have the weapon in the house. King said very little to Carol about the pistol, noting that he did not want to worry her. Throughout the case, whenever the authorities were at a dead end in all their other accusations against King, they would return to his missing weapon. They insisted a retired police officer would never voluntarily throw away his gun, a memento of his years of service. It was his power, his protector, his profession.

But King was not emotionally connected to his weapon. He had first discovered the cracked cylinder while cleaning the gun after shooting it at a firing range during the time he worked as a guard at the United Bank. When he pondered trading the weapon for a Glock 17 or 19, the gun dealer would not take the broken-down old revolver in trade. Realizing it would cost him far more to fix the cracked cylinder than he originally paid for the gun, King, who saw no future need for the damaged, dangerous weapon, dismantled the revolver and threw it in the trash shortly after he left his post at the United Bank. He had told this to the FBI during the initial interview on June 24 before he contacted me.

Besides focusing on the gun, the district attorney pointed to the type of bullets found at the crime scene. They were 110-grain semi-jacketed +P ammunition, hollow-point bullets manufactured by Remington Arms and used by the Denver Police Department in the mid-1980s when King was on the force. As a police officer, King was given this ammunition though it did not work ideally in his Colt revolver. It was a "hot load," bullets with possibly more explosive capacity than the gun was designed to handle. Shooting such ammunition in a revolver is a sure means of causing the timing to go out and the cylinder to crack.

The authorities insisted that the +P bullets were key in pinpointing King's guilt. According to them, the +Ps had been specifically manufactured only for the Denver Police Department. Since King had kept 18 rounds of +Ps after he left the force, it was suspicious that 18 shots had been fired during the murders. They must have been the same bullets which had been issued to King. Nobody but a Denver police officer would have had access to this ammunition.

The fact that a Colt revolver had been used to kill the guards was central to the prosecution's case. One reason, according to Deputy District Attorney Bill Buckley, that the former guard accused in the theft from the automated teller, Paul Yocum, could not have committed the murders was because he had a .357 Smith & Wesson revolver and his speed loaders were only for Smith & Wessons. Apparently, this meant that Yocum could never have had access to a Colt or a Colt speed loader. Only King, the police and district attorney implied, could have ever possessed the Colt and +Ps used to kill the guards.

Also questionable were King's whereabouts during the robbery. He stated that he had awakened at around 8:00 that Sunday morning and decided it was time for him to get back in the swing of playing over-the-board chess. He had given up tournament chess in 1981 when he had been transferred to the midnight shift at the airport and the quality of his over-the-board play had declined. King continued to play informally, including with Tom Coogan, the man who served as police chief between 1983 and 1987. King had occasionally still come to the Denver Chess Club at the Capitol Hill Community Center next to Cheesman Park for non-rated games until about 1984 or 1985.

Between 1985 and 1989, King had been an avid postal chess player. A national association matched him with opponents to whom he sent his moves by mail. At one time, he had 18 games going simultaneously. King had played 244 officially sanctioned correspondence games during this time.

Photo by Phil Goodstein

The Capitol Hill Community Center was the home of the Denver Chess Club during most of the 1980s. It was where Jim King sought a chess game when the United Bank was robbed on the morning of Father's Day, 1991.

By the summer of 1989, King had tired of postal chess. He felt that his opponents were feeding the moves into elaborate computer programs. His last postal game was on September 7, 1989. King missed the give-and-take of live chess. For some months before Father's Day, he planned that he would again become an active face-to-face chess player.

Shortly before Father's Day, Carol asked Jim what he would like to do for that occasion. He noted it was high time he did something about his chess itch. His family did not need to do anything special for him on Father's Day. He decided he would celebrate Father's Day by going out that morning to play at the chess club as he did several years ago.

During the 1980s, the Denver Chess Club rented space in the Capitol Hill Community Center at 1290 Williams Street. A primary purpose of having its quarters in this centrally located facility adjacent to Cheesman Park was that anybody seeking a game could go there and find an opponent. Chess players showed up at the club, which was located in room four in the basement of the mansion that was the home of the community center, in the middle of the night and on holidays. Members got into the house by using two keys that were in a combination lock box attached to the rear basement door. One key was to the house, the other was to the chess club's room. The combination had been R-K-R, rook-king-rook.

King had previously played at the chess club in the community center on Sunday mornings. Most of his games at it were non-rated speed or five-minute chess. In such a game, a player must make all his moves within five minutes or he loses on time. A specially designed clock is used to time the games.

Some around the community center complained about the late hours of the chess players. The leaders of the community center also argued that the comings and goings from the chess club meant that sometimes the basement door to the community center was not secure, making the center as a whole unsafe. The unfriendly attitude of the center's management to the chess club, combined with financial problems of paying the rent, had led the chess club to vacate the community center approximately three years before the Father's Day Massacre. After it left the community center, the chess club did not have 24-hour-a-day accessibility. It moved its weekly sessions to Post No. 1 of the Veterans of Foreign Wars at West Ninth Avenue and Bannock Street, a building five blocks from the courthouse. About nine months before the Father's Day Massacre, it had relocated to VFW Post No. 501 at 4747 West Colfax Avenue.

The retired police sergeant, who had not been active in the chess club for six or so years, and who had let his membership in the United States Chess Federation lapse, did not know this. Believing that the chess club was still flourishing at the Capitol Hill Community Center and that it was the best place to find a good chess game, at about 9:15-9:30 on Father's Day morning, King left his house and drove the 12 or so miles to the community center. He went up Sixth Avenue to Josephine Street to 13th Avenue to the house at the southeast corner of 13th Avenue and Williams Street. Prior to going to the community center, King had tried to call for information about the chess club. The club did not have a specifically listed number and no one had answered the phone at the community center. The former police sergeant assumed that nothing had changed to force the club to vacate that ideal location.

King parked in a driveway near the rear of the community center. As he started to go down the steps to the basement entrance, he noticed that the combination lock box was not there. Its absence implied that the chess club could be gone. Consequently, he did not go down the stairs.

Still, he hoped to learn something about the fate of the chess club. He walked around the community center, along 13th Avenue, to the front door. At the bottom of the stairs leading to the front porch, he noticed a well-dressed man. The latter stated he knew nothing about the chess club. When King went up to the front door, the building was locked and there was no indication that the chess club was still in the community center. King realized that there was no hope for a chess game. Returning to his car the same way he had come, King drove home. He had only been at the community center for two or three minutes.

The Capitol Hill Community Center is about one and a half miles from the United Bank of Denver. For the police, that was enough to put King in the vicinity of the robbery. King, though, insisted, that he had returned home at approximately 10:00 AM. After changing his shoes and doing some more yard work with Carol, he left with his wife.

The couple went to Mount Olivet Cemetery to visit the graves of Carol's parents, grandparents, and other relatives. She and Jim often visited the cemetery, usually about once a month. Carol wanted to get to the graveyard, which is located about four miles north of her and Jim's house, to see how some geraniums she had planted that spring were doing. There had been a severe hail storm on June 1 which had badly damaged the Kings' house and had caused leaks everywhere. Carol feared that the flowers at the cemetery might have been destroyed by the hail. After stopping at a Dairy Queen for frozen yogurt, the couple returned home around one to two o'clock. King washed his car later that afternoon.

The retired police sergeant first learned about the United Bank robbery while watching television at about 6:00 that evening. He did not remember what program he had on when Carol called out, telling him she had just heard the news. He turned the channel to try to learn more. His immediate reaction was sorrow and a fear that guards he knew and had worked with had been murdered.

Later, seeking to counter King's alibi that he had been at Mount Olivet after his chess trip, the police searched the cemetery, looking for evidence. Divers went into the graveyard's lakes. Once more, they failed to find anything connected to the bank robbery.

Meanwhile, the district attorney's office sought to make King responsible for all deficiencies in the United Bank's security system. The police learned that King had discussed with his fellow guards how someone could rob the bank. One thing which guards and police officers always talk about is crime and the way a smart criminal can attempt to beat the system. Despite this, the district attorney's office was arguing that King was the only guard who ever considered such nefarious activities. Simply thinking about robbing the bank, according to the authorities, was suspicious. In the eyes of the district attorney's office and the media, King had actually been working as a security guard to case out the bank for the robbery. They also noted that King wore a pedometer which showed the distances he walked while on duty as a bank guard.

The middle-aged, retired police officer had a problem with cholesterol and needed to exercise. His doctor ordered him to walk

Photo by Phil Goodstein

The section of Mount Olivet Cemetery where Carol King's parents are buried.

vigorously for at least 30 minutes a day. Carol encouraged him to follow these instructions, frequently walking with him. She had given him the pedometer so he would have an idea of how far he walked during his bank rounds. Strolling through the numerous corridors of the bank was one way he could get the needed exercise. The pedometer showed he averaged five to seven miles a shift. Seen in this light, he told his wife that the guard's job was an exercise godsend.

While serving as a police sergeant at Stapleton Airport, King had prowled along the roofs and hallways to make sure nothing was amiss. He did the same thing at the United Bank. Like other guards, he was given maps of the bank. He studied them so he would know where to go when asked to inspect an area of the bank or make a delivery.

During the search of King's house, the police found four one-page maps of sections of the United Bank in a file folder marked "plans" in his cluttered study. Among them was a sketch of the concourse level, specifying the location of the elevators, vault, and monitor room. The district attorney readily broadcast, and the media repeated, this was definitive evidence that King had plotted the robbery.

Guard supervisor Jim Prado, when interviewed, noted that all guards were given such maps and that they were welcome to keep them. He had drawn a couple of special points on the map. Three of the four pages had nothing to do with the area of the bank which was robbed. Nothing was marked "confidential" on the plans. The 1989 map of the concourse level which King had been given during his days as a bank guard was obsolete by 1991.

The Suspicious Safe-Deposit Box

Another item that cast suspicion upon King was his safe-deposit box. He and his wife kept the usual items in it: financial records, baptism, birth, and marriage certificates, insurance policies, mortgage schedules, valued personal keepsakes, and so forth. By June 1991, the box was getting crammed since it also included some of their children's records and many car titles. King also wanted to put back-up floppy disks from his writing in the safe-deposit box which would not fit in his small existing box. On June 17, King got a larger box. He told the bank official that the $10-a-year additional fee was no big thing. It was worth having the larger box to contain his valuables.

This, the authorities charged, was further evidence of King's well-calculated efforts to conceal the loot. The FBI, in fact, announced that the new box was just about the right size to stash away $200,000 in cash. The authorities searched it. To give the search greater sensationalism, instead of asking for King's key, they had a locksmith break into the box on July 5. The first locksmith did not have the proper tools to do the job. Only after a second locksmith had been called in to assist were the authorities able to crack the safe-deposit box.

There was no missing money, gun, stolen videotapes, bank keys, walkie-talkies, log sheets, or any other evidence of the robbery in the safe-deposit box. Occupying a good deal of space was a hand notary seal. There was also a storage box in which one could place computer floppy disks. The most incriminating materials in the safe-deposit box were six allegedly bogus police ID cards.

King had previously worked in the identification division of the police department. During the search of the safe-deposit box, the authorities discovered six police ID cards with King's photo. One had the wrong date of King's birth. Another had his birth name, James W. Ette, rather than his adopted named on it. A third had the name of William Keplinger after his mother's maiden name. Other cards were in the name of William Scott Goody and Oren W. Marshall. (The last was the name of a man who had sold King a house in 1980.) Supposedly, these cards showed King's criminal disposition.

The bogus ID cards received immense publicity. Television reporters spelled out the names of the purported aliases and asked viewers to call the police or FBI if they knew anything about someone ever using such names. The police and FBI systematically investigated 119 separate banks and savings and loans in addition to credit unions in the Denver metropolitan area to discover if King had some secret account, hidden safe-deposit box, or whether the banks had an account in the name of one of the aliases.

Working with the FBI, the police also sought out such accounts in the names of King's wife, sons, and alternate suspect Mike

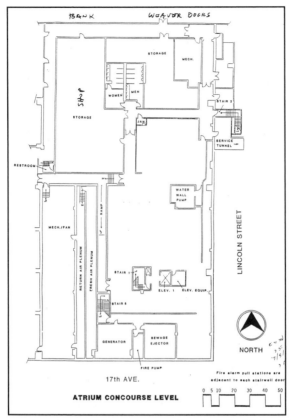

A map of sections of the concourse level of the United Bank was found in King's house in a folder marked "plans."

McKown. The authorities further investigated banks in Mesa, Arizona, where King's mother lived. Once more, they found nothing. Nor did they discover anything when they vigorously searched storage facilities throughout the Denver area, including rental lockers at Stapleton Airport.

The prosecution pointed out that King had visited his safe-deposit box frequently since Father's Day. This was evidence that he had moved cash in and out of the new box. But if King had been out to carefully destroy all evidence of his staging the bank robbery, it was a wonder he did not also destroy the ID cards. Besides, where

Photo by Phil Goodstein

King had his safe-deposit box at the 1stBank of Westland.

was the money if it was not in the box? The authorities claimed that King had rented the larger safe-deposit box to secure the $200,000. Where's the beef?

Nonetheless, the district attorney and police heavily stressed the ID cards as examples of King's nefarious criminal mind. Similarly, taking no account of the earnings of King's wife, authorities claimed to have discovered a "mystery" deposit and withdrawal of $4,250 from King's banking account on August 17, 1990. Somehow, this was linked to the robbery of the United Bank despite the fact it had occurred nearly a year before the Father's Day Massacre.

And so it went. On issue after issue, there was just enough evidence to *suspect* that King might have been involved, but there was nothing to provide evidence beyond a reasonable doubt that he was guilty of the crime. "There's nothing there," I told the media. "There's no loot, there's nothing."

Despite this, on the afternoon of July 8, District Attorney Norm Early held a widely publicized press conference. He stated he was sure that King was guilty and that he would formally file charges against him the next day. Mr. Early was naturally eager to claim credit for the arrest and prosecution. He had recently lost a close runoff election for mayor. Apparently, he wanted to bury his defeat

by forcefully demonstrating that he was the city's fighting district
attorney who had solved the robbery-quadruple homicide.

King was officially accused on July 9 of 15 felony counts,
including eight counts of first-degree murder. Not only was King
accused of premeditatedly executing the four bank guards, but he
was also charged with murdering them while committing the felony
of aggravated robbery—a crime known as felony murder. (The
defendant could only be convicted of one count of first-degree or
felony murder against each of the guards.) The former police
sergeant was also accused of aggravated robbery, and six counts of
menacing for each of the six employees who were present when the
armed gunman pointed his weapon at them. Federal officials
announced they were pondering charging King with bank robbery.
Coincidentally, about this time, Denver Police Chief Ari Zavaras,
who had defamed King, announced his retirement. The next stage
of the case was about to begin.

5

The Request
for a Gag Order

Day after day, television stations and newspapers defamed James King, repeating every rumor emanating from the police and district attorney's office. Starved for specifics, the media hinted about "tightly held" evidence that will "tighten the noose" on Jim King.

The major Denver media are all owned by national corporations including Scripps-Howard, Gannett, McGraw-Hill, General Electric, and Westinghouse. Their foremost goal is increasing their profits by selling newspapers and boosting television ratings. Even so, their lack of critical reporting standards was appalling. Continually, on seemingly every rumor, such as that of King's two non-existent criminal "brothers," they eagerly and unquestioningly repeated the statements of the authorities. At best, it was as if the media were a well-rehearsed chorus carefully repeating the district attorney's lines. At worst, they were the prosecution's barking and running dogs.

A defense lawyer must prepare for all contingencies in a case. As long as the police and district attorney's office seek to try it in the media, he must fight back. Over the years, I have often needed to match the authorities blow for blow in trying to present the defense's side to the media. Ironically, biased press coverage helped me first establish my reputation as a criminal defense attorney.

After I was admitted to the bar in 1956, Francis P. O'Neill hired me as his assistant. A veteran local attorney for whom I had done some research while I was in law school, he was a Denver native and former member of the Colorado General Assembly. His main areas of expertise were criminal law and representing insurance companies in the defense of claims. One of his brothers was with the FBI; another was a Denver police officer. They referred him a good deal of criminal work.

I originally wanted to go into labor law, but there were no openings in that field when I was admitted to the bar. O'Neill assigned me many of his criminal cases. Often they made the news, especially the *Denver Post*.

Zeke Scher was the paper's court reporter. He had followed O'Neill around the courts and frequently covered his cases. Scher also wrote up the cases I handled for O'Neill.

Scher, then attending law school at night, subsequently became an attorney. As a reporter, he always slanted his stories in favor of the prosecution. In great detail, he would spell out the specifics of the crime and the claims of the police and district attorney. His stories failed to mention any damaging cross-examination or the nature of the defense's case. When my clients would be found not guilty, despite the tone of Scher's stories which implied that they were guilty, people who judged the cases based on the newspaper stories figured that I must be a great lawyer to win the acquittals. Scher's stories taught me the power of the press and the need to be on top of the media coverage of my cases.

Knowing that an unbiased jury would never be found for King if I did not combat the massive prejudicial publicity against him, I angrily told the media on the morning when King was officially charged that the case reminded me of a soap opera. "It's like the press and media are cheerleaders . . . as to what is going to turn up next. The press is part of an orchestra playing the DA's song. . . . There will be a 37-percent eclipse of the sun today," I continued, noting the astronomical phenomenon. Unfortunately, due to the way the district attorney's office had violated judicial and bar canons against trying the case in the media and had failed to control the irresponsible and prejudicial statements of the police, combined with the uncritical reportage of the media, "there is a 100-percent eclipse of justice going on now." The solution was a gag order.

A gag order is a dictate by the court that no one involved in the case can give opinions on it, especially attorneys or witnesses. The court can similarly seal records and prevent the media from broadcasting or publishing materials pertaining to a case. Usually, for example, the court will order that names and photos of jurors not be released. The courts have sought to protect the identity of women who have been the victims of sexual assaults. Still, at first glance, gag orders reek of a prior restraint of the press and have the aura of being a direct violation of the First Amendment and the right of free speech. Naturally, such gag orders should only be used to prevent a greater evil—the denial of a fair trial.

I have never been comfortable calling for gag orders, although I have requested a few over the years when massive prejudicial publicity is virtually destroying any hope my client has for a fair trial. What I urge the courts to gag is not a free press, but irresponsible statements which are deliberately made to bias the prospective jury pool. The principle of the gag order is that the question of guilt is to be determined in the courtroom by an unbiased jury of the defendant's peers. Such a trial is to critically examine all of the evidence and accusations against the defendant. He and his lawyer are entitled to inspect the evidence and cross-examine hostile witnesses. The only way the jury can determine the guilt of the defendant is by listening to the complete testimony and arguments in court. Jurors are not to come into court having already formed an opinion on the case based on slanted media reportage.

To be sure, the right of free speech is a most precious possession. All too often, governments and special interests have sought to violate it and stifle dissent. I have fought this during my entire career. The American Civil Liberties Union, the Anti-Defamation League, and other organizations have honored me for doing so.

I particularly recall one case involving free speech. It was when I defended three members of the San Francisco Mime Troupe in February 1967, because they spoke out against the establishment during a play. The city specifically accused them of performing "an indecent and lascivious act" in public, committing an "indecent and

Photo by Bill Peters

Three members of the San Francisco Mime Troupe, in blackface, were arrested on September 28, 1966, for staging a play in Denver that denounced the Vietnam War. I defended them without charge in my fight against censorship and political repression. Gag orders, such as the one I sought in the King case, have nothing in common with such censorship. Robert Slattery is the man at the left. I served with him in the Army during World War II. By coincidence, he was the interlocutor of the Mime Troupe's A Minstrel Show or Civil Rights in a Cracker Barrel. *He was not arrested that evening though he wished to be. Sitting directly next to him in blackface is future Hollywood star Peter Coyote.*

filthy action" with "obscene gestures" in public, and uttering "filthy words" and using abusive language in public in September 1966, when they performed *A Minstrel Show or Civil Rights in a Cracker Barrel* in Denver. The play criticized the Vietnam War, dealt with black-white relations, and reflected on the growing tensions between middle-class and lower-class blacks in the civil rights movement. I gained the actors' acquittal after a ten-day, three-night trial.

A gag order has nothing to do with such censorship. In England and Canada, when a person is arrested, the media are only allowed to report the arrest and the crime, but nothing more. The specifics of the case are spelled out in the courtroom, not on the ten o'clock news. In such circumstances, the First Amendment must be balanced by the Fifth, Sixth, Eighth, and Fourteenth amendments which guarantee the accused a fair trial, due process, an impartial jury, and prohibit cruel and unusual punishment. In view of the massive media smears of King, which had been made from the time of his arrest with the direct connivance of the police and the district attorney's office, I was simply trying to see that King had a fighting chance when I asked for a gag order. Something, I announced, had to be done to stop the "false guerrilla tactics" and hysteria campaign conducted against King.

Enter the Governor

The executive branch of the government entered the fray in the persona of Colorado Governor Roy Romer. Right about the time King was formally charged, on July 9, the Colorado Supreme Court struck down the state's amended death penalty. In 1988, the General Assembly decided that the existing death penalty, which the Court had previously found to be constitutional, was not harsh enough. In order to make it easier for the state to execute people, the legislature ordered that if, after declaring the defendant guilty, the jury found that the aggravating factors in a murder outweighed any possible mitigating factors in behalf of the defendant, the accused was automatically to be put to death. Writing for the Court, Justice George Lohr, in *People v. Young*, 814 P.2d 834, ruled that the old procedure, where the jury was still to weigh whether death was the appropriate penalty even in face of the preponderance of aggravating factors, protected against an arbitrary abridgment of due process and the imposition of cruel and unusual punishment. Since the new law did not, it was unconstitutional.

It was unclear whether this ruling invalidated the state's total death penalty. Nevertheless, the prosecutors demanded King's execution in the wake of the Supreme Court's decision. Governor Romer joined them. Insisting that Colorado had to have this means of human sacrifice, he stated that it "is tragic that it may not be possible for the death penalty to be applied" in the King case. The implication was that King had already been proven guilty. To make sure the state could legally kill him and more people, the governor announced that the death penalty would be part of his call for a special session of the General Assembly. On September 19, 1991, the legislature reinstituted the previous death penalty law.

The way the governor called for King's death was illustrative of the unfair rush to judgment I was trying to prevent in my efforts to get a gag order. Given the choice between trial by media and a fair trial in a court of law, there is nothing to decide. All that are gagged are sensational opinions and statements concerning the case by the police and attorneys.

Illustrative of how a gag order can work was another development in the case. About a month before King went to trial, one of the deputy district attorneys prosecuting him was arrested for shoplifting. Under great stress from a heavy court load, the prosecutor was taking medication for severe headaches. He was

Affidavit of Detective Jon Priest requesting the arrest and search warrants for Jim King.

District Attorney Norm Early

also having problems with a defective hair dryer he had previously purchased. The prosecutor had taken the broken machine into the store and, without making an effort to exchange it, sought to leave the store with a new one.

The police, district attorney's office, and the courts all kept the prosecutor's arrest under wraps pending the trial. The fear was that if the news got out, the jury pool would be tainted, necessitating a new prosecutor. This would considerably delay the trial. Only after the verdict did news of the deputy district attorney's misdemeanor come out. While I did not know about the shoplifting charge until it was publicly announced, the courts did the right thing in gagging the announcement of this news.

For almost a month, I was engaged in a game of touch and go with the media over the gag order. The prosecution wanted carefully to time the release of the warrants and affidavits of July 3 to get the most mileage out of them. Indeed, it was not I, but the district attorney's office, which had initially moved for a gag order.

The morning after King's arrest, on Independence Day, July 4, King was called into court for an advisement of his rights by County

Court Judge Larry Bohning. Chief Deputy District Attorney Craig Silverman represented the state. He was a win-at-any-cost prosecutor who was frequently reversed on appeal on account of his prejudicial comments and actions. Though he was ready to use the media to influence future jurors, he wanted to make sure that the district attorney's office did not make any mistakes that morning leading to an appellate reversal of a conviction in this case he eagerly hoped to try. Mr. Silverman moved that cameras be banned from the court, fearing that the publication of King's photo before a lineup would hopelessly taint the case.

I seconded Mr. Silverman's prophylactic motion. It was probably, I told the court, going to be the first and last time that the prosecution and I agreed on anything in the proceeding. Judge Bohning granted Mr. Silverman's motion, but would not prohibit the media from publishing or broadcasting any image of King that they might have acquired from other means.

I was again in court before Judge Bohning on July 5. Within the intervening 24 hours, King had been accused and convicted by the media. Television stations repeatedly interrupted their programs with specials to report the latest rumors on the case. The front pages of the July 5 *Denver Post* and *Rocky Mountain News* carried banner headlines announcing that King was doubtlessly the killer. District Attorney Norm Early took to the airwaves. Rather than explaining how King had come to be a suspect, he gave a speech fully worthy of the opening statement of a slashing prosecutor in a murder trial.

According to legal ethics, the district attorney's office is not supposed to release prejudicial information or try a suspect in the media. That, though, did not dissuade the authorities in this case. Throughout July 1991, leaks were so omnipresent that it was obvious that high officials in the police department or the district attorney's office had to be feeding the press materials designed to vilify King and prevent him from receiving a fair trial; hence the stories about King's "brothers," about him violating bank rules by wearing his gun on duty as a guard, and about the police identifying the composite drawing as looking like a former police sergeant.

To make matters worse, I did not really know what was going on during the first week after King's arrest. The district attorney is only required to turn over materials to the defense once a suspect is formally charged. Before then, King and I were in something of a twilight zone where we were not allowed access to the police reports, warrants, and affidavits. All I had to go on were King's statements to me that none of the prosecution and media assertions were true.

I knew I had to act. If this wave of unsubstantiated, prejudicial publicity against King were to go unchallenged, King would never get a fair trial. I therefore asked Judge Bohning to prohibit the authorities from releasing to the media any materials which they might have improperly obtained. "This is a request not to publish libelous, inadmissible material that may or may not be admitted in the courtroom, and that would be devastatingly prejudicial to my client. That's all we're asking," I told the court.

Sometimes during my argument, I spoke directly to the media. Facing them rather than Judge Bohning, I wanted to make sure they reported the defense's version of the case. Judge Bohning, however, refused to go along with my plea. He ruled that the media were to be allowed to continue their field day of reporting any gossip and dirt they could dig up against Jim King.

The Publication of the Warrants and Affidavits

The prosecution initially sought to seal the publication of the warrants and affidavits of July 3, which the police had used to arrest King. On July 8, it told the court that these documents contained secret information whose publication would harm the investigation. County Court Judge Brian T. Campbell granted the prosecution's request. Shortly thereafter, having gathered what initial material it could against King, the district attorney's office was ready for the affidavits and warrants to be published. By then, it had leaked most of the supposedly secret information to the media in its efforts to convict King by negative publicity.

Throughout July, I was before judges Bohning and Campbell trying to limit the thoroughly outrageous and irresponsible trial by media against King. When the district attorney's office suddenly wanted to release the warrants and affidavits, I sought to prevent their publication. The warrants and affidavits stated merely the rumors, suspicions, and coincidences that seemed to implicate King in the Father's Day Massacre. Even without releasing these documents, the authorities had already told, and the media had faithfully reported, most of the innuendoes.

The way the district attorney's office was using the media to declare King guilty without a fair trial, I stated during one television interview, smacks of "a stench of weakness in the case when they [the authorities] start utilizing and manipulating the media to enlist the prospective jurors to be biased against my client." They are "inoculating the jurors with a virus," I informed Judge Bohning.

Courtesy Judge Larry Bohning

Judge Larry Bohning presided at King's advisement and the hearing on the gag order.

The continual media allegations that King must have done it made it unlikely an unbiased jury could ever be found.

Consequently, I told the court, it should restrain the media from irresponsibly reporting every police canard and instruct the district attorney's office to obey legal proprieties by not releasing the materials to the press. Opposed to this, media attorneys hysterically screamed about the "public's right to know." "Right to know

The media went out of their way to show a shackled Jim King being led into the courtroom.

what?" I asked. "Illegal evidence? Prejudice? Lies? Slander?" Outside the courtroom I openly told the media that "you're making millions by inflaming the public."

One hearing on the motion to suppress the publication of the warrants and affidavits was continued for a couple of days on account of King's clothes. I insist that my clients have the right to be dressed as everyday people when they come into court, not as prisoners in jailhouse garb who are visibly manacled. Jurors and potential jurors automatically assume that the defendant is shackled for good reason and that, since he is in prison clothing, he must have done something wrong. Because jurors might judge a defendant by his dress, it is incumbent that the accused be allowed to wear appropriate clothing for a court hearing—"the presumption of innocence must carry the garb of innocence." Judge Bohning ordered that henceforth King was to be permitted to wear civilian clothes for all court appearances. Despite this, time after time, television stations broadcast footage of a handcuffed King being escorted into the courtroom.

Finally, after a number of continuances, on July 29, Judge Bohning agreed to a closed hearing on the question of unsealing the inflammatory warrants and affidavits. It was a two-and-a-half-hour secret proceeding. I had requested it because we sought to discuss the exact nature of the evidence. Judge Bohning, however, denied my motion to keep the affidavits and warrants sealed. Noting that most of the material in them had already been made public, he did not think that the case would be tainted by the release of these documents. He gave me a three-day stay to appeal his order. Denver District Court Judge Richard Spriggs denied my appeal and the Colorado Supreme Court refused to act. Therefore, the documents were published on August 2.

The release of the warrants led to a new attempt to besmirch King. All the charges and aspersions which had dominated the reportage throughout July were repeated, but there was nothing new in the information released in the warrants and affidavits. Skeptics pointed out that no physical evidence had been uncovered. The publication of the warrants and affidavits was anti-climatic. Much of the public greeted their release by asking: "Is that all?"

By focusing on these rumor-filled documents, I was able to get thinking people and potential jurors to see that the case against King was hollow—it was nothing more than a big balloon filled with the hot air of the police, district attorney's office, and media frenzy. By making the publication of the warrants and affidavits a front-page story, I deflated some of the prosecution's case, helping assure King would get a fair trial.

Meanwhile, yet more coincidences haunted the case. On June 27, a New York bank was robbed during which three people were shot. The composite drawing of the suspect showed a man wearing a hat and sunglasses. It looked a good deal like the sketch of a bank robber in Garden City Park, New York, who had staged a holdup there on November 29, 1990. Initially, the police were sure there was a connection between that crime and the events in Denver.

On August 23, the television show "America's Most Wanted" focused on Paul Alsbury. He was a former San Antonio police officer who had been convicted of the armed robbery of a Denver armored truck terminal, and who was suspected of the armed robbery of a guard servicing an automated teller machine in a Denver suburb in 1989. The media seized upon all this to show that King had to be involved, since the description of the New York robber was vaguely like the Denver culprit, while a former police officer with Denver ties was sought by "American's Most Wanted."

Two Slashing Prosecutors

As King proceeded on the path to justice, I faced two of the region's best prosecutors: Bill Buckley and Lamar Sims.

Mr. Buckley was born in Chicago on March 14, 1940. He had come to Denver to go to college, had worked as a probation officer while attending the University of Denver School of Law, and had joined the district attorney's office about the time he passed the bar in 1971.

Mr. Buckley's brother, a corrections officer in Arizona, had been killed during a prison break in the 1960s. He had dedicated himself to seeking justice by becoming a career prosecutor. Over the years, he had emerged as a cold, logically calculating, tough adversary in court. For some time, he had specialized in murder cases. During a pretrial hearing in November 1991, the judge referred to Mr. Buckley as the attorney who had probably prosecuted more murder cases than anyone else in Colorado history.

In his youth, Mr. Buckley had been caught up in the folk music revival. He once helped finance a local folk music nightclub and sang part-time in a folk band. During trials, he would entertain the media by playing recordings of him singing the "Wild Irish Rover." Somehow, the message of Joe Hill, Woody Guthrie, Malvina Reynolds, Pete Seeger, Paul Robeson, U. Utah Phillips, and other great folk singers about the need to fight against injustice and for the underdog was not heard by Mr. Buckley. A rather visible character in his own right, he sought to portray himself as a cool, quiet operator against a flamboyant defense attorney who was milking the media in the case.

Lamar Sims was born in New York on May 28, 1953. After graduating from Harvard University Law School, he had spent two years in private practice before joining the district attorney's office in 1981. A handsome man, Mr. Sims had worked in the past as a fashion model and was an outstanding orator and athlete. Sometimes, his addresses to the jury sounded like the cascading cadences of a preacher. Mr. Sims and Mr. Buckley worked as a team and were frequently assigned high-profile murder cases.

Bill Buckley led the prosecution against King.

With these two skilled and determined prosecutors, I had to do anything and everything to assure that my client would get a fair trial. As I denounced the prejudicial publicity, Mr. Buckley flayed me for grandstanding before the media. He specifically cited the claim that I was pondering withdrawing from the case.

I entered the case by accident, at the behest of a fellow chess player whom I thought needed some basic legal advice. Before I realized it, I was plunged into a case as controversial as any in my career. King had given me a very small retainer, and I knew he had little money to pay the massive expenses his defense would entail. I estimated that court costs, the hiring of investigators, and paying for expert witnesses could easily exceed $50,000 in addition to the everyday costs of running a law office. The fee I would usually charge in a case like this was $150,000 to $300,000. One of my partners jogged my memory about the financial realities of practicing law.

Like everything else, justice has a price. While an indigent defendant is entitled to a public defender or a court-appointed attorney free of charge, an individual with limited resources, like

King, is expected to pay the costs of his own defense even if he is ultimately vindicated. King, moreover, had financial problems. Other than for his police pension and his wife's minimal monthly earnings, he had virtually no assets.

The media, in turn, found a new sensation in the rumor that I was going to withdraw from the case. Once more the papers grossly exaggerated the developments. As they did with everything else concerning the Father's Day Massacre and the accusations against King, they blew my pondering the economics of the case out of proportion.

Whether King was rich or poor, he deserved as good a defense as possible. I wanted to defend him. The chess connection called me into action—a keynote of the game is the defense of the king. I was also outraged by the media vilifications of King, particularly the fabricated article about his non-existent robber "brothers." Therefore, after meeting with my partners Scott Robinson and Chris Miranda, I dedicated myself anew to defending King.

In light of the mounting costs of the case, I eventually managed to get the court to appropriate $5,000 for an investigator for us since

Lamar Sims joined Bill Buckley in prosecuting King.

King was financially insolvent. Most of this sum went to a special investigator to defend on the death penalty should King be convicted. My good friend and longtime investigator, Tony DiVirgilio, a retired police officer, donated most of his time in not only investigating, but also assisting in the courtroom during the many hearings and the trial itself.

In early 1992, Scott Robinson joined me as co-counsel in the case. A Colorado native who was born on February 8, 1950, he had grown up in the western Denver suburbs. A Phi Beta Kappa, he had obtained his bachelor's degree from the University of Denver in 1972 after having previously attended Colorado College in Colorado Springs. Scott earned his law degree from the University of Colorado in 1975 where he had edited the law review. I had hired him in 1977 after he had spent two years as a law clerk for the Colorado Court of Appeals. In the intervening years, Scott had emerged as an accomplished lawyer who was especially skilled in appellate work. By the time of the King case, he had assisted me in a number of high-profile cases in which we had a winning tradition.

Working with Jim King

It was a pleasure working with King. He was cooperative and fully understood the operations of the legal system. He spent a great deal of time helping me review the police and FBI reports. In a careful, very legible handwriting, he made comments about the reports and evidence which I found valuable. During the course of the preparation for the trial, I visited him 23 times in jail. My trips to see him were always productive. They also were necessary to calm him, encourage him, and deal with his fears.

While I was fighting for King in court, he had problems in jail. He was initially incarcerated in an isolation cell at the Denver City Jail. The authorities immediately announced that he had been placed on a suicide watch where bright lights were shined in his cell, preventing him from sleeping. The claim that he was suicidal was another calumny, an excuse for placing King in such atrocious conditions. I managed to get the deputies to turn down the lights.

The courts refused to grant King bond, and he was moved to solitary confinement in the infirmary of the Denver County Jail. I feared for his safety there. As a former police officer, there was

Scott Robinson was my associate in defending Jim King.

always the possibility that he would encounter convicted defendants whom he had arrested or testified against. For his own safety, he was isolated from other prisoners in what the sheriff's department called "administrative segregation." Unfortunately, the authorities overdid it, resulting in extremely harsh, punitive treatment.

King was placed in a ten-by-ten foot cell where there was no television, radio, or any other entertainment. He was not permitted to have a chess set or a deck of cards. The prisoner was only allowed to use the gymnasium three times a week when nobody else was around. Deputy sheriffs escorted him to the showers every other day. Carol usually visited him three times a week.

Most of King's time was spent reading. Even at that, the Denver County Jail has a notoriously bad library, while friends and family of prisoners are not allowed to bring books, newspapers, or magazines into the jail. A prisoner was able to get books directly from the publisher or a bookstore. King read a lot of science fiction while incarcerated. I tried to cheer him up when I saw him in jail. I sometimes brought a chess set with me and might play him a game or two during my visits.

The guard supervising the infirmary allowed prisoners visiting the nurse to stare at King or shout at him. He was not at all comfortable with this. At one point, King sent me a clipping of a newspaper article which reported that a prisoner had been accused of a new crime on the basis of a statement he allegedly told another inmate. Written on it, King asked me: "How do you prevent this? Everyone here tries to talk to me." I advised him not to discuss the case with anybody. I further warned him to take care about any tricks the deputy sheriffs might pull. Mr. Buckley, I informed him, had the habit of using jailhouse snitches in the cases he was trying.

The deputy sheriffs placed another prisoner near King's cell who would often turn his television to full blast or sing an obnoxious ditty which inmates called the "James King death row song." It included the verse, "King, you're going to the chair."

Some deputies harassed him, awakening him every 20 minutes. They also turned up the air conditioning in the infirmary to the point he was freezing—his clothes and blankets did not help keep him warm. Sometimes, King shook uncontrollably. Other guards were very nice and helpful.

In March 1992, the jailers' policy toward King changed. He was informed that another inmate, a trustee, was eager to play chess with him. While I told my client he was free to play chess with his fellow prisoner, he should have the trustee sign an agreement stating that all he was doing was playing chess with King. I again reminded Jim not to talk about the case with his fellow chess player or anybody else.

The trustee, apparently, was not a very skilled chess player. A newspaper account noted that King usually gave his opponent queen's odds and still easily won all the games. That the retired police sergeant had good reason not to trust the jailers and the trustee came out about a year after the trial. I got a call from a public defender. He informed me that he was representing that prisoner, who had since been released and accused of a new crime. The defendant was seeking a plea bargain. Included in the evidence he cited to mitigate his sentence was that he had been a snoop and informant for the FBI on Jim King when the two played chess together at the Denver County Jail.

The revelation of this piece of dirty business was another compliment to King's ability to hang tough in jail. The months of isolation naturally affected him. At the most, he was permitted out of his cell for two-hour breaks twice a day. He found the jail food so atrocious that he started losing weight. Later, Deputy District Attorney Buckley claimed that King deliberately sought to lose weight in jail to alter his appearance before the eyewitnesses and the jury.

A personal side of King was revealed when I allowed him to answer a questionnaire submitted by a television station. He told viewers that the authors he liked best included Tony Hillerman, C. S. Forester, Alexander Dumas, Tom Clancy, and Louis L'Amour. The *William Tell Overture* was his favorite work of classical music. He also enjoyed country and western music and listened a good deal to Colorado Public Radio. The man he most wanted to meet was Jesus.

6

The Preliminary Hearing

Every defendant has the right to a speedy trial. Sometimes, however, the prosecution wants too speedy a process. Before the defense has a chance to thoroughly investigate the case, the prosecution, with the assistance of the police and FBI, has a head start in preparing for the trial. Consequently, it is frequently necessary for the defense to ask for delays. I did so concerning the preliminary hearing.

When someone is accused by information—a paper filed by the district attorney's office as opposed to a grand jury indictment—the defendant has the right to a preliminary hearing on the charges against him. There the prosecution must establish probable cause that the accused committed the crime. The law only requires the state to produce some evidence against the defendant; it does not have to prove its charges beyond a responsible doubt. The court is to view the evidence in the light most favorable to the district attorney.

The defense can waive the preliminary hearing. I, however, usually insist on one. It gives me the chance to see and cross-examine the prosecution's key witnesses and have an eye-opener on the nature of the state's evidence. It also gives me an idea of the prosecution's strategy and tactics.

The preliminary hearing for King was scheduled for mid-August. On August 14, Judge Brian T. Campbell granted my motion to continue it until Tuesday, October 1. The judge ruled that the defense could present evidence that the presumption of guilt was not clear nor was the evidence great that the defendant had committed the murders. This would impact his decision as to whether King should be granted bail. During the preliminary hearing the outlines of both the state's case and the defense became clear.

Central to the prosecution was the testimony of two of the victims of the bloody bank heist, David Barranco and Kenetha Whisler. This was their first face-to-face confrontation with King in court. During direct examination, both specifically stated that the retired police sergeant was the robber.

I knew that if I did not eventually impeach the eyewitnesses, a jury would likely find King guilty. Therefore, I asked them about their initial statements to the police and how it was that they had failed to identify King when first shown his photo on June 20, four days after the robbery. I also got the eyewitnesses to admit that the robber had been wearing a disguise which covered his head and eyes.

The tall, suave, 25-year-old Barranco told how he was officially the "Team Leader II—Cash Vault Manager." His job was to supervise other employees as they counted receipts in the vault. "I have really never worked Sundays," he noted. Father's Day was only the third time he had ever worked that post on a Sunday. Turning to the crime, he described how the robber wore clothes which looked as if they came from the Salvation Army. The gunman had a clear complexion. He did not notice any moles on the robber.

The moles were crucial. From the time of the robbery, law enforcement personnel had repeatedly asked the tellers whether the gunman had any facial blemishes. One and all denied anything outstanding or unusual about the robber's face. This was to shape the heart of my defense—the dubious and polluted eyewitness identifications.

King has a number of visible moles on his somewhat lumpy, asymmetrical face. One is a couple of inches above his right eyebrow. Three are directly above his nose on his forehead. Four

Photo by Phil Goodstein

Judge Brian Campbell presided at the preliminary hearing.

are on his left cheek, including one at the fold of the mouth. The largest mole on his left cheek can be seen at upwards of 20 feet away. While the tellers reported that the gunman had been wearing an adhesive strip on his left cheek, they did not place it in a position where it would hide King's most noticeable mole. There were no moles on the composite drawing of the suspect.

King's flesh-colored moles do not easily show up in photos of the retired sergeant. Only those who have personally seen him readily notice the facial blemishes. Consequently, someone who had only been shown a picture of King would not describe him as having moles.

To emphasize the defendant's moles, I had King stand. When Barranco admitted that he had no trouble viewing the defendant, I pointed to the moles on the retired officer's left cheek. The witness conceded that he could easily see them. Barranco further admitted that he had not identified King as the robber prior to July 5 when he was shown the doctored photo. In this area, his testimony was nailed down for the trial.

In her initial statement to the police shortly after the robbery, 35-year-old Kenetha "Kay" Whisler explained how she had been working in station three of the cash vault that Sunday morning.

Suddenly, over the noise of the machines and the sound of a radio in the background, she heard a distinctive click. When she turned around, she saw the gunman pointing his weapon at her. Nobody else was around. The robber was extremely well dressed and looked like a businessman. Still, his mustache appeared to be phony and something seemed to be wrong with the nosepiece of his sunglasses. She noticed pink tape on the glasses which had dark, plastic frames. Perhaps they were flip-up sunglasses.

The five-foot, two-inch-tall, 185-pound Whisler observed that the robber was taller and heavier than her husband. Her spouse was five-foot-six and weighed about 210-220 pounds. She guessed that the gunman stood six-foot-one to six-foot-two, weighed 240 to 250 pounds, and had a potbelly. The robber was not muscular, but he was not flabby. He had on black shoes.

Whisler admitted that she had not had that good a look at the robber. She had mostly focused on his gun. It was a small weapon that fit easily into his hand. It had a short barrel that was maybe three to five inches long. Even at that, when she first saw the intruder, she thought it was a joke, that the gunman was an assistant manager, Greg, in disguise. In response, she had stated, "What is this? A joke or what?" The gunman immediately ordered her to "shut up!" Only when she heard the robber's voice, which was totally different from Greg's, did she realize that a crime was in progress.

Finally, Whisler conceded that she was not sure she would be able to recognize the gunman again. He had on a "really good disguise," she told the police. She had failed to identify King during the June 20 photo study. At that time she had noted that three men in the photo books looked somewhat like the gunman. Number one, Ralph Allison, had a mustache identical to the robber's, but other features were wrong. Photo eight, John Perpetua, had cheeks comparable to the gunman's, but the mouth was wrong. Number ten, Robert Hoffman, had a face similar to the man who had robbed her, but his cheeks were too full. She had said nothing about photo number 16, Jim King.

In great detail, I had reviewed Whisler's statements to the police and FBI prior to the preliminary hearing. It was obvious that I had good cause for my preparation once Whisler took the stand. In a histrionic tone, she claimed that she would "never forget his face,"

Kenetha Whisler

referring to the robber. "The instant he [the FBI agent supervising the July 5 photo lineup] laid it [the picture of King] in front of me, I told him I knew who it was. . . . Just looking at the picture, I was scared." She had no doubt that King was the gunman.

Whisler's testimony seemed too pat. During cross-examination, I tried to explore how she came to be so sure King was the intruder. If she would never forget the robber's face, why did she fail to pick out King when she was first shown his photo? Whisler denied having been shown the photo in the first lineup on June 20. To impeach her, I called the FBI agent who had overseen the lineup. He conceded that King's photo was shown to Whisler on June 20.

I reminded her of the admission of June 16 that "I'm not sure if I could recognize" the robber. Nor did she remember seeing any moles on the gunman. I contrasted her previous statement that the robber had on a "really good disguise" with her current insistence that the disguise had not affected her ability to identify King. To make sure she had a good look at King, I had him approach the witness. I put one arm over King's forehead, simulating the hat the robber had been wearing. My other arm was thrown over his eyes, to represent the intruder's sunglasses.

The sunglasses reflected on another part of Whisler's story. In the wake of the robbery, the bank had arranged for post-trauma stress counseling for the tellers. During one such session, Whisler told the police, she had noticed a pair of flip-up sunglasses that looked identical to those of the robber. She immediately became frightened and upset.

So how much credence should be given to her statement "I'll never forget his face"? Was this convenient thinking? Was it that, desperate to find a suspect, the authorities had conveniently induced her to identify King? Or had she only identified King because she had already been shown his picture on June 20?

During redirect examination, Whisler insisted that she also would never forget the robber's voice. If she could only hear him speak, she would know for sure whether King was the man. The witness had been insistent on this point from the time of the crime.

On July 1, the authorities were still intensively investigating Paul Yocum. When they again showed Whisler his picture, she noted he might be the robber with a lot of a makeup. But before she could identify him, she first wanted to hear his voice. Whisler also wanted to hear King speak. She vividly remembered the gunman telling her to "Get out and go lie with the others."

Deputy District Attorney Sims thereupon ordered King to stand up and state "Get out and go lie with the others." I immediately objected, announcing my client would say nothing. What Mr. Sims wanted was a melodramatic act of self-incrimination. Moreover, the law provided for a specific means of a voice lineup. It was to be done in a carefully staged setting with comparable voices. When Judge Campbell asked Mr. Sims for his response to my objection, the district attorney retreated, stating he would hold the issue of a voice lineup in abeyance for a future evidentiary hearing. Though no such voice lineup was ever held, the question of King's voice was to haunt us during Kenetha Whisler's testimony at a motions hearing and the trial.

Besides the two eyewitnesses, the prosecution also called numerous police officers and FBI agents at the preliminary hearing. These were the officers who had been involved in the investigation. Preeminent was the testimony of Detective Jon Priest. A 13-year veteran of the department who had been a detective for ten years, he

Detective Jon Priest was the lead police investigator in the case.

had served on the homicide bureau for the past two years. Promoted to sergeant shortly after the King case, Detective Priest was the police department's lead investigator in the Father's Day Massacre. Prior to the preliminary hearing, he had given me a personal tour of the bank, explaining his theory of the case. Detective Priest repeated this to the court, telling why he believed that the robbery and murders were a one-man job. During cross-examination, I had him admit that the authorities had yet to produce any physical evidence against King.

Priest was insistent that King did not live "very far" from the United Bank. The defendant's house was in the far western suburbs, 11.4 miles from the bank. But, he contended, this was only a short drive on a Sunday morning. The detective testified at great length how he and other police officers had driven all the routes King might have taken to and from the bank. They had timed these commutes, including round-about ways of getting to the bank. According to Priest, it only took him 12 minutes to make the drive in one test and 15 minutes in another. It was therefore possible for a witness to have seen King at home at 9:00, while King rang for admission at the bank as Bob Bardwell at 9:14. In response to these claims, which took no account of the many stoplights from the freeway to the bank or the time the robber must have spent entering and exiting from the seventh floor of the parking garage, I began to call Detective Priest "Speedy" Priest and "Race Car Driver" Priest.

Mr. Buckley and Mr. Sims also contended that only 18 bullets had been fired during the murders. The ammunition recovered at the crime scene was identical to the +P bullets which King had been issued during his day as a police officer. The prosecutors further sought to make a good deal about King's past employment at the bank. They showed he had mentioned to other guards that it would be easy for a criminal to rob the bank. King's disposal of his weapon, shaved mustache, and new safe-deposit box were also listed as evidence of King's involvement in the murders.

I called some witnesses on King's behalf, including police officers and FBI agents. I wanted to establish that the prosecution's case was a house of cards. This poignantly came out in the ballistic evidence. Little was to be made, my witnesses told Judge Campbell, that +P bullets had been found in the bodies of the murdered men. Other police departments besides Denver's used +P bullets. An official of the Remington Arms Company stated that +P bullets had been introduced in 1979 and were fully available to the general public. FBI tests demonstrated that three separate types of ammunition had been used in the crime, including projectiles manufactured by Winchester and Federal. The bullets that killed guards Mankoff and Wilson were not comparable to the +Ps issued to Denver police officers when King was on the force. This might indicate that at least two gunmen had been involved in the murders.

A police witness noted how the description of the robber changed between the first police radio broadcast of the robbery at about 11:00 AM and a subsequent simulcast shortly after noon on Father's Day. This reflected that the initial statements of the eyewitnesses were confused and in conflict.

In an unusual move, I placed an alibi witness on the stand, David Lee Bell, King's next-door neighbor. The defense rarely calls any crucial witnesses during a preliminary hearing. Why give the prosecution a shot at them, especially if it did not know of them or have a statement from them? But I was afraid that the prosecution, which had been the first to talk to Bell, would try to get him to change his story before the trial. This way I would have his solid, sworn testimony for King on the court record. Also, having him

None of the eyewitnesses described the robber as having moles. By pointing to King's moles, I hoped to show the dubious nature of the tellers' identification of my client.

take the stand would force the media to report some of the defense's contentions as opposed to the steady drumbeat of the prosecution which could easily prejudice future jurors.

Bell told the court that he had seen King drive up to 665 Juniper Street and get out of his car around 10:00 AM on Father's Day. King was wearing shorts. Bell's testimony showed that King could not have been robbing the bank if he was back at home right about the time the robber was *leaving* the bank. We further introduced police and FBI reports about another neighbor's statement that she had seen King at his home around 9:00 AM. I put a city employee on the stand who worked at the airport to tell the court about the strange doings of a character who vaguely resembled the suspect at the airport shortly after noon on Father's Day.

Nor was there anything inherently implausible about King's assertion he was looking for a chess game at the Capitol Hill Community Center on Father's Day morning. To prove this point, I called the caretaker of the Capitol Hill Community Center, Edward L. Huntington. He lived in a camper trailer in an unpaved lot behind the mansion which was the home of the community center.

The police had been the first to speak with Huntington when King explained that he had been looking for a chess game at the community center. Huntington, who was from Manzanola, Colorado, and whose family still lived there, had worked for about five years at the community center. The 66-year-old caretaker had never had any previous encounters with the law and was quite shy about discussing the case. When he was shown a photo of King, Huntington denied that he had ever seen the man.

The police had tried to get all they could out of Huntington. They videotaped an interview of him. In the course of it, they asked him a number of leading questions about the chess club. Among them was whether he could remember if there was some attorney involved in that outfit. He stated he had heard such allegations, but could not recall the lawyer's name. Still, Huntington seemed an impressive prosecution witness in the videotape when he insisted that he would have seen anybody who had come to the community center between nine and ten o'clock on Father's Day morning. The prosecution hoped to keep him in reserve for the trial as an important witness who would disprove King's alibi.

Ed Huntington was the caretaker of the Capitol Hill Community Center.

However, when my investigator talked to Huntington, he learned that the caretaker's statement to the police was only part of the story. There had been a big wedding at the annex of the center the previous evening. Besides drinking coffee with a buddy, Gary Hendry, on Father's Day morning, Huntington had updated the center's bulletin board and cleaned up from the wedding. In the course of doing the latter, he had moved upwards of a hundred chairs and three or four large tables between the two buildings. His procedure was to load the chairs on a dolly, push them out of the front door of the annex, lock up that building, and haul the furniture to storage space inside the front door of the mansion. Each trip took somewhere between five and 15 minutes and he had made six or seven such trips that morning, hauling 13 chairs at a time. It was very possible that he had been in the annex or putting the furniture away at the time King had briefly been at the community center.

Huntington further conceded that people were always coming and going at the center. Though the chess club had moved out approximately three and a half years before, individuals looking for chess games still occasionally showed up at the community center. He did not see everybody who came by the building. When it was not in use, he made sure the house was locked up tightly. This included times when he would be leaving the mansion for less than five minutes to transfer the chairs and tables from the annex to the house on a Sunday morning. Therefore, Huntington admitted, it would have been possible for someone to come to the center, find it locked, and see that the chess club was no longer there without him having observed the visitor on Father's Day.

The preliminary hearing continued beyond the four days for which it had been scheduled. We concluded it on Monday, October 7, in a different courtroom. After calling four more witnesses, it was time for final arguments.

Mr. Sims emphasized that the eyewitness identifications of King were automatically evidence enough to bind the defendant over on the murder charges. "I don't think there's any real question regarding the issue of probable cause as to the counts of murder, as to the aggravated robbery, as to the menacing." The bulk of his argument did not concern whether the prosecution had established probable cause, but whether there was any reason for the court to grant King bond. He raised this point even before I had the chance to establish my case that the there were such gaping problems with the prosecution's evidence that King should be released on bond pending the trial.

Mr. Sims' strategy was logical. Neither he nor I seriously doubted that Judge Campbell would bind King over for trial. The major purpose of the preliminary hearing had been the discovery of the state's evidence.

I hoped to show in my closing argument that there was no "proof evident or the presumption great" (the test of setting bond in a first-degree murder case) that King had committed the crimes. Toward this end, I focused on the dubious eyewitness identifications of King. While it was lamentable, I informed the court, that there had been no live lineup and that I had not be allowed to attend the photo lineup to ensure that the authorities said or did nothing to prejudice the witnesses, the problems with the identifications went beyond that. "What we know that happened is that all of them [the eyewitnesses] saw King's photograph before, and none of the other people that they picked out were ever part of the lineup." King looked familiar simply because the eyewitnesses had been shown his picture before. The photo lineup was tainted.

Nor should much be made of the fact that King had discussed how easy it was to rob the bank with other guards. All the guards did this. They played war games. This was vital "to develop prophylactic techniques to prevent the robbery. This is their job. This is what they think of. Police officers think about how crimes could be committed so they can guard against [them], . . . so they can theorize how they take place—that's precisely what the guards had done."

The problematic nature of the prosecution's case, combined with the questionable eyewitness identifications, greatly impacted the question of whether King should be granted bond. The eyewitnesses only claimed to have seen the defendant committing the aggravated robbery. There was nothing to connect the retired police sergeant with the murders. "I think if the court is objective on the issue of homicide, there are no witnesses, there are no confessions, there's no scientific evidence." Add to this "so-called eyewitness testimony that has been impeached heavily," how "every item of

The police administration building is on the left; the Denver City Jail is on the right.

scientific evidence has been negative as to my client," and how I had produced alibi witnesses for King, "the proof is not evident or the presumption great that my client would be convicted of first-degree murder." Therefore bond should be granted even if the prosecution's case is allowed to proceed.

Mr. Buckley continually interrupted me during my closing statement. He finally had a chance to have his say during his rebuttal argument. Here he spelled out in great detail the prosecution's entire case. The 11.4 miles between King's house and the United Bank were nothing, a very short commute on a Sunday morning. Whisler did not identify King during the June 20 lineup because the FBI agent was so unobservant that he had allowed her to skip a page in the photo album he was showing her. Every innuendo, coincidence, error, and unexplained factor in the investigation of the crime became in Mr. Buckley's summation concrete evidence that King was a master criminal.

Finally, Judge Campbell issued his ruling. He agreed with Mr. Sims that the eyewitness identifications alone were enough to establish probable cause and bind King over for trial. Discussing his finding, the judge readily admitted that "the lack of evidence, the location of the murder weapons, the location of the money, [and] things of that nature are troublesome." But, he continued, as he reflected upon the situation, he "increasingly came to the position that: what would one expect? This was not a half-baked plan. This was a plan that required a great deal of thought and a great deal of planning." Therefore, "it would be natural to expect that some of these items that . . . [the] prosecution would hope to have included in its case might not be here."

The bottom line, Judge Campbell concluded, is "that this is a case for a jury. This is a case . . . that involves a devastating crime against four members of our society and members of their families. It was a difficult crime against those that remained. And it is truly a crime that must be passed upon by 12 collective minds with unique backgrounds hearing all of the facts." Since this was a capital charge, the defendant was denied bond. Finally, Judge Campbell admitted his doubts about the strength of the prosecution's case. He noted that he did not want anyone to be misled that his ruling meant that King was guilty.

I took this as a positive sign from an objective, non-biased judge. There seemed to be enough reasonable doubt upon which I could build for the trial. The preliminary hearing had been valuable in that it allowed me to learn more about the prosecution's case. It also gave me a record of the statements of the witnesses under oath and a peek at their personalities and demeanors. I would carefully check whether they had given different versions of their testimony in previous reports to the police and FBI. Their testimony was established for the trial. In light of what they had sworn during the preliminary hearing, I would call them to account if their memories miraculously improved or changed in the intervening months before the trial.

7

A Colorful Judge

Shortly after King was bound over for trial, the defense faced another problem: which judge should try the case. By rotation, the case was assigned to District Court Judge Federico Alvarez. He had served as a county court judge from 1987 until 1990, when he was elevated to the district bench. I did not have any experience trying cases before him. Judge Alvarez had close ties with an official of the United Bank of Denver. Upon applying to become a district judge, he had had the bank official write the governor a letter of recommendation. Judge Alvarez also had an account at the United Bank.

I only learned this on October 31. I was taking a deposition in a civil case when I received a message that it was urgent I call Judge Alvarez. He was in his chambers with Deputy District Attorney Sims. Over the phone, Judge Alvarez informed me of his links with the United Bank. He noted he had been thinking of disclosing them from virtually the time he had been assigned the case. On this basis, on November 12, I moved that Judge Alvarez recuse himself.

Most judges try to be fair. They realize their immense powers and rarely attempt to do or say anything which would taint the fairness of a trial or lead to a reversal on appeal. While Judge Alvarez had candidly and honestly disclosed his ties with the bank and insisted that they would not influence his rulings in court, he knew that the very fact that he had these ties might tarnish the proceedings. "It is clear that the judge should not remain when there is any appearance of impropriety," he conceded. Consequently, he stepped aside on November 14.

By lottery, the case was next assigned to the chief judge of the Denver District Court, Robert P. Fullerton. He, however, had a full docket, including two impending murder trials. On November 18, he therefore passed the King case on to the next judge in the rotation, Richard T. Spriggs.

A former deputy district attorney, the 57-year-old Judge Spriggs had grown up in Rome, New York, received a bachelor's degree in English literature, served as a paratrooper, and earned his law degree from Cornell University in 1961. Shortly thereafter, he came to Colorado where he was admitted to the Centennial State's bar. Besides serving in the district attorney's office, Mr. Spriggs had worked as an Assistant United States Attorney, Assistant Colorado Attorney General, and had briefly left Denver to serve as a prosecutor for the federal Organized Crime Strike Force in Philadelphia in the late 1960s.

As a deputy district attorney, Mr. Spriggs had specialized in fighting white-collar crime. Through the 1970s, he was a close friend of District Attorney Dale Tooley. In 1983, Mr. Spriggs had been the chief rival of Norm Early to be named district attorney when a vacancy occurred in that office upon Mr. Tooley's resignation. When he was away from the courtroom, the judge relaxed as a fly fisherman.

Judge Spriggs had already been marginally involved in the King case when he denied my appeal of Judge Bohning's order permitting the release of the warrants and affidavits. Judge Spriggs and I had many interesting encounters while he had been a prosecutor. Foremost of them was the case of Franke E. "Kiko" Martinez.

Kiko, as we all called the defendant, was a young, socially conscious attorney from southwestern Colorado whom the authorities claimed had sent three politically ominous mail bombs to opponents of Chicano liberation in October 1973. An incredible wave of prejudicial publicity labeled Kiko Denver's mad bomber. Fearing that a fair trial was impossible and that the system was out to get him, Martinez fled into exile in Mexico. He remained out of

Photo by Phil Goodstein

The Honorable Richard T. Spriggs

sight until he was arrested trying to re-enter the United States at Nogales, Arizona, in September 1980.

The Chicano activist faced both state and federal charges. During a federal trial on one of the letter bombs, held in Pueblo, Colorado, in late January 1981, the Chief Judge for the District of Colorado, the Honorable Fred Winner, conspired to obstruct justice when he held secret meetings with the Assistant United States Attorneys trying the case. His goal was to force a mistrial so that the prosecution, having learned the defense's strategy, evidence, and the character of its witnesses, would be better prepared for the retrial. Eventually this was exposed. So was the fact that the police destroyed evidence of one of the letter bombs which might have exonerated Kiko. In light of this, Deputy District Attorney Spriggs, who was prosecuting Kiko on the state charges, dropped the Colorado case against Martinez. The federal prosecutors, though, were not about to quit. They vindictively pursued Kiko for years. Not until April 6, 1989, after he was acquitted and cleared of all federal and state charges, was he was readmitted to the bar.

Deputy District Attorney Spriggs and I also previously clashed in the trial of members of Motion Picture Machine Operators Union No. 230. From about September 1977 until January 1978, a number of non-union movie theaters were vandalized, fire bombed, or bombs were discovered on their premises in Denver, Greeley, Fort Collins, and Loveland, Colorado. The obvious suspects were members of the Motion Picture Machine Operators Union. It was an old craft union which protected its members' professionalism at theaters. The projectionist's job was not only to show the pictures, but also to splice damaged films, open and close the curtains, and ensure that patrons received the best image of the show. By the late 1970s, new devices were increasingly making the jobs of the skilled union members obsolete. Management continually attempted to cut corners and save costs by displacing members of the Motion Picture Machine Operators Union. It was alleged that some workers sought to protect their jobs by sabotage.

Jim King's letter of application to work as a part-time guard at the United Bank.

As the theater attacks continued, the police turned their attention to John William Ford III. He had a long criminal record and had twice been fired from local cinemas. On the side, he had worked as a stripper at a gay nightclub. Ford also sought to be a tough guy and was prone to violence. When he appeared to be definitely involved in the bombings, he was given immunity from prosecution in exchange for his testimony before a grand jury. Based on Ford's confession that he had planted a number of bombs and vandalized theaters at the behest of leaders of the Motion Picture Machine Operators Union, the grand jury handed down an eleven-count indictment against seven union members on March 30, 1978.

District Attorney Spriggs prosecuted the case before the Honorable Henry Santo, a judge who always gave me a very rough time. The trial against four defendants was held in February 1979. In the interim, one of the defendants pleaded guilty to reduced charges. Another, who had actually joined with Ford in criminal actions, committed suicide. The trial against the seventh defendant was severed and slated to be held in March.

The prosecution's case depended on the testimony of the colorful John William Ford. Over the years, he had had many run-ins with the police. He also trumpeted his skills in martial arts, knowledge of explosives, and ways to wreak havoc. I focused on them when I cross-examined him.

Ford readily admitted that he did not have the best reputation for veracity. He had repeatedly lied in court in the past. Yes, he agreed, he would lie again to stay out of jail. Similarly, he confessed that he was a thief. At various times he had stolen from his mother and had stolen a camper in Nevada. That was only the beginning.

Playing on Ford's vanity, I asked him about his prowess in the martial arts. He boasted he had a black belt in karate. He took great pride in his skill with numchuks. These are hand-to-hand combat weapons which consist of two short hardwood sticks combined by a chain. At first glance, it is hard to see how they are a weapon, but they are deadly in the hands of a skilled user. I had the witness demonstrate why black belts love the tool.

With the numchuks in his hand, Ford became a man possessed. Standing in the witness box, he was shouting and threatening as he waved the numchuks. Each time he swung them, I stepped back,

OFFICIAL COMMENDATION.

TO   Office of the Chief of Police

Date ___May 25, 1973___

FROM: _TRAFFIC OPERATIONS_____
          Division – District – Bureau

I wish to commend Officer ___James W. King___ , Serial No. ___61-45___ ,
who is presently assigned to ___Parking and Point Control___
for the following:

     ☒ Outstanding Police Action   ☐ Act Beyond the Call of Duty
     ☐ Unusual Bravery   ☐ Unusual Attention to Duty
     ☐ Citizen Praise or Compliment   ☐ Other Meritorious Act

WHEREAS it is realized that the great bulk of police work is done routinely by good policemen,
let it be known that the above-named officer displayed initiative and alertness decidedly in excess
of the norm in this particular instance.

Fact Situation: ___On April 2, 1973 Officer King while employed off-duty at the___
___Bank of Denver, observed one Jerome Paul Koppi in the act of robbing the bank.___
___Officer King immediately apprehended the suspect. The quick, decisive and___
___efficient manner in which the arrest was effected not only caused no injuries___
___to bank personnel or customers, no momentary loss to the bank, but resulted___
___in the suspect being convicted in U.S. District Court.___
___Louis A. Giovanetti, Special Agent in charge Federal Bureau of Investigation___
___in a letter to Chief A. Dill, credits the conviction and sentencing to 15 years___
___of the suspect to the quick and efficient manner in which Officer King conducted___

Commending Officer _____ 52-16

Command Officer's Approval _____ 47-43

Read and Approved _____
                              Division Chief
        Arthur H. Dill
                              Chief of Police

The commendation awarded to Jim King for stopping a bank robbery in 1973.

ducking behind the lectern. The jury could easily see how dangerous the witness and his weapon were.

Martial arts were not the witness's only specialty. He also noted that he could easily bleed at his gums. I asked him to demonstrate. Suddenly, his mouth was foaming with blood. When he put a handkerchief to his mouth, it was immediately thoroughly soaked with blood. Ford admitted that this was a carnival trick, one which he had used over the years to terrify adversaries. The informant's demonstration shocked and nauseated the jury.

Ford further claimed a mastery of yoga and an ability to meditate. More than that, he could communicate with the dead and said that his grandfather occasionally levitated. Jurors and spectators were smirking, smiling, and snickering at his outrageous assertions.

Upon the conclusion of Ford's testimony, I moved for a dismissal of the charges. Judge Santo took it under advisement while he granted a verdict of acquittal for one of the defendants. Meanwhile, Mr. Spriggs, seeking to bolster Ford's veracity, called Ford's girlfriend, Luann Price. She was supposed to prove his assertions. However, when asked for specifics, she continually replied "I don't remember." Consequently, when she left the stand, I renewed the motion for an acquittal.

This time Judge Santo was fully receptive. Ruling that Ford was "a liar, perjurer, thief, and criminal," who readily admitted that he would lie to stay out of jail, the judge concluded that Ford's testimony was inherently unbelievable. But without Ford's testimony, the prosecution had no case. Therefore, all charges against the defendants were dismissed.

I recalled this and other cases we had tried when I learned that Judge Spriggs would preside at the King trial. This was my first case before him since he had been named to the bench in 1988. Though I knew he had an innate decency and fairness, I still feared that, as a former district attorney, he would tend to side with the prosecution. I discovered that while Judge Spriggs was occasionally apt to yell at me and sometimes appeared to be quite crabby, I knew he could be counted upon to conduct a fair and orderly trial.

Pretrial Rulings

Having a good judge is vital. Prior to the trial, there are numerous hearings and motions. Lawyers cannot arbitrarily call any witnesses they wish, introduce evidence, or employ legal strategies at the spur of a moment. Rules require that they must inform the court and opposing counsel of any witnesses they plan to call. It is up to the judge to determine if various defenses can be employed, and whether certain expert witnesses can testify. Most of all, the judge decides what evidence is admissible, whereby he establishes the essential framework of the trial.

King was formally arraigned before Judge Spriggs on November 25. The defendant pleaded not guilty and the trial was scheduled to begin on May 11. Judge Spriggs ordered the prosecution to inform the court within ten days as to whether it would seek the death penalty. The prosecution was also instructed to give the court a detailed list of witnesses it planned to call. We, in turn, were ordered to inform the court by December 20 about what witnesses we planned to call and whether we would employ what is known as an affirmative defense in claiming that King had an alibi.

We filed such a pleading: King could not have killed the guards because he was either at the Capitol Hill Community Center, or on his way home, at the time the crime was committed. The prosecutors sought to taint the defense with the use of the alibi. But "alibi" in the courts is a simple descriptive term to note that the defendant could not have committed the crime because he was elsewhere when the offense occurred. The prosecution must disprove this defense beyond a reasonable doubt.

Finally, Judge Spriggs' ruling of November 25 ordered that the media were not to intervene in the pleadings of the case. He limited all briefs to a maximum of ten pages. This was only the beginning.

In the months leading to the trial, Judge Spriggs was continually dealing with evidentiary questions. For example, he granted my motion to quash the testimony of Frank Gentry of Burlington, North Carolina. This was another example of the prosecution's attempt to convict King by using highly speculative and remote evidence where its prejudicial impact far outweighed its relevancy.

Gentry attended military police school with King at Fort Gordon, Georgia, in 1954. The two men subsequently served together as MPs at Camp Kilmer, New Jersey, and Siegelsbach, Germany. Gentry told the authorities that King had had an obsession with bank robberies. He had discussed bank robberies as if they were his favorite hobby. King had neither actually proposed robbing a bank nor attempted to do so, but, as a military policeman, King had abstractly speculated on the matter. At the most, Gentry had dismissed King's talk of bank robberies as a sign of King's immaturity. Now, however, the prosecution sought to allow Gentry to be called as a witness to prove King's 37-year-long premeditation. I argued that this had absolutely no relevance to the doings of King on Father's Day 1991. Judge Spriggs agreed, and Gentry disappeared from the case.

I also persuaded Judge Spriggs to suppress as evidence the bogus ID cards found in King's safe-deposit box. There was nothing in the search warrant that stated the authorities were looking for them.

Judge Spriggs presides as I ponder a point in court

Nor did the ID cards prove very much. There was no indication that King had ever tried using them or passed himself off to the world as anybody but James William King. The cards were nothing more than his dabbling about during a few spare moments when he was on the ID bureau. Nothing connected them to the bank robbery.

Judge Spriggs likewise prohibited the prosecution from introducing any evidence that King was in anyway involved with the theft from the automated teller at the United Bank on Memorial Day weekend 1990. King had never been accused of this crime and there was no evidence against him. The police, for instance, showed King's photo to the witness who had claimed to have seen Paul Yocum exiting from the room next to the automated teller machines. But that individual was unable to identify King. Any mention of the automated teller heist would be nothing more than an improper tactic by the prosecution in its effort to taint King through guilt by mere association with prior crimes.

I also moved that King's statements to the police on July 2 and July 3 be suppressed for use as evidence. July 2 was the day when, after the police and FBI approached him, King initially stated that he did not wish to speak with them without an attorney present.

Only after the law enforcement officials had assured him that he was *not* a suspect, and that they urgently needed his help as an ex-police officer and bank guard, did he talk to them. All the while, the police well knew King was a suspect. The affidavits for the search and arrest warrants specifically relied on King's statement of July 2. By telling him he was not a suspect so that he would possibly implicate himself, the authorities had violated King's constitutional right against self-incrimination.

This question and other matters of procedure and evidence were the subject of a three-day motions hearing before Judge Spriggs on March 3-5, 1992. I particularly used it to attack the Achilles' heel of the prosecution's case—the tainted eyewitness identifications. I hoped to get the court to suppress them. No fair live lineup had been made. On the contrary, in a number of photo lineups, the eyewitnesses had made vastly different statements. Therefore, far from being conclusive evidence that King was the robber, the unreasonably suggestive way the tellers were induced to identify King was so improper and poisoned that the eyewitness identifications should not be allowed in court.

As the party moving to suppress the evidence, we had to go first, calling the eyewitnesses to impeach the dubious nature of their identifications of King. This again gave me a chance to review the demeanor and stories of all six of the bank vault employees under oath in a court setting. I questioned them closely, comparing their answers with past statements to the police and courts.

I did not want to hurt or embarrass these victims of the crime. The point was to make sure their testimony accurately reflected their memories of the robbery. The victims get no revenge and justice is not served by the conviction of an innocent defendant.

Police officers and FBI agents were subpoenaed to testify about the various statements the tellers had made prior to the July 3-5 identifications of King. Even if the authorities had not done anything improper in obtaining the identifications of King, the defense's goal was to show that the eyewitnesses' initial identifications of King were so nebulous as to be meaningless. Therefore, the robbed tellers should not to be allowed to testify at the trial.

When I sought to establish the above, the question of King's voice came up once more. When the issue of King's voice was raised at the preliminary hearing, Mr. Sims promised he would bring it up at the appropriate time. Now, he claimed, a statement made during the preliminary hearing showed that eyewitness Kenetha Whisler could recognize King by his voice. I also moved to suppress this so-called evidence.

During her redirect examination at the preliminary hearing, Whisler mentioned something that surprised me. I had turned to one of my cohorts at the defense table and whispered "Where did that come from?" Whisler claimed to have heard this, insisting that it was King who had said "Where did that come from?" to me while we huddled at the defense table. She recalled that King was quite animated at the time. He had sat impassively during most of her testimony. But as soon as she heard "Where did that come from?" she was sure the voice was identical with that of the robber. To rebut her assertion, I called other people who had been at the defense table and the court reporter to note that there was no record of such a statement being made by King at the preliminary hearing.

The trial by innuendo of the district attorney's office was also apparent during the evidentiary hearing. Mr. Buckley insisted that

Shoeprints were found on the cardboard in the domestic water room in the subbasement comparable to those discovered near William McCullom's body.

King's statements to the police on July 2 and 3 were essential to the case. After all, during one of them King had noted how guards would be called to let unidentified people into secured areas. "You wouldn't know if it were a vice president or a secretary," King told the investigators on July 2.

This, according to Mr. Buckley, showed King's criminal mind. The name the intruder used to get the guard to come to the elevator was that of Bob Bardwell, a bank vice president. By mentioning that a vice president might ring for admission, King obviously knew that the robber used the vice president's name. That showed he must have committed the crimes. During his rebuttal argument at the preliminary hearing, Mr. Buckley had so focused on this fact that it sounded as if Bardwell was the only vice president of the bank. Therefore, King's mention that a vice president might ring for admission was unquestioned proof of his guilt.

This was absurd. We obtained a list of the vice presidents of the bank. The document was more than a page long, showing upwards of a hundred vice presidents. All King was noting was the poor security at the bank. Because he said the same thing that other guards did, the prosecution was accusing him of responsibility for the Father's Day Massacre. This evidence should obviously be quashed.

Judge Spriggs, however, ruled against us. He agreed that the eyewitness identifications were weak, but they had not been deliberately tainted. It was not for him, but for a jury to decide the truthfulness of their statements. The jury was also called upon to determine whether Whisler had heard King's voice at the preliminary hearing.

The judge further ruled that, since King was a former police officer who had previously consulted with an attorney, the defendant knew what he was doing when he continued to discuss the case with the police. This was crystal clear because King had first told them that I had advised him not to speak with the authorities without the presence of a lawyer. King was not in custody during these conversations and there was no evidence that his remarks were coerced. The police also had the right to use strategic deception in getting suspects to talk. Again, it was up to the jury to determine if there was anything inculpating him in something like his statement about the vice presidents of the bank.

Finally, Judge Spriggs ruled against my motion for a change of venue. I had filed it, fearing that the massive prejudicial publicity made it impossible to get an unbiased jury pool. But Judge Spriggs was not sure of this point. Not until we actually got to jury selection, he observed, would we be able to get a feel of how much the publicity had impacted the members of the community called for jury duty. Besides, from past experience, Judge Spriggs noted that changing venue was often more trouble than it was worth. In many ways, I agreed with Judge Spriggs. The hysterical publicity against King had been so great that it had permeated all corners of Colorado. I had only asked for the change of venue for the record so that I could point to it on appeal if I indeed found it was impossible to get a fair jury.

Additional motions were made prior to the trial. In early April, Judge Spriggs permitted me to call a witness at the trial who was an expert on the problems of eyewitness identification. That was crucial because without the fuzzy eyewitness identifications of King, the prosecution had no case. I wanted to be able to rebut the tellers' testimony by showing that sometimes eyewitness identification is unreliable. The judge further granted my motion that I could point to other suspects in the robbery as part of the defense.

Alternate Suspects

A defense attorney is rarely Perry Mason. His job is to defend his client, not to solve the crime or do the work of the police in finding the murderer. The rule of the court is that a defendant is innocent until he is found guilty by evidence presented to convict him of the crime beyond a reasonable doubt. The law does not state that the defense lawyer must show who committed the crime if reasonable doubt exists about his client's guilt.

Still, by pointing to alternate suspects, I wanted to show the jury that, comparatively, there was more evidence against other men than the defendant. Take, for example, former bank guard Paul Yocum. He had vowed his revenge against the United Bank after his acquittal of the charge he had stolen money from the automated teller. With his obvious animus and his storehouse of weapons, he was a most plausible suspect. This did not mean that he was guilty, but given the meager evidence against King, Yocum could just as easily have been charged with the murders as King.

The same was true of Harry Glass, the former guard whose fingerprint had been found on the Mountain Dew can propping open what should have been a locked door. He had no supportable alibi for where he was during the robbery and had quit the day after the murders.

In December 1991, I learned about 38-year-old Dewey Calvin Baker. His uncle described Baker as "bad news." A man with a large mole on his left cheek, he had worn a mustache for years. The mole was situated right about the spot where the eyewitnesses claimed that the intruder had worn an adhesive strip. On May 2, 1991, about six weeks before the Father's Day Massacre, Baker had been paroled from a federal prison in Wisconsin where he had been serving time for four over-the-counter bank robberies. The suspect had shaved off his mustache in the early fall of 1991, shortly before he was arrested in California on four counts of bank robbery and one count of the aggravated robbery of a post office. Baker was incarcerated as a federal prisoner in the Santa Clara County Jail in northern California when I learned that he was hinting that he had committed the Father's Day Massacre.

Baker had been in Denver in May 1991. Phone records showed that he had called both the Colorado State Penitentiary and the Colorado State Reformatory from Denver. He had further visited an ex-convict in Pueblo from whom he had stolen a .22 revolver. He stated he had tried to enlist that man in a robbery in Denver, but something had gone wrong.

My investigators were not exactly sure of Baker's location in June, but the convict resembled the physical description of the robber and the man who had been reported trying to rent a car at the city's soon-to-be closed Stapleton Airport on Father's Day. The police and FBI claimed to be fully aware of Baker. They had investigated him, clearing him of the Father's Day Massacre.

At first, Baker only hinted at a connection with the crimes. He stated that he hoped that "they" did not try to pin the Denver job on him. But he implied that he had been involved in "dusting" four bank guards. Obviously, his involvement in the case needed to be probed further.

Convicts have a notorious reputation for boasting of their dirty deeds and can rarely be trusted in a case like this. Baker stated that

Dewey Baker

he figured he would likely spend the rest of his life in prison and had
little to lose by the confession. The physical evidence against Baker
was just as strong as it was against King. Had the bank employees
been previously shown a photo of him, rather than King, they might
well have identified Baker as the robber.

To counteract all the negative publicity against King, I told the
media about Baker. I hoped to point out the incriminating evidence
against Yocum, Glass, and Baker to the jury. In this manner, I would
show how speculative the prosecution's case was against King.

The Death Penalty

By the time that Judge Spriggs permitted me to employ the
defense of alternate suspects, the case was literally a matter of life
and death. From the time of King's arrest, the district attorney's
office demanded capital punishment. Despite the recent Colorado
Supreme Court decision striking down the state's amended death
penalty, on December 4, District Attorney Norm Early personally
signed the motion stating that the prosecution would request the
death penalty should King be convicted of first-degree murder. I
immediately denounced this move.

There is no evidence that the death penalty has any impact in reducing crime or making society a safer, more civilized place. States which do not have the death penalty have a lower murder rate than those where the death penalty is the ultimate punishment. Nor is the death penalty equally enforced. Invariably, the poor and members of minority groups are the only people who are executed. The death penalty is a legacy of wars, colonialism, slavery, racism, and the class bias of the courts. Worst of all, mistakes are frequently made in capital cases.

Nonetheless, something about this barbaric, immoral punishment which has a morbid attraction for certain people: a belief that if criminals are murdered by the state, their deaths will atone for or revenge other murders. Calling for the death penalty also heightens the stakes in a case and increases the media sensationalism.

Not only pervasive, violence sells. It is exploited by Hollywood directors to pace movies. Vicious hits are celebrated in sports. Often homes are battlefields with battered spouses and children. Veterans, who have been taught to kill, are frequently violent to their loved ones. Far from condemning such crude physical force, the death penalty affirms that violence is at the heart of the state.

Despite defending more than 100 defendants facing murder charges, I have never had a death conviction against any of my clients during my 41 years as a lawyer. Indeed, only two of my clients have ever been found guilty of first-degree murder. In one case, the defendant killed another person in a bar during a robbery and was subdued by irate patrons. (He escaped from the penitentiary one and a half years later, never to be found.) In the other, the accused was a battered woman who, in a state of desperation, killed her husband while he was sleeping after he had repeatedly raped and beaten her during their three-year marriage. She then faked a burglary of their residence while she celebrated her tormentor's death by going out with her sister to a dance hall.

Despite my claim that the death penalty was inapplicable in this case, at a December 23 hearing, Judge Spriggs granted the prosecution's motion that it could ask for death should King be convicted. I immediately appealed to the Colorado Supreme Court, noting that the effort to invoke the death penalty was actually ex post facto legislation. The court refused to hear my appeal in January. This meant King's life would be on the line.

Father Jim Sunderland led the Colorado Coalition against the Death Penalty. He advised me on how to fight that punishment while he visited King in jail where he was the Catholic chaplain.

One break I got shortly before the trial was when Judge Spriggs dismissed the menacing counts against King on April 30, 1992. These stemmed from the allegation that the robber had pointed a gun at the six people in the cash vault. The district attorney had added them to the charges of murder and robbery. Since nothing was to be gained by including them in the trial, they were dropped.

Meanwhile, the unending prejudicial publicity against King continued. Among those aiding it were the so-called victim advocates. These are employees of the district attorney's office who are assigned to assist those who have been the victims of crimes and their families overcome the trauma of the felonies. Far from acting as independent counselors who help the victims understand the full workings of the criminal justice system, the victim advocates can be shills for the prosecution. Often they sit near the district attorney's table at hearings and seemingly share inside information with the victims. On occasion, they have interfered with my witnesses and have testified against my clients. Their entire operation implies that the accused is automatically guilty. This can seem to mean that helping the victims demands the conviction of the defendant regardless of evidence.

Pictures of the families of the slain guards were frequently shown and family members interviewed throughout the case. The obvious message was that a conviction was necessary to appease the furies of the survivors. At times, it even appeared that the media wanted to turn the King case into an inflammatory circus. Toward this end, the Colorado Broadcasters Association moved that live television coverage be allowed in the courtroom.

I opposed this move. This trial was literally a matter of life and death. It was not something to be trivialized as a commercial opportunity whereby testimony would be interspersed with advertisements for kitchen gadgets, fat reducing techniques, and old westerns. Besides, I feared that expanded media coverage would mean further echoing of prosecution slanders and innuendoes against my client.

During broadcasts of and about trials, so-called experts—academic law professors and media attorneys who have never tried an important case—pontificate on court tactics and clever common strategies. Their comments, along with the atmosphere of a media circus, would naturally prejudice jurors and potential jurors. Even worse, in case of a mistrial, they would have so biased the community that a fair trial would be virtually impossible.

Again, Judge Spriggs ruled against me. While he ordered that no pictures were to be published or broadcast of the jurors or the eyewitnesses, he otherwise granted expanded media coverage on May 5. Among those picking up on it was Court TV. It announced plans to broadcast the case nationally. In response, to guard the jurors from slanted television exposure and common fare, I asked that the court sequester the jury during the trial. This motion was also denied. With such a deck stacked against me, I knew I faced a tremendous fight when the trial of the People versus James W. King began on Monday, May 11, 1992.

8

Selecting the Jury

The first day of the trial, case 91CR2686, in Courtroom 16 of the Denver City & County Building, was hectic. A pool of 236 people had been called from which we were to select the jury. Not all those called for jury duty, much less members of the media and spectators, could fit into the courtroom. Judge Spriggs had already had a bad day, a pigeon having soiled his jacket. Nor was he used to Courtroom 16 since he usually presided in Courtroom 11. (His regular courtroom was not large enough to accommodate all who were interested in the trial.) To make matters worse, the air conditioning broke down in the packed courtroom. The computer used to generate juror lists similarly went on the blink. With the potential jurors standing in the aisles and sitting on the floor, the court moved the first session of the trial to the more commodious city council chambers.

Judge Spriggs was blunt about the jury's role. "This is a very serious case, a very important case," he informed the men and women who would sit in judgment of the former police sergeant. "Jury service of any kind is work. Jury service in a murder case is hard work. Jury service in a death penalty case is very hard work."

The judge conceded that not all on the panel were happy to have been called for jury duty. "Getting a summons for jury service is like being hit by a freight train." Many naturally sought to be dismissed from the panel. During the first day, for example, about

25 potential jurors were excused for assorted reasons including health problems, travel plans, or some connection with the legal establishment. To assure the convenience of the jurors, Judge Spriggs banned cameras from the hallways surrounding the courtroom. He feared that otherwise the media sensationalism about the case would turn into "a bunch of lunacy."

Otherwise, the expanded media coverage proceeded apace. Local lawyers were hired as expert commentators. Some even traveled to New York to be guests on Court TV. That network tended to cover the case like a football game where the announcer sometimes interrupted the testimony to explain what he thought was happening. The result was to give viewers a disjointed feel for what was actually occurring in the courtroom.

The Conscience of the Community

Selecting the jury is the most important part of a trial. A jury trial is the quintessence of democracy. It is a living example of participatory democracy—the jury is the most democratic institution in America. On a jury, ordinary, everyday citizens are called upon to help decide the destiny of their fellows, making life and death decisions that shape the fabric of the community. The jury serves as a buffer for the accused from the state and prosecution. To ensure that it fulfills this role, a jury of one's peers must be drawn from a panel of people from all racial, cultural, and class backgrounds.

One of my early appellate victories was *Montoya v. Colorado*, 345 P.2d 1062. The Colorado Supreme Court ruled, in November 1959, that jury pools must be selected from the whole of the community as opposed to efforts to systematically exclude people with Spanish surnames from jury lists. In this manner, I helped democratize the jury system.

The only case I have ever argued before the United States Supreme Court is *Test v. United States*, 420 US 28. On January 27, 1975, the Court upheld my contention that an attorney has the right to inspect the jury list to see that it is a true, mirrored cross section of the citizenry. This is vital to assure that anyone—black, Hispanic, or white—is judged by a jury selected from the whole of the community, not a selected group of white property owners.

Photo by Phil Goodstein

The trial of Jim King was held in Courtroom 16 on the top floor on the right hand side of the Denver City & County Building.

Historically, jury lists were manipulated. Sometimes senior citizens, who knew the jury commissioner, would be permanently placed on jury lists. These retired individuals looked forward to court service, while the jury pay supplemented their income. Other times, repeat jurors would be big property owners or prominent, conservative businessmen. The prosecution liked these repeat jurors since it knew they generally sided with the state.

It is not simply the nit-picking and hairsplitting of an attorney which insists on a representative jury list. The jury is the linchpin of fair trials. Time and again, since the first Anglo-Saxon juries appeared a millennium ago, governments have sought to use the courts to jail or kill their opponents. The jury system is based on the principle that the population stands above and beyond the powers of the state. The jury is the bulwark of the people against the executive and legislative branches. The jury system assures that before the government can deprive an individual of life, liberty, or property, it must be able to convince a jury of the defendant's peers that the accused is, beyond a reasonable doubt, guilty of the crime with which he is charged.

Some do not like the jury system because juries are notoriously independent. In the courtroom, the judge is in complete command. By a wink, nod of his head, or tone of his voice, he can indicate what he thinks about the entire proceeding. The judge can limit the scope of testimony, cut off witnesses, and keep out or admit evidence. This is seldom a question of the personalities of diverse judges, but of the nature of the system. Judges, by virtue of their backgrounds, class standing, education, ideology, and the way in which they come to be judges, tend to be part and parcel of the status quo. As employees of the state, consciously or unconsciously, they see the role of the courts is to uphold and defend the establishment.

As distinguished from judges, jurors are everyday citizens. Members of juries take their responsibilities quite seriously. The members of a 12-person jury will usually represent the collective wisdom and experience of 500 years. I would guess that the jury makes the right decision 90 percent of the time. The lawyer must focus his courtroom tactics on the jury. It is his main audience. His every action is geared toward it so that it will find in favor of his client.

At the conclusion of testimony, the judge delivers his charge to the jury. He informs it of the nature of the evidence and the law, giving the jury specific instructions as to what verdicts it may reach. The judge can do almost anything in conducting the trial and spelling out his instructions except tell the jury what verdict it must reach. That is why the authoritarian-minded personality so hates juries—these randomly selected democratic bodies are apt to believe their fellow citizens over district attorneys, the government, and reporters who usually faithfully echo the assertions of the police and prosecution.

Since the decision of the jury will determine the defendant's fate, the attorney must be most careful about who is on the final panel. The potential jurors, the venire, are drawn from the master jury wheel by lot. Once in the courtroom, the judge briefly informs them of the nature of the case and introduces the attorneys and the defendant. If a potential juror knows any of the people involved in the case, including possible witnesses, he is usually automatically excused from the panel.

Voir Dire

Voir dire follows. Voir dire is a medieval French term literally meaning "to say the truth." This is where the judge and the attorneys question prospective jurors. Not only do I try to learn about the potential jurors during voir dire, but I also use it to educate the panel about the nature of due process and the presumption of innocence. Though I might ask only one member a specific question, I try to observe how others in the venire react to it. For example, I will inquire if a prospective juror agrees that it is absolutely necessary that the state prove its case beyond a reasonable doubt lest we teeter on the verge of a dictatorship. Time and again, I remind the men and women who have been randomly selected to judge my client, that the jury system is our safeguard against despotism. I try to get them to agree that the jury is vitally necessary, that this cross section of humanity is the best body to decide the fate of any human being.

When I speak to continuing legal education classes or write for law periodicals and books, I always discuss the Big Four of due process. These are the points I attempt to get across to the jury during voir dire. Number one is that the defendant is presumed to be not guilty. Second, the burden of proof is on the prosecution and never shifts to the defense. Third, the prosecution must prove the defendant's guilt beyond a reasonable doubt. Finally, the defendant need not testify or present any evidence.

Sometimes, I expand this to the Big Five. I do so, as in this case, if I should employ what is called an affirmative defense. This is where I show that the defendant was misidentified, acted in self-defense, was insane or the victim of disease, the crime was caused by an accident, or the defendant was justified in breaking the law. The prosecution must *disprove* such a defense beyond a reasonable doubt.

There is a good deal of theater in court. A trial is a morality play acted out in the Temple of Justice. From the start, the prosecutor seeks to depict the defendant as a villain, an immoral creature who is already guilty. The defense counsel must sell the jury panel the Big Five. Specifically, he must get across to the men and women who are to judge his client that the presumption of innocence and the burden of the prosecution presenting evidence beyond a reasonable doubt against the defendant are *not just jingles*. They are vital to

PEOPLE v. JAMES WILLIAM KING - - VENUE / TELE SURVEY MAR 1992

QUESTIONS

INTRODUCTION: Hello, my name is _____. I am conducting a
                    survey on a Denver District Court case.

(Proceed immediately to question #1 - - no hesitation.)

QUESTION #1:   ARE YOU OVER 18 YEARS OLD AND A RESIDENT OF THE CITY AND COUNTY OF
                    DENVER?

127   74.27%   Yes - - proceed to question #2
 44   25.73%   No - - discontinue survey
171 100.00%   ? - - discontinue survey

QUESTION #2   DO YOU KNOW ABOUT THE CASE WHERE JAMES WILLIAM KING IS CHARGED WITH
                    THE JUNE 16TH, 1991, FATHER'S DAY MURDER/ROBBERY OF THE UNITED BANK OF
                    DENVER?

100   70.74%   Yes - - proceed to question #3
 27   21.26%   No - - discontinue survey
127 100.00%   ? - - discontinue survey

QUESTION #3   BASED MERELY ON WHAT YOU HAVE READ OR HEARD ABOUT THIS CASE, DO YOU
                    FEEL AT THIS MOMENT THAT THE EVIDENCE AGAINST JAMES WILLIAM KING IS:

 21   21.00%   (A)   STRONG
  5   5.00%   (B)   VERY STRONG
 20   20.00%   (C)   WEAK
  2   2.00%   (D)   VERY WEAK
                    ----
 52   52.00%   (E)   DON'T KNOW (do not volunteer this answer)
100 100.00%   --
                    Continue to question #4

QUESTION #4   BASED MERELY ON WHAT YOU HAVE READ OR HEARD, IS IT YOUR IMPRESSION
                    THAT JAMES WILLIAM KING IS:

 33   33.00%   (A)   PROBABLY GUILTY
  4   4.00%   (B)   CERTAINLY GUILTY
 15   15.00%   (C)   PROBABLY NOT GUILTY
  4   4.00%   (D)   CERTAINLY NOT GUILTY
                    ----
 44   44.00%   (E)   DON'T KNOW (do not volunteer this answer)
100 100.00%   --
                    Continue to question #5

QUESTION #5   BASED MERELY ON YOUR DISCUSSIONS WITH OTHER PEOPLE IN THE CITY AND
                    COUNTY OF DENVER, DO YOU BELIEVE OTHER PEOPLE'S OPINIONS ARE:

 42   42.00%   (A)   VERY TYPICAL OF YOUR OPINION
 14   14.00%   (B)   NOT VERY TYPICAL OF YOUR OPINION
                    ----
 44   44.00%   (C)   DON'T KNOW (do not volunteer this answer)
100 100.00%   --

END OF SURVEY - - THANK YOU

*The results of a telephone poll I commissioned on public views of the
King case.*

preserve the liberties of all. A defense lawyer must be unrelenting
during voir dire in his efforts to win the jury over to the principles
of the Big Five.

Obviously, we could not thoroughly question one by one each of
the 236 potential jurors in the King case. The venire were asked to

fill in questionnaires, giving basic information about themselves: Where were they born? Where did they work? Were they home-owners or renters? Did they have children? What did they know about the case? Did they know anybody who worked in law enforcement? Anybody at the United Bank? Had they ever done business with the bank?

Prior to the trial, I had submitted a 12-page-long draft question-naire. Judge Spriggs only adopted a superficial, two-and-a-half page questionnaire that had 28 queries. It asked about the educa-tion, homes, and families of the potential jurors. They were also quizzed if they had ever previously been the victim of a crime, testified in court, or had served on a jury.

By reviewing these questionnaires, I could at least get a slight feel for the people who would be sitting in judgment of Jim King. I was also encouraged by a telephone poll I had taken on the subject: nearly half of those asked whether they thought King was guilty replied that they did not believe King guilty or had not formed an opinion about the case.

Death Qualifying the Jury

The most complicated part of selecting a jury in a capital case is what is called "death qualifying" the jurors. Should King be found guilty, the jury would be asked to decide whether he should be sentenced to death. In all other cases, it is up to the judge, not the jury, to impose the sentence. However, since death is the ultimate penalty, for years the jury, as the conscience of the community, was charged with the task of reaching this decision. The jury had to unanimously agree on the death penalty; otherwise, the defendant received a mandatory life sentence.

(In 1995, lamenting that the State of Colorado had not legally murdered anyone since 1967, the legislature removed the death decision from the jury. Hoping to have more executions, the lawmakers gave this power of life and death to a three-member panel of judges. Two of the judges who were to deliberate on the death penalty were to be called in specially for that part of the trial. They were not to have sat in on the guilt-determination phase of the proceeding where the evidence was presented against the defen-dant. Not having heard or seen the witnesses, they could only rely on a review of a cold, dry transcript before listening to the testimony about whether the death penalty should be invoked.)

Since the jury, upon a murder conviction, would be required to decide the question of life and death, only people willing to impose the death penalty could serve. This is an extreme advantage to the prosecution. Usually those who oppose the death penalty are citizens who have questioned the morality of taking one life for another. As such, I want them on my juries since they are people who will carefully sift the evidence. By asking for death, the prosecution assured that these individuals would be dismissed from the King panel. Those who believe that death should be automatic in case of a conviction were also dismissed from the panel.

The death penalty presents the defense with an extra burden during voir dire. Not only does a lawyer need to select persons whom he believes are favorable to his client, but he simultaneously has to reflect upon how these jurors might vote on the question of life and death. Sometimes, consequently, I might elect to keep a person on the panel who has a good profile on the death penalty whom I would challenge if it were not a capital case.

Rather than asking jurors' views on the death penalty in open court, the jurors were divided into groups, members of which were ordered to report to court at a certain time. They were called individually into Judge Spriggs' chambers to discuss their feelings on capital punishment, any qualms they had about serving on the case, and how they had been affected by the prejudicial publicity about King. (No cameras were allowed in chambers and the media were not allowed to publish photos of potential jurors.)

Typical were the views of a potential juror who noted that, as an insurance adjuster, he would weigh the cost-benefit ratio of executing a criminal. Since he was not categorically opposed to the death penalty, he was qualified to serve. The same was true of a college professor who did not think anything would be accomplished by the execution of a convict in his 60s even though she might vote for the death of a younger murderer. The public defender's office, which tries many death penalty cases, greatly assisted me in providing legal research and background materials I could use in formulating my arguments against the death penalty, helping me sharpen my questions on this matter.

David Wymore, a Colorado public defender specializing in death penalty cases, has developed a rating system, increasingly used nationally, between one and six to evaluate potential jurors' views on the death penalty. A one is categorical opposition to it. A six is an individual who advocates its automatic imposition. Defense attorneys usually prefer jurors who rank as twos and threes. Sometimes I might accept a four or five if the member of the venire shows himself to be skeptical of the prosecution's case and is insistent that he will hew the line of demanding evidence beyond a reasonable doubt before voting to find my client guilty.

A Biased Juror?

It took us about a week to question the jurors in chambers on both the death penalty, and how they had been effected by the prejudicial

---

DISTRICT COURT, CITY AND COUNTY OF DENVER, STATE OF COLORADO

Case No. 91CR2686   Courtroom 11

JURY QUESTIONNAIRE

THE PEOPLE OF THE STATE OF COLORADO,

vs .

JAMES WILLIAM KING,

Defendant.

This jury questionnaire is being used to save time in the selection of the jury to try this case. You are to answer the questions truthfully and completely. The questions are designed to obtain information concerning your ability to serve as a juror who can be fair to both sides of this case. Therefore, even though you may feel the questions are personal, you should provide the information requested. You are expected to sign your questionnaire and your answers will have the same effect as a statement given in Court under oath. If there is insufficient space to write your full answer, continue on the back of the sheet.

THE INFORMATION WHICH YOU GIVE IN THIS QUESTIONNAIRE WILL BE USED ONLY BY THE COURT AND THE LAWYERS TO SELECT A QUALIFIED JURY.

ALL COPIES OF THE RESPONSES WILL BE RETAINED BY THE COURT AND KEPT IN CONFIDENCE. THE ATTORNEYS ARE UNDER ORDER OF THIS COURT TO MAINTAIN THE CONFIDENTIALITY OF ANY INFORMATION THEY LEARN IN THE COURSE OF REVIEWING THESE QUESTIONNAIRES.

YOU ARE DIRECTED NOT TO DISCUSS THIS CASE WITH ANY OTHER PROSPECTIVE JUROR OR ANYONE ELSE AND YOU ARE DIRECTED NOT TO LISTEN TO OR READ ANY NEWS ACCOUNTS OF THIS CASE DURING THE JURY SELECTION PROCESS.

BY THE COURT:

_____
Richard T. Spriggs
District Court Judge

The first page of the jury questionnaire.

pretrial publicity. Often, I, the prosecutors, and Judge Spriggs were at dagger's end during these proceedings. From the outset, this was war. My co-counsel, Scott Robinson, and I clashed with Mr. Buckley and Mr. Sims on virtually every point. Judge Spriggs and I quarreled throughout the proceedings. Actions were then taken which determined the shape of the trial.

During the death-qualifying phase of voir dire, I received anonymous phone calls from both a deputy sheriff and the wife of a deputy informing me that a potential juror was greatly prejudiced against King. This member of the venire had been heard to tell her co-workers at an airline kitchen that she was sure King was guilty.

When questioned, however, the potential juror swore that she had an open mind. "I don't believe everything I read in the paper or see on TV. With all the things I've read and heard, I haven't heard enough to make a decision," was her response to my question about whether she had formed an opinion on the case and if the prejudicial media coverage had impacted her ability to be a fair judge of the defendant. She likewise showed herself to be hesitant about imposing the death penalty. Still, I was worried about the allegations concerning her bias.

I reported the calls to the court. In response, the prosecutors promised that they would check on the charges. They arranged to have an investigator go to the potential juror's workplace. The investigator said that the story was merely a rumor that could not be confirmed. On this basis, Judge Spriggs rejected my motion to dismiss the juror for cause. I did not want to spend a peremptory challenge on her. She was selected for the jury—an event that would haunt us until the announcement of the verdict.

This juror illustrated why I was so concerned about how the massive prejudicial publicity about the case had impacted all on the jury panel. I specifically examined the venire about it. What did the potential jurors know about the case? Had they been closely following it in the news? Would they be biased by the previous media reportage? Would they judge the defendant based only on the evidence introduced in court? I also wanted to ask them about Rodney King.

This was one more coincidence in the case. Another man named King, Rodney King, had been viciously beaten by California police

If yes, please state what you have heard and the source of your information. _____

_____

_____

    50. Based on what you have heard or read, have you formed any opinion as to the guilt or innocence of the defendant? _____

    51. Is there any reason why you couldn't be an impartial juror on either side?

_____

_____

ATTITUDES REGARDING DEATH PENALTY

    The Court is asking the following questions regarding your feelings about the death penalty because one of the possible sentences for a person convicted of a First Degree Murder is the death penalty. Therefore, the Court must know whether you could be fair to both the prosecution and the defendant on the issue of punishment. The fact that these questions regarding death penalty are being asked does not mean that you should infer the defendant is guilty of first degree murder.

    52. What are your **general feelings** regarding the death penalty?

    53. What are your feelings on the following specific questions:

        a. Do you feel that the death penalty is used too often? Too seldom? Randomly?

        Please explain: _____

        b. Do you belong to any group(s) that advocate the increased use or the abolition of the death penalty? (Check one)

            Yes _____

            No _____

        i. What group(s)? _____

6

I tried to draw out the views of potential jurors about the death penalty in the draft of the questionnaire I submitted to the court.

officers in 1991. Their brutal deed was captured on videotape. Despite this, shortly before Jim King went on trial, the four accused police officers were acquitted of battering Rodney King. A civil uprising had ensued in Los Angeles in the wake of the verdict where mostly black citizens protested what they perceived to be the biased, racist nature of the police and justice system.

So what did the venire think about this? Would they be extra cautious in acquitting a former police officer since they did not want a repeat of Los Angeles in Denver? Or would they ignore the Rodney King factor in their deliberations? Did they think it might be a telling coincidence that the big-name case in Los Angeles then involved somebody named King, the same way they were to sit in judgment of a defendant named King in Denver?

What made this even more poignant was a further coincidence. Right about the time that we were selecting the jury, there were three absolutely bizarre shootings, one after another, involving local law enforcement personnel. It was also revealed that there was misconduct in the property bureau of the Denver Police Department in dealing with guns. In such circumstances, it was vital that the attorneys be able to sound out any biases the venire might have about past and present police officers. Judge Spriggs, however, refused to allow me to raise this line of inquiry when we questioned the venire in his chambers. Fortunately, as I discovered during the general voir dire, none of the venire thought there was a prejudicial connection between the Jim and Rodney King cases.

The judge also cut me off when I sought to enlighten the potential jurors about the case. I wanted to make sure they fully understood what the death penalty was about and what the prosecution was asking of them. "Mr. Buckley is in love with death," I noted. Judge Spriggs angrily cut me off. "I'm warning you, you are going to play by the rules. If there is any more of it, we are going to have a real problem. Just stick to the script, will you?" he ordered me, ruling that I did not have the right to make sure that the venire knew that it was the prosecution, not the court, which was demanding death. Such exchanges punctuated the whole of the death-qualifying voir dire.

Judge Spriggs has an impatient side. He is constantly after the attorneys to get on with the case and sometimes tries to rush things. During a pretrial hearing on May 5, he had announced that he would personally conduct voir dire on the questions of death, whether potential jurors had been impacted by the prejudicial publicity of the case, and if jury service would impose an extreme hardship on them. I objected. Unlike the lawyers, who had been intently studying the case for months, Judge Spriggs—like all judges— lacked the specific knowledge of certain nuances of the case needed to bring out the quirks and leanings of the venire.

Scott Robinson repeated my objection on May 8, when Judge Spriggs was forced to reconsider the matter. In light of Supreme Court rulings we cited, the judge conceded that counsel had the right to examine the jurors during the death-qualifying phase of voir dire. However, once the actual questioning of the sequestered jurors was underway, Judge Spriggs again announced, two days into voir dire, over my objections, that he would personally question the venire. There is nothing to show that voir dire by the judge expedites a trial in the slightest. Even if it does, that is still no excuse to rush this most vital part of the proceedings.

Judge Spriggs originally only allocated two days for death-qualifying the jurors. He told the media that the jury selection process would not be a "Cecil B. DeMille production." Time and again, he cut me off during voir dire because he was impatient to get on with the trial. "Counsel is asking repetitive, redundant, and sometimes wholly incomprehensible questions," he stated in response to my efforts to get a full grasp of the feelings, prejudices, and inclinations of the potential jurors.

I constantly had the feeling that Judge Spriggs was needlessly trying to cram the proceedings into an arbitrary schedule. With the death penalty looming and battling the prosecution for hours on end, I would sometimes get tense. Once, when I challenged one of Judge Spriggs' rulings, he noted: "Let the record reflect that Mr. Gerash is bellowing." "My client's life is in the balance," was my impassioned rejoinder.

A trial demands the full attention of the lawyer. Not only are you continually in court from about eight to five, but you have to spend additional time preparing for any and all contingencies and double-checking facts, the law, and previous testimony. It was not unusual for Judge Spriggs to expect the attorneys to put in 12-hour days during the trial. Asking for a break, I noted that the pace was getting to me. "The court is rushing to injustice because it's putting pressure on the lawyers. We have to sleep. We have to eat. I'm single now. I have to cook," I informed him. In response to this statement, which was broadcast on national Court TV, I received several proposals of marriage after the trial.

Judge Spriggs' courtroom demeanor led to yet another coincidence in the case. Among his favorite aphorisms when lawyers were clashing before him is that he might consider their point valid "when pigs fly." To accentuate this, he had a picture of a pig with wings which he would flash at the attorneys as a sign that he was frustrated by their behavior.

Right about the time the trial was getting underway, Norwest Banks, which had by then taken over and changed the name of United Banks, launched an advertising campaign featuring a free checking program with the slogan "when pigs fly." Scott Robinson asked that Judge Spriggs ground the flying pigs for the duration of the trial. This was vitally necessary, I added, "especially since some people refer to my client's profession as pigs." The pigs flew away from the case and back into the pigsty.

Other tensions flared during jury selection. For a while, I thought somebody was spying on me at my house. As I backed out of my garage to drive to court on Thursday, May 14, I noticed two men sitting in a parked car near my driveway closely watching me. As I left, the vehicle, which had Washington license plates—I was not sure if it was from Washington, D.C., or from Washington state—suddenly took off. Deputy District Attorney Buckley denied that the police or his office were snooping on me. "For the record, we're not staking out his house," he told the court. Perhaps it was another coincidence, or it might have been what I described as a "normal, healthy burglary." Fortunately, nothing more came of this.

A few days later, however, after testimony had begun, Carol King informed me that her nephew's car had been burglarized. We had asked him to gather photos of Jim King over the years, showing that the defendant had periodically worn and shaved off his mustache. The burglar had not taken any valuables from the nephew's car. But the photo collection was missing. When I informed the court of this, Judge Spriggs made fun of it by stating, "Mr. Buckley, return the photos to Mr. Gerash."

Incidents like this accentuated my belief that I had to be on guard against hidden animosity on the part of potential jurors to King. For example, while I was in Judge Spriggs' chambers during a conference with him and the other attorneys, I learned that a member of the venire had shown his disdain for the defendant by twice wadding up some paper, coming over to the defense table, and tossing the paper into King's water cup. King's wife and sister witnessed this.

Similarly, other factors were present which might bias the jury. Notably, a copy of the composite drawing of the bank robber was posted on a custodian's locker in the basement of the City & County Building near a public cafeteria where potential jurors might go to lunch. King's sister Myra discovered this and called it to my attention. The prosecution claimed no knowledge of it. Judge Spriggs ordered that the drawing be removed.

The United Bank Tower as seen from the City & County Building where Jim King was tried. Shortly before the trial, the financial institution changed its name to Norwest Banks.

By airing our disputes and tensions in Judge Spriggs' chambers during voir dire, he, Scott and I, and the prosecutors reached a mode of understanding. We had vented enough steam at this time and had learned how we all operated whereby we could settle into a somewhat civil relationship for the duration of the trial—it was a triple catharsis.

A Portrait of the Jury

After a week's sequestered examination concerning publicity and the death penalty, 80 potential jurors were selected as death-qualified for the final panel. Both sides were granted a dozen peremptory challenges. On Monday, May 18, we began the next phase of voir dire in open court.

Initially, 38 names were drawn from the 80 potential jurors. In addition to the 12 jurors, there were to be two alternates. Added to the 24 who might be dismissed by the peremptory challenges, this made up the 38 people who were first impaneled. Judge Spriggs limited us to two hours to thoroughly question them. Should a potential juror be dismissed for cause, we only had five more minutes to question his or her replacement.

Mr. Sims was the incarnation of charm and friendliness during his examination of the jurors. He asked them about their favorite television shows, hobbies, and philosophy. Still, he reminded them, "this is deadly serious business." He pleaded that the jurors focus on facts, not external appearances. He used the cliché "don't judge a book by its cover" to establish this point.

I intently probed possible biases of the potential jurors. I wanted to know their thoughts about the criminal justice system. "The issue is identity—whether this man committed these horrible crimes," I told the panel. I especially wanted to establish that it is easy to forget everyday facts and experiences. I brought this out by such questions as which way is Lincoln facing on a penny? Who is the president on a nickel? Which way is he facing? Where is the word "Liberty" on the coin? What are the letters for number two on a phone? For number seven? What color of tie was Mr. Buckley wearing yesterday?

I also like to learn about the personal backgrounds of the people who serve on the jury. This led me to supposedly perform a wedding during voir dire. I was asking a potential juror about his wife. He insisted he was not married, but lived with his girlfriend and the child he had by her. "Then you're married, congratulations!" I responded, noting that he was married under Colorado common law. "Thank you, Reverend Gerash," quipped Judge Spriggs.

Richard Crawford advised me on selecting the jury. He is a jury consultant—there is a whole field of people who specialize in trying to read the traits and personalities of potential jurors. A non-lawyer, Crawford has closely studied the jury system and is the author of an excellent book on it, *The Persuasion Edge*.

I naturally let my personal feelings influence who I select for the jury. In this case, for example, I was drawn to a member of the venire who was from Boston. He had clashed with his parents and had run away from home. Seeking an emancipated lifestyle, the 41-year-old man lived in a bohemian section of Denver. By the time of the trial, he was an unemployed actor and comic who sometimes performed at the Mercury Cafe, the city's distinctive alternative nightclub. He was also something of a baseball freak. He promised he would critically evaluate all the evidence. I was glad that the prosecution did not challenge him whereby he was seated on the jury. My instinct was wrong.

On Tuesday morning, May 19, after being further rushed by Judge Spriggs, we selected a jury of seven men and five women plus two alternates. Scott and I, the prosecutors, and Judge Spriggs knew who the alternates were by the time the jury was seated. However, so there would be no distinction among the jurors and members would pay equal attention to the testimony, the alternates were only identified when the jury began its deliberations.

The jury was a mixed bag. It included a mechanic who worked on small aircraft and loved to ride motorcycles and jump out of airplanes; he was joined by another mechanic who worked for Continental Airlines—a naturalized American citizen from Iran who had moved to the United States 18 years earlier; a man who had worked for Coors Brewery for 18 years; a self-employed electrician; a woman who worked in the food service kitchen for United Airlines—the juror about whom I had heard the rumors of her bias; an architect who used to work near the United Bank; the unemployed actor; an avid golfer who was a counselor; a factory representative for Ford; an administrative assistant at the airport; and an inventory control specialist/accountant for Coca-Cola. A lively, efficient 38-year-old, who had previously worked in the oil business, and now managed a real estate office, was selected by her fellow jurors as the foreperson. The alternates were a customer service representative for a vacuum cleaner company, and a nurse who managed a chiropractor's office. The jury was well integrated, including blacks, Chicanos, and whites. One of the jurors, by coincidence, was named King. Two jurors were chess players who sometimes spent spare moments during the trial playing one another. This was the body that was to decide Jim King's fate. We made our opening statements to it on Tuesday afternoon.

9

Opening Statements

Next to selecting the jury, the opening statement is the most important part of the trial. Ostensibly a road map, where each side tells the jury what it will prove, the opening statement, properly handled, is much more. It should be an opening *argument*.

I want my opening statement to be a fireside chat, a compelling narrative that defines the defense's entire theory of the case. In a convincing manner, I try to put the jurors in the defendant's shoes. To make the opening statement an enticing story that tells the jury what actually happened, I quote or paraphrase what the witnesses and experts will say. My goal is to expose the weaknesses of the prosecution and clearly define the defense.

In the opening, I repeatedly return to the principles of the Big Four of due process. I continually remind the jury that the burden is always on the prosecution. The state must prove each and every one of its contentions beyond a reasonable doubt before the defendant can be convicted. The defense does not need to prove anything. This safety net is vital to prevent the state from imprisoning people based on suspicion or conjecture. It guards us all from arbitrary, spiteful, and wanton prosecutions.

Studies have shown that more than 70 percent of the time the jury has already made up its mind by the end of the opening statements before any evidence has been presented. Since the district attorney goes first, I always want to be ready to answer him and present a different picture of what happened. I seek, with a passion, to show my firm belief that the defendant is not guilty. Specifically, I like to encapsulate the entire case in the first 90 seconds of my speech. I try to give the trial a catchy moniker, such as in this instance calling it "The Case of the Quest for a Chess Game Turning into a Nightmare of Murder Charges."

Deputy District Attorney Buckley delivered the opening statement for the prosecution, setting the pace for the state's case. Repeating a theme Mr. Sims had raised during voir dire, he told the jury: "Don't judge a book by its cover." True, King might appear to be a mild, quiet man. This, however, was the cloak of a cold, calculating killer. Everything pointed to the fact that the robbery and murders were an inside job. They were committed by a man who entered the bank by trickery and murdered the four guards in cold blood, driven by his insatiable greed.

The way the killer had been able to fire off 18 shots in a short period, Mr. Buckley insisted, showed that the criminal had an excellent knowledge and command of firearms. The bloody bank heist was "militaristic and well planned," executed with the "precision of a 'Mission Impossible' plan." The crimes required detailed training and skill by the perpetrator. The culprit possessed "too much insider knowledge" for him not recently to have worked as a guard. Most likely, the murders were committed by someone who had the discipline instilled by service in the military and as a police officer. It was done by a former guard who had shown an "inordinate, excessive interest in learning" all the nooks and crannies of the bank, one who patrolled it far beyond the duties of a weekend guard. Only one man fit all the counts: James William King.

Mr. Buckley turned to specifics. He described the crime, including how the intruder had kicked at the door to a room where the bank had once stored ammunition and guns for the guards. But the killer did not need such ammunition since he had already murdered the four guards, using bullets identical to police issue.

Interest in the trial was so great that people lined up for admission to the court. Sometimes they had to draw lots to sit in on the case.

The prosecutor traced how the police had come to identify the defendant as a suspect. He was a former guard, a veteran, and police officer familiar with guns who did not have a good alibi of his whereabouts during the robbery. King had carried a .38 Colt revolver as a police officer—the same type of weapon used in the murders. It was no accident that King could not produce his gun, his protection as a police officer. He destroyed this crucial weapon which revealed his guilt. This was just the beginning of the massive evidence which pointed to King. The prosecution would expand on it as it proved that King was the killer.

Could anybody believe that King was simply the victim of all sorts of coincidences? That he just happened to shave his mustache after the murders, lose his driver's license, get a new and larger, safe-deposit box, discover that the chess club had moved after it had been closed for more than three years, and be near the United Bank right when the facility was robbed? Could anybody believe that King conveniently disposed of his trusted Colt revolver which he had always carried as a police officer and a guard? Was it sheer coincidence that ammunition identical to police issue was used to murder the victims? No, these are not coincidences, but proof of King's guilt.

If this is not enough, Mr. Buckley continued, for crushing proof, five eyewitnesses will tell you that they saw King robbing them that day. Circumstantial evidence will be presented to show that King had the knowledge and ability to commit the crimes. Forensic experts will tell you that the defendant carried hollow-point bullets identical to those found in the bodies of the four murdered guards.

Moreover, King's statements confirm his guilt. Thirty minutes after the FBI had first questioned him, James William King confessed to a cohort that he was scared because he did not have a good alibi for his whereabouts on Father's Day morning. The retired police sergeant similarly told FBI agents and police officers contradictory stories about his activities that day. Even worse, his alibi was contradicted by his wife and son. This is indicative of the massive evidence which points to King's guilt in murdering the guards and robbing the bank.

Mr. Buckley engaged in numerous preemptive strikes during his opening, trying to rebut our assertions before we had even made them. There was, for example, the question of the cracked cylinder on King's revolver. Replacing a cracked cylinder, according to the prosecutor, was a very easy repair. King, for instance, had had the cylinder of another handgun previously fixed. The only reason he did not do so with his .38 Colt Trooper was because it was the murder weapon.

King took great pride in his career as a police officer, Mr. Buckley continued. Evidence will be presented that King had a trophy case which included his stripes, handcuffs, and police identification cards. Why, then, should he have disposed of his most valuable possession as a police officer, his revolver? This was another indication of his guilt.

A pair of shoes was found in King's house that were comparable to those which left the shoeprints at the scene of the crimes. While it was true that the FBI could not identify them as the shoes worn by the killer and they were probably not the murderer's shoes, still it was suspicious that such a pair was discovered in King's house. Maybe he had a similar pair of which he had disposed.

Likewise, was it sheer coincidence that the retired police sergeant got a new and larger safe-deposit box on June 17, the day after the murders? Why did he visit it repeatedly in the week after the crime? He had no use for such a box except that he was using it to hide the loot. But this was to be expected from a cynical former guard who had "wandered all over the bank" and gone to "unique places of the bank." So when all the evidence is in, there will be no question that James William King is guilty on all counts with which he is charged.

While Mr. Buckley was speaking, a strange sound could be heard in the background. Somehow, with all the recording equipment and cameras in the courtroom, part of the public address system picked up echoes of the microphones from the traffic court. Possibly, this reflected that there were a lot of shadowy accusations and innuendoes which had yet to be fully aired in the case.

Scott's Opening

After drafting a possible opening statement and comparing notes with Scott Robinson, I assigned Scott the task of delivering our opening statement. I was drained from voir dire and did not have the time to polish my speech. Scott, in turn, was eager to make the opening statement. I coached him to be strong on the initial remarks to the jury. "On Father's Day last year, Jim King did not get up from bed, eat breakfast, dress, drive to the United Bank of Denver, murder four security guards, and steal $200,000," Scott began his fighting, affirmative talk.

"During the next few weeks, you . . . will hear the facts of what really happened at the United Bank last year when this brutal, disgusting crime was committed. You will learn that Jim King did not commit this horrendous crime. Yet he sits just a trial away from conviction and possibly death for a crime he did not commit. His innocence will be proven by the scientific evidence. . . .

"You will not only be jurors," Scott continued, "but you will also be witnesses to what happens to a man who is unjustly charged. You will not learn, however, who killed the guards or even how many people were involved." On this basis, my co-counsel reviewed the details of the case.

He noted how the authorities had sought to investigate the crime. They talked to whomever they could, past and present employees, drivers of armored cars, people who had passed by the bank that morning, and anyone else who might know something about the murders and robbery or had even noticed anything unusual occur-

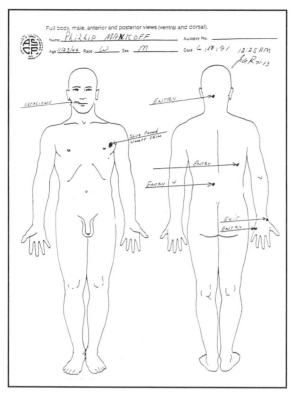

The autopsy report of Phillip Mankoff shows where he was shot.

ring last Father's Day. All the evidence indicated the gruesome crime was an inside job. The police focused on past and present guards. This led them to compose two photo books which consisted of the driver's license pictures of 50 current and former guards.

On June 20, one by one, five of the eyewitnesses were called to meet with FBI Special Agent John Kirk. He showed them these photos. The law enforcement expert had the robbed tellers take their time in reviewing the pictures, having the witnesses turn the pages of two three-ringed notebooks containing the pictures—there was one photo per page. Agent Kirk asked the victims of the crime to focus on features that cannot be changed, specifically on the shape of the nose, chin, and ears. None of the eyewitnesses identified King; hence, he was not the robber. This lineup exonerated our client.

Meanwhile, mysteries abounded at the United Bank. The robber had left behind fingerprints, palmprints, and shoeprints. The authorities had yet to identify them. But they were obviously those of "one of the murderers." Scott kept referring to the "murderer or murderers" and the "man or the men" who were responsible for this heinous deed. His intent was to show that the evidence was so nebulous that the authorities could not really tell if one or more people had been involved. Even at that, all of the scientific evidence was negative to King. This "evidence exonerates James King."

Scott told how, beginning on Father's Day, King innocently did a number of things, actions "which will haunt him the rest of his life, actions which he will always regret." One was leaving his house at about 9:15 to seek a chess game. King had been planning to return to head-to-head chess for some time and was looking for a chess game that Sunday morning. Prior to leaving for the Capitol Hill Community Center, King had encountered his neighbors between 8:00 and 9:00 that morning, changed his clothes, and drove to the what he thought was still the home of the Denver Chess Club. After he failed to find a game, he returned home around ten o'clock, having been gone approximately 45 minutes. A neighbor saw King drive up to his house at about 10:00, four minutes after the robber had left the vault. This was crucial because King's house is at least a 15-minute drive from the bank. After visiting the cemetery with his wife, King spent a quiet afternoon at home.

The next day, "the worst possible day," King got a new safe-deposit box. He visited it a number of times during the next week because he was trying to arrange the materials in it and sort out his valuables. This too was to haunt him.

So was the fact that he had disposed of his police revolver. The gun, for King, was a tool of the trade. After he retired as a bank guard, he had no use for the dangerous, defective weapon. If the gun had not been broken, he would have kept it. But since it had a cracked cylinder, he disposed of it. Yet another innocent act had woven a web of suspicion.

As a former bank guard who had complained about the institution's poor security, King naturally followed the case closely in the media. After a few days, he wondered why the police and FBI had not called on him. His past role at the bank had been discovered by a reporter for the *Rocky Mountain News*. King freely and openly spoke with the journalist and later with the authorities.

As the police urgently sought an arrest, King noted that the bank was vehemently blaming ex-guards for the crime. He realized that the police were suspicious of him because he did not have a strong alibi for his actions during Father's Day morning. "James King had been horrified by the robbery and the murders." Having worked at the bank, gotten rid of his revolver, and having planned to go to Las Vegas, he feared the authorities might suspect him. "Just what he had feared would happen had happened, and from the reports that he was reading in the newspaper, it didn't look like the police were making much progress with the investigation," Scott intoned.

King knew that the police were desperate to make an arrest for the murders. "After talking with the two FBI agents on June 24, King was troubled by the fact that he did not really have a strong alibi. . . . Jim King's worst fears were soon realized. He was questioned not once, but twice more by police detectives and FBI agents. On each occasion he talked with them about his whereabouts on Father's Day, what he had done with his gun, his knowledge of shortcomings in United Bank security, answering whatever questions were asked of him."

After his first interview with the FBI, King shaved off his mustache. He was bothered by pimples under it. This had been a recurring problem and he had shaved off the mustache in the past. He knew that the FBI agents would have reported that he wore a mustache on June 24, but he did not care. He did not consciously think that shaving his mustache would implicate him in the murders "because he knew he was innocent." But once more, this unpremeditated act haunts him. "He threw away his gun, shaved off his mustache, and traded in his safe-deposit box . . . and here he is."

More than two weeks after the Father's Day Massacre, "on July 3, when his wife and son returned home after work, both shared with him the fact that they had been contacted by the FBI at their places of employment. None of them dreamed, however, that that would be Jim King's last night at home before his nightmare began."

Scott described King's arrest on the evening of July 3. "How did all this happen? What led the police to suspect and charge Jim King with the cold-blooded murder of the four security guards?"

Using these queries as his pivot, Scott turned to the scene of the crime. He noted that a mysterious alarm had gone off at the bank at 5:04 AM, and other strange happenings on Father's Day morning. Right in the middle of the crime, the alarm was reset at 9:33. "Why? We don't know."

This unanswered question is typical of the fact that the night before the murders was not a normal night. The evidence will prove this. We will call, for example, a witness who will tell you about seeing a big man in his 40s, with silver-flecked hair, wearing a fedora with a yellow feather in it, erratically driving by the bank somewhere around 7:00 that morning. We will point out that a virtual arsenal was seized from another former guard, Paul Yocum. We will note that unidentified palmprints have been found near the scene of the murders. No physical evidence, however, exists linking King to the robbery.

Scott talked about the evidence found in the monitor room. There the killer "covered up his tracks—but not his footprints. They were left." This allowed my co-counsel to tell more about the mysterious shoeprints, prints which do not match any of King's shoes, prints which exonerate Jim King.

We will also call witnesses from Stapleton Airport. They will tell you about an unusual man who was seeking to rent a car with only cash shortly after noon on Father's Day. The man they will describe looked a good deal like the man identified by the tellers. All, however, agree that the man at the airport was not Jim King.

Alternate suspects abound in the case. Not only is there Paul Yocum, but there is also Mike McKown. Many around the bank initially thought that the latter committed the crime. Doug Bagley was a fired guard who had previously propped open a door leading to the monitor room with a pop can just as occurred during the Father's Day Massacre.

My associate proceeded to trace King's life, his duty on the police force, the nature of the crime, and the way the police had conducted photo lineups both before and after accusing King. Nor was much to be made of the fact that a Colt revolver was used in the killings. Half of the police force carried Colts. Thousands of others in the Denver area also owned Colt revolvers. King did not identify his police career with his gun; rather, he took pride in his badge and

Photo by Phil Goodstein

Jim King was given a commendation when he stopped a bank robbery while working as a guard at the Bank of Denver in 1973.

his ability to maintain the peace without resorting to violent force. King was a "law enforcer, not a law breaker."

So why did the authorities zero in on King? All they have is a string of coincidences against him. Nor should you unquestioningly accept the claims of the eyewitnesses that King was the robber. We will show that the eyewitnesses were not at all clear about identifying King. All of them, in fact, failed to identify King when first shown his picture.

The defendant, as we will prove by calling numerous reputation witnesses, was a non-violent, non-aggressive person. Moreover, "the scientific evidence will convince you Jim King was neither the robber nor murderer. Jim King's neighbors know he was not leaving that bank vault at 10:00 AM. People who know him will tell you he is not a savage, cold-blooded murderer."

You will see that this is a case where the authorities have continually tried to carve, shape, and shove evidence into holes to try to make it appear that Jim King committed these hideous crimes. For example, the police got quite excited about King's moles when they noted that the eyewitnesses saw a small bandage on the face of the robber. But all the eyewitnesses positioned the adhesive strip in such a place that it did not cover King's moles. None of the eyewitnesses identified the gunman as having any moles.

Seeking to make the lack of evidence in the case crystal clear, Scott recalled how, upon learning that King had been at Mount Olivet Cemetery on Father's Day, the authorities "had underwater divers go in there [in the graveyard's lakes] to look for loot or any connection with the robbery and it also proved negative. They went to every bank. They dug up the lawn around the house. They searched the house on two separate occasions for five hours each, and found nothing.

"Jim King drives a 1978 Ford car. He lives in a modest house, has had a modest life, served honorably as a police officer for 25 years, has no history of brutality, no history of being sued for brutality, and indeed, his only connection with a robbery was when he stopped one and was given a commendation by the Denver Police Department and the FBI. This is how a man is rewarded for 25 years of honorable service to the City and County of Denver."

An expert witness, Scott promised the jury, will rebut the prosecution's bogus eyewitness identifications. She will tell you about the problems with false convictions, and how sometimes eyewitnesses invent data. Experts in firearms will discuss the nature of Colt revolvers and +P ammunition. Finally, we will call neighbors and, of course, Jim King.

All the authorities have against King is a tragic set of coincidences. This, however, is not a crime. The evidence does not justify accusing Jim King of the robbery and murders at the United Bank. So listen to the evidence. When you do, you will return a verdict of not guilty.

10

The Prosecution's Case

Lacking any scientific or physical evidence against King, the heart of the prosecution's case was the five eyewitnesses who had identified him. This was extremely damning. Juries give more credence to eyewitness testimony than to anything else. Unfortunately, eyewitness identification is none too reliable.

Being the victim of a violent crime can be a very traumatic event. Naturally, a victim is frightened. Over the years, the law has developed an elaborate set of procedures and tests to try to prevent victims from being influenced by police suggestions. Otherwise, they might testify against whomever is accused in the belief that they are furthering the cause of justice. We had to make sure the jury understood this point. It was even more apparent when the eyewitnesses took the stand.

The tone of the case was set by the first prosecution witness, vault manager David Barranco. The tall, earnest, clean-cut, dark-haired young man was sworn in at about 8:45 on the morning of May 20. The 25-year-old Denver native had a degree in marketing from the University of Arizona. He had been employed by the bank for approximately nine months prior to the robbery. During that time, he had worked in its various vaults. About three weeks before the robbery, he had qualified to be manager of the "armored vault."

That was the technical description of the vault which had been robbed on Father's Day. The employees were the "armored tellers." They were so known because they received the deposits brought in by the armored car couriers.

The witness informed the jury of how he needed both an access card and the knowledge of a four-number cipher code to enter the vault through a mantrap. The access card was specifically called a "markey" card. Each card was programmed so that employees could only enter doors where they belonged. Using a pointer, Barranco showed the jury precisely where the various events occurred on a map of the vault.

Having established this background, Mr. Buckley got the witness to tell precisely what he remembered about the robbery. Barranco related that he had noticed the intruder in the vault at about 9:45 AM. He gave his description of the robber. "It will be a long time before I forget that face," he stated as he identified King as the gunman. This gave him a chance to tell how he had pinpointed King as the robber during the July 5 lineup.

Barranco had been out enjoying himself on the Fourth of July. When he returned home in the evening, he discovered messages from the police both on his door and answering machine: They cautioned that he should not watch the news or read the paper until the authorities could talk to him. It was quite late by then and he had no trouble obeying those instructions. Knowing that something vital had happened in the case, early the next morning, before 8:00, he was called into a bank conference room where he was shown the six-person photo lineup that included King. He swore that he "immediately" identified the former police sergeant as the robber.

In the course of Barranco's testimony, the prosecution naturally introduced into evidence the six-man photo lineup of July 5. It also placed into evidence the two notebooks containing the photos of 50 past and present guards which had been shown to Barranco on June 20. Included was the picture of King which Barranco had failed to identify that day. A touched-up copy of this photo, with a hat added, the mustache accentuated, and sunglasses over the eyes, was blown up and placed right next to an enlarged picture of the composite drawing of the robber. The doctored photo of King looked a good deal like the composite drawing—enough to alarm us.

Sketch by Lucas Boyd

David Barranco

I had pinned Barranco down during the preliminary hearing when I got him to admit that he had not been able to identify King as the robber during the initial phases of the investigation. He had also conceded that he had not described the intruder as having any visible moles. In light of this, I figured I would subject him to a change of pace at the trial. I therefore assigned Scott Robinson, who had previously published articles on eyewitness identification, to cross-examine the prosecution's lead-off witness. During his early statements to the police, Barranco admitted that while he thought King looked a good deal like the robber, he was not absolutely sure. He had also stated that he believed that the robber's mustache might have been a fake.

Still, of all the eyewitnesses, he was the only one to indicate during the June 20 photo lineup that picture number 16—King— looked at all like the robber. But, Barranco told the FBI agent supervising the lineup, number 16 was *not* the man. While the guard in the photo had a mustache and hair like the robber's, the gunman had a fuller face than number 16. Barranco noted that another guard, photo number eight—John J. Perpetua—had a face similar to the robber, but the hair and mustache were incorrect. The witness also claimed that photo number 17—Loid Luscomb—looked more like the robber than did number 16. (The five-foot-ten, 260-pound Luscomb had a salt-and-pepper mustache. He had worked as a guard from October 1985 until December 1986. By the time of the robbery, Luscomb was living in Austin, Texas.)

Even when Barranco was again shown the photo of King on July 5, he only stated that King was "very similar" to the robber. He qualified his identification by telling the authorities that the touched-up photo of the retired police officer was the man "I believe robbed the United Bank of Denver."

Scott turned to specifics of the eyewitness identification. He got Barranco to admit that he was distracted by the gunman's reflective sunglasses, how the disguise had confused him, and that he was scared facing the armed robber. In great detail, Scott had Barranco tell that the clear adhesive strip on the robber's left cheek would not have hidden or cloaked King's moles. Once more the vault manager conceded that he had never described the robber as having moles. To emphasize this point and how anybody who had ever seen King would note the moles, Scott went over to King and pointed out his visible moles. Barranco admitted that he could see them 20 feet away from the witness stand. The cash vault manager, as did the other eyewitnesses, noted that he had frequently seen photos of King in the newspapers and on television since the robbery, pictures which confirmed his belief that King was the man he had encountered on Father's Day.

My associate pointed out how elaborate Barranco's description of the robber was, with his detailed portrait of the gunman's clothing and face. Barranco also immediately claimed to have noticed the gun, the hat, the coat, the sunglasses, and the shoes. The last were of black leather and looked fairly new. The robber was not wearing gloves and there was no jewelry on his hands.

The witness did not remember any distinctive odor about the gunman. Nor did any of the other tellers. This was a prelude to a point we were to bring out when we examined the firearms experts. Someone who has just fired a revolver exudes the scent of gunpowder. Since the intruder in the vault had no such odor, could it be that the robber was a different man than the killer?

The district attorney had Jim King's driver's license photo touched up to look like the man in the composite drawing.

Barranco further stated that there was nothing noteworthy about the walk of the robber. Scott contrasted this to the witness's earlier statement to the police that the gunman might have had a limp as he toddled along with a somewhat unusual step. Besides, according to the police, the robber had just violently kicked at the wall and Plexiglas window in the monitor room. Might he have injured his foot in the process? But, Barranco told the jury, the gunman had approached him so quickly that he did not have time to notice if the intruder had a limp or particular walking style. He had primarily focused on the gun.

In previous statements to the police, Barranco had described the robber as having a revolver with an eight- to ten-inch barrel. He modified this in court to a six- to eight-inch barrel. Just as in old westerns, the gunman immediately cocked the hammer. Barranco admitted that he did not know much about guns. He was not aware, in Scott's term, that it was a "no-no" for a police officer or security guard to walk around waving a revolver with a cocked hammer.

Scott guided the witness through the various photo lineups he had seen. On June 17, Barranco had been shown a six-person photo lineup including Mike McKown—the initial suspect in the case. The vault manager had noted that numbers one, two, and four looked somewhat like the robber, but he was not positive enough to identify any of them. (McKown was number four.) Barranco swore that he did not want to be the cause of a false arrest.

My co-counsel went over Barranco's previous testimony at the preliminary and evidentiary hearings. He stressed its inconsistencies. Despite the fact that Barranco could not really remember if the gunman had on a tie or if his shirt was dark or light, the witness insisted he had a crystal-clear vision of precisely what the gunman looked like. "It is incredible what you remember" during such a trauma, he explained. That is how he remembered "exactly" what had happened. It seemed that the further the robbery receded into the past, the better the witness's memory became.

Four tellers stated that John Perpetua looked somewhat like the man who robbed them. The poor quality of this picture reflects the shadowy images shown the bank employees.

Scott asked Barranco if he had identified King during the June 20 parade of photos. The witness conceded he did not. Nor did he specifically focus on any of the gunman's unchangeable facial features such as his nose, ears, and chin. Then, catching us by surprise, Barranco asserted that while he failed to pinpoint King on June 20, he had actually picked King out that day, two weeks before King had been arrested or been publicly mentioned as a suspect. Noting that he had stated that photo number 16 looked somewhat like the robber, Barranco exclaimed: "I really haven't said this before, but at that time, it was my gut feeling that this [King] was the man. I don't know to this day what held me back from saying that. . . . I was hoping this FBI agent could read me well enough to investigate the matter further."

Later, outside the presence of the jury, I objected to Barranco's statement. If this is what Barranco thought, we should have been informed of it during discovery. "If any other witness has second or third thoughts," I told Judge Spriggs, "we'd like to hear about it."

Judge Spriggs, as I expected, overruled my objection. Sarcastically, he noted: "There isn't a script for this, you know. One of the prices you pay for asking questions is that witnesses get to answer them."

Actually, in some ways we were very glad to hear Barranco's surprise answer. It showed how flimsy the identifications were. While his firm statement that he was sure that King was the robber could easily be a key nail in King's coffin, it might also be a great help to the defense. One reason attorneys continually review the records of a case and previous testimony is so that no surprises ensnare them during a trial.

Barranco's statement that he had identified King during the June 20 lineup was evidence that he had conveniently invented this memory in the belief that it would help convict King. Though he insisted that he immediately had second thoughts about not identifying King when he was first shown the retired sergeant's photo, he never told them to the police or FBI. If he had been so sure that King was the man, he would have stated as much earlier. If we could bring this out, it would create reasonable doubt in the jurors' minds. They might not automatically believe the eyewitness's claims if they grasped that Barranco had suddenly remembered something he had never stated before.

To demonstrate this point, Scott questioned the witness in great detail about the hours and hours he had spent discussing the case with the police and FBI in the days that followed the robbery and June 20 lineup. For instance, on June 21, Barranco had spent 90 minutes talking about the robbery with the police, telling them all sorts of details about the heist. But he had said nothing about his second thoughts concerning the June 20 photo lineup. Shortly after that discussion with the police, Barranco was asked to pick out a .38 Colt revolver from three Smith & Wesson revolvers. Once more he had an ideal opportunity to tell the authorities about his "second thoughts." Again, he failed to mention anything.

Other conversations with the police and FBI followed. On June 28, Barranco spent nearly four hours with FBI visual information specialist George Nobel, the man who sketched the composite drawing. The vault manager again remained silent about his "second thoughts." In other words, Scott's cross-examination showed that Barranco had numerous opportunities to finger King if he had truly made an identification.

Still, the reason I objected was for the record. Besides doing your all during a trial to gain the acquittal of your client, you are also closely monitoring and placing on the record all the developments in the courtroom and making objections. Should the jury convict your client, you must have previously made these objections in order to use them as error on appeal. Nor is it unusual, during the course of a trial, for a defense lawyer to move more than once for a mistrial in the hope of preserving error for appeal.

Scott continued to cut away at Barranco's diverse statements to the police and previous testimony. He brought out that the July 5 picture of King had a slightly different texture than did the photo Barranco had been shown on June 20. In the interim, the police had highlighted the King photo. It stood out far more than did the other five pictures in the lineup. The witness conceded that he had previously seen it and had never before viewed the other five photos.

Sometimes it was hard to hear what Barranco was saying. Time and again, Judge Spriggs had to order the witness to speak up and not talk so fast. Apparently, Barranco was quite nervous, especially with his newly revealed, sensational testimony. At one point, the witness muttered: "Too many days, too many people."

Judge Spriggs' intervention highlighted the poor design of Courtroom 16. Rather than being right next to the jury, the witness box was across the room from it. Jurors did not get a good view of the witness. To see him 30 or so feet away, they had to look through the court reporter and evidence table. The distance meant they could not properly observe the reactions of the witness, whether he was sweating, breathing unduly, and the character of his body language. This made it even more incumbent upon us to bring out the problematic testimony of the prosecution's first witness.

The Overlays

Barranco's revelation also provided us with a great opening for a cross-examination testing exercise I had prepared for the trial: photos of President George Bush, movie star Harrison Ford, and other prominent public figures disguised under overlays with a hat, mustache, and sunglasses resembling the composite drawing of the suspect. (Ford was selected because he was at the peak of his fame. Polls showed that he had as high a recognition rate as did the president.) Graphic artist Teresa Banta designed the overlays.

I first got the idea of creating the overlays at a conference of an organization of which I once served as president, the American Board of Criminal Lawyers. The desirability of a testing tactic was aired during a round-table discussion I had with fellow defense attorneys. They suggested the use of overlays for cross-examination. After being convinced that such a test was needed to illustrate to the jury the limits of eyewitness identification, I called a psychologist, Dr. Edith Greene of the University of Colorado at Colorado Springs.

She had received her doctorate from the University of Washington in Seattle in 1983, studying under a national authority on eyewitness psychology and identification, Dr. Elizabeth Loftus. Since gaining her degree, Dr. Greene had published several articles on eyewitness identification. Her professional specialty was psychology and the legal system, especially the way eyewitnesses make identifications and juries reach verdicts. Dr. Greene had

*Eyewitness David Barranco was asked if he could
identify the man behind the disguise.*

previously testified in courts in California, Arizona, Washington,
Nevada, Minnesota, and elsewhere on the problems of this crucial
topic. I had used her services in 1990 in the court-martial of the Case
of the Gay Colonel at Fort Carson, near Colorado Springs, concerning eyewitness identification.

The defendant was a 42-year-old Army dental surgeon who,
since 1985, had been struggling with his sexual identity. After years
of doubt and consultations with his wife, a psychologist, a psychiatrist, and a priest, the Colonel realized that he was a homosexual. To
help raise funds to combat AIDS, he once performed in women's
clothing on the stage of a Colorado Springs gay bar.

The military learned of this through a fellow officer, Captain X,
who had been arrested for soliciting an undercover MP and who had
advertised for sex on the walls of public lavatories. The witness was
given immunity from prosecution in exchange for him identifying

other possibly gay officers. The informer was further allowed to resign from the Army.

Based on the revelations of Captain X, the military vindictively prosecuted the dental surgeon. When he realized that his homosexuality was causing problems, the Colonel offered to resign his commission in the summer of 1990. A supervisor, who wanted to see the defendant imprisoned because he was a homosexual, blocked this move. The dentist was consequently charged with ten counts of conduct unbecoming an officer.

The charges were an outright witch-hunt against an officer who was on trial simply because he was gay. To cloak this, the court-martial included accusations that the Colonel had, while wearing women's clothing in public, exposed himself to two women and an 11-year-old girl in Colorado Springs laundromats. The police had had the eyewitnesses identify the dentist in two photo lineups. Here I turned to Dr. Greene for assistance.

She thoroughly reviewed the evidence. The psychologist noted that there were severe problems with the photo lineups and identifications. In one of the photo lineups, five light-skinned individuals were placed next to the darker skinned Colonel. In the other, the five other suspects were much younger than the defendant. Dr. Greene so convinced the court that the eyewitness identifications were of dubious merit. Thanks to her testimony, the dentist was acquitted of the charges that he had exposed himself. Nonetheless, the jury found him guilty on the other eight counts only because he was a homosexual. He was sentenced to nine months in a military prison (he could have received a maximum sentence of 40 years), and was dismissed from the Army.

Remembering how effective a witness Dr. Greene had been in the Case of the Gay Colonel, I consulted her about the identification of King. Our goal was to show that individuals, even when not facing an armed robber, have difficulties identifying a well-known person in disguise. She and I prepared overlays of six different famous people: Jack Nicholson, Lee Iacocca, Marlon Brando, Robert Duvall, Harrison Ford, and George Bush. Dr. Greene had experimentally used these pictures in a psychology class to determine the percentage of recognition. We prepared to use the overlays to cross-examine the eyewitnesses in the King case.

With this background, Scott pulled out one of the overlays for the cross-examination of Barranco. He showed the witness a photo of a famous person disguised by a hat, sunglasses, and a mustache. As I held the picture up so Barranco and the jury could clearly see it, Scott asked: "Can you identify it?" When the witness said no, Scott urged him to "take as much time as you want. Anybody you know?" Barranco again immediately stated he could not identify the man. Scott continued: "It could have been anyone, couldn't it?" Once more, Barranco stated he did not know who was behind the disguise.

Barranco's answer established our point—the witness was confused by a disguise comparable to that worn by the bank robber. Therefore, the vault manager's long, drawn-out identification of King at the inducement of the police with their tainted photo lineup must be doubted. All Scott needed to do to clinch this point was to lift up the overlay and show who was hiding behind it.

Rather than doing this and letting the record show that Barranco could not identify the man behind the disguise, to my frightened surprise, Scott led Barranco on. Had the witness ever seen *Presumed Innocent*? Barranco had not. How about such films as the *Raiders of the Lost Ark* or *Indiana Jones and the Temple of Doom*? Thank the heavens that Barranco stated he had, but did not get the clue. He was still unable to identify the man behind the disguise. Scott thereupon lifted up the overlay, revealing a picture of Harrison Ford.

Judge Spriggs diverted attention from the witness's inability to identify the well-known actor when he quipped "it looks like Mr. Gerash in his youth. . . . I had never noticed the resemblance before." In other words, the eyewitness identification of the man in the disguise was so nebulous that I could have been the suspect!

Barranco lamented that he would have been able to recognize a "real photo" of Ford beneath the disguise, not one with "some cheesy picture on top of it," a picture that was only a "caricature." Scott fell into the witness's hands. Not content to let go of the overlays, Scott continued to push his luck by holding up another of the disguised overlays. This time he struck out when Barranco immediately identified the suspect as a picture of President Bush. Scott muttered, "Good for you. You see how this works." The jury was intently interested in the overlays, trying to guess who was

Harrison Ford lurked behind the
overlay shown David Barranco.

hiding beneath the mask. Meanwhile, realizing he had overplayed his hand, Scott concluded his cross-examination by noting, "I don't think you really want me to keep going on."

The prosecutors had said nothing when Scott produced the overlays. Only after Scott had used them to impeach Barranco's testimony did Judge Spriggs take it upon himself to question whether the overlays were admissible evidence since they had not been previously endorsed as exhibits. The district attorney thereupon picked up the judge's aggressive ruling against us.

We noted that we did not need to endorse the overlays since they were not specific items of evidence, but only testing devices. Moreover, Judge Spriggs had not prohibited the state from seeking to bias the witnesses and jury when he allowed the prosecution to place a huge blowup of the cropped photo of the mustached King wearing a hat and sunglasses right in front of the jury box. Despite this, outside the presence of the jury, Judge Spriggs lambasted us for "trial by ambush. . . . I view your neglect [to inform the court about the overlays] to be something less than accidental. I don't want any more surprises." I thought that he, as a former prosecutor, was siding with the district attorney. Nonetheless, after sternly warning us about the tactic and announcing we were not to be allowed to produce any more non-endorsed exhibits to test the other eyewitnesses, Judge Spriggs permitted the already used overlays to remain in evidence.

It was questionable whether the overlays would have had the same impact with the other eyewitnesses as they did with Barranco. Though the eyewitnesses were sequestered—they could not sit in court or view the proceedings on television prior to testifying— word of mouth about the overlays would doubtlessly have gotten to them by the time they took the stand. Combined with Judge Spriggs' ruling, this meant we had to focus on their earlier statements to show the nebulous character of their identifications of King. This came out during the testimony of the state's second eyewitness, Maria Kay Christian.

The Testimony of Maria Christian

Born in Denver in August 1970, the five-foot-seven, 225-pound Christian had initially described the robber as relatively short, being between five-foot-five and five-foot-nine. He was wearing a black gangster hat, a "shady looking kind of hat," with a gray jacket, dark black or navy blue pants, and a "weird" striped tie. When the

Sketch by Lucas Boyd

Maria Christian

gunman had asked "Who is the cashier?" and silence descended on the employees, Christian had pointed to Barranco.

The witness recalled that while she and the other employees were down on the floor, the robber had cocked his revolver and stated: "Keep your eyes closed. I don't want you to feel it." Christian assumed that this meant he was going to kill them. She obeyed orders, and had later been afraid to get up in the mantrap. Still, she was sure she could easily identify the gunman if she saw him again as she pinpointed King as the robber.

She was the first eyewitness called in by the police after King's arrest. At around 3:00 PM on July 4, she identified him in the six-man photo lineup. Even then, however, she was not 100-percent positive that King was the man, since she noted that suspect number five as well as suspect number two—King—might have been the robber. During the evidentiary hearing in March, when we had argued that the photo lineup was impermissibly suggestive, Christian had sworn, "I wasn't definite, but I thought it [photo number two] could be the robber." But the gunman's face, she continued, was a little rounder, more like photo number five. Mr. Sims, however, got her to state that she had no doubt that King was the gunman. "He looked like the man I saw that day. . . . That was the man who robbed me."

When I cross-examined Christian, she admitted that she was near-sighted, but had not had her glasses on at the time of the robbery. Her glasses had been prescribed about a year before the Father's Day Massacre. She did not wear them all the time. In fact, she stated she did not need the glasses to see in the distance. So do you need the glasses to drive? I asked. She denied that she did. I thereupon produced her driver's license which required her to wear the glasses while behind the wheel. Christian was forced to concede that she did not really get a good look at the robber. Indeed, when she initially saw the intruder while talking with David Barranco and David Twist, she thought he was a guard and had not paid much attention to him.

At the most, the witness admitted only having about a five-second face-to-face glance at the robber. In her initial description of him, she insisted he had a clear complexion and a double chin. She further conceded that she had not seen any acne, pimples, scars, or moles on the robber. In response, I had King stand and approach the witness. He stopped about three feet away from Christian, the distance she described as being the space separating her from the gunman. Pointing to King's moles, she admitted she could see them.

"You didn't see any moles on the robber, did you?" I inquired. She admitted: "No, I didn't really notice any moles. I don't remember all the moles." The witness further conceded that she had frequently seen King's picture on television. The repeated viewing of his visage had strengthened her belief that he was the robber.

In court, Christian was "definite" that King was the intruder. Looking at my notes, I called attention to her previous statement at the evidentiary hearing in March that "I wasn't definite, but I thought it [photo number two] could be the robber." The witness also conceded the gunman seemed familiar. He might have been a guard whom she had previously encountered while working at the bank.

Christian had been employed by the financial institution since June 22, 1990. This was shortly before King quit. But, the witness admitted, she had no conversations with the guards who came through the vault. Nor had Christian worked weekends during the period her employment overlapped with King at the bank. No evidence was introduced that she had ever previously encountered King.

The timing of King's employment was also crucial concerning another of the prosecution's claims. It admitted that, possibly, the guards had been less cautious than they should have been that Sunday morning because they knew the intruder as a former employee. The district attorney conceded that sometimes friends and family of the guards were allowed into secured areas. But none of the murdered guards had worked with King and there was no evidence that he knew them. It was not impossible that McCullom knew the man who had called at the elevator. Perhaps, that was why there was no sign of any resistance on McCullom's part when the intruder entered the elevator. Maybe the whole police scenario of the crime was fundamentally flawed.

The fact that the robber might not have been the sophisticated insider alleged by the prosecution came out in another statement by

President George Bush disguised to look like the robber of the United Bank.

Christian. As had all the accosted tellers, she had made a videotaped statement to the police immediately after the robbery. Both there and in her testimony she insisted that after the gunman had ordered her and her fellow employees to lie on the floor, he asked: "Who is the cashier?" This was significant because the vault did not have a cashier—anyone working in that area of the bank would know so.

Likewise, there was the question of whether the intruder had ordered the employees into the mantrap or the "little room." Some of the witnesses claimed he had said "mantrap." Others were insistent that he had not. In her recollections of the robbery, Christian vacillated over whether the gunman had said "mantrap." She explained that she had learned that term on her first day on the job. All the tellers, guards, and couriers referred to the little room as the "mantrap." The place where she and the other tellers were imprisoned was one of three mantraps around the vault.

The robber was also apparently unaware that the armored vault contained two safes filled with cash. He did not question Barranco's claim that two visible safes in what was called the "Saturday vault" only contained "paperwork." Actually, that was the site of the richest currency holdings in the vault. The fact that the gunman was so easily dissuaded from taking more cash, along with his use of "cashier" and "little room" might well indicate that the gunman was *not* someone who intricately knew the workings of the United Bank. Could it be that the intruder was not an insider? Could he be a collaborator of an insider? Did not his lack of bank terminology show that something was missing from the state's portrait of the culprit and the crime?

Police Witnesses

Before putting the other eyewitnesses on the stand, the prosecution called a wide array of police officers, FBI agents, and bank security officials involved in investigating the robbery. In the lead was 32-year-old Danell M. Taylor, a general investigator for the bank's risk and security department. To catch up on her work, she had come to the bank at about 10:12 on Father's Day morning. Her office was near the guard shack. The bank officer had attempted to gain admission to the concourse level by calling on the guard phone, but she was surprised to get no answer. She was likewise surprised that a front door to the bank was open, using it to get into the financial institution.

"I had no idea anything had happened at this point," she told the court. When she first went to her office, she noticed nothing amiss other than that the guards were not around. After a bit, she went to the main floor security station in the hope of finding a guard. (The security personnel there were hired by the management company that ran the United Bank office complex, but were not bank guards.) Right about then, when she was in the bank atrium, "suddenly the cash-vault tellers came running into the lobby, yelling and screaming, that they had just been robbed. They were very upset, shaking, scared to death." She called in the news of the robbery and led the police into the vault.

Others who had been working in the bank, including those on the concourse level, did not realize what had happened while they were on the job. Taylor, meanwhile, made it sound as if she were the lead investigator in the case. Besides describing the horrendous murder scene, she threw out broad generalities without substantiation.

The prosecution hoped to inflame the jury by showing it gruesome photos of the murdered guards such as this shot of Scott McCarthy.

There was, for instance, the question of whether the guards parked on the seventh level of the garage where the locked elevator was discovered. She was insistent that guards parked there. So who did? we asked on cross-examination. She was unable to provide specific names and dates.

Taylor's testimony hinted at another unanswered mystery about the robbery. According to the prosecution, the gunman had to flee before 10:00 when employees from the proof department came to the armored vault to pick up checks delivered by the armored car couriers. Did such people come by on Father's Day? What happened when they rang for admission and received no answer? Did they then contact the guards? Again, what did they do when no guards responded to their calls? Why did they not immediately contact a security supervisor or the police? Could someone from the proof department have been involved in the crimes? These questions were not satisfactorily addressed during the trial.

Police officer after police officer took the stand. They and FBI agents told how they had investigated the robbery and murders and what they had found at the crime scene. On cross-examination, all were forced to confess their failure to find any physical, scientific, or circumstantial evidence against King. This was not for lack of trying. The Mountain Dew can which had been propping open the door to the control room, for example, was introduced into evidence. But nothing linked it to King. In fact, the jury learned, the fingerprint of guard Harry Glass was on it.

The prosecution called Detective Jon Priest, the police department's lead investigator in the case. He told the jury about the authorities' theory of how the murders had been perpetrated and why only one man was involved. After his initial testimony, Detective Priest frequently returned to the stand to explain mysteries and fill in missing parts in the prosecution's case. As he had at the preliminary hearing, he boasted of his prowess in being able to drive the 11.4 miles from King's house to the United Bank in 12 minutes on a Sunday morning. When not on the witness stand, Speedy Priest sat at the district attorney's table as the prosecution's special consulting expert.

The district attorney proceeded to wave the bloody shirt. While we conceded that four gruesome murders had been committed on Father's Day, the prosecution sought to inflame the jury against King by showing it horrendous photos of the murdered guards lying in pools of blood. The state accentuated this by screening a video of the crime scene. Drs. Thomas E. Henry and K. Alan Stormo, the two medical examiners who had performed the autopsies, testified. They used four bone-white Styrofoam models of the heads of the executed guards. The skulls were pierced with long, skinny, haunting knitting needles to show where the men had been shot and the precise direction of the bullets causing their deaths. The physicians noted that they wore surgical gloves while examining the bodies at the bank.

The prosecution also called a crime scene investigator who told about the evidence he had discovered during his sweep of the United Bank. Of primary importance was a pair of latex gloves that he had found in the trash on the seventh-level of the parking garage where the killer apparently made his getaway. Such gloves were compa-

Styrofoam heads of the slain guards were pierced with knitting needles to show the direction of the bullets fired by the killer. The primary intent of this exhibit was to inflame the jury.

rable to those issued to the police. He admitted on cross-examination that none of the witnesses had seen the robber wearing gloves. All tests failed to link these gloves to King, and there was no trace of nitrates on them as would have been on the gloves of anybody who had worn them while firing a revolver. Nor was anything else found on floor L-7 connected to King.

In face of this, Judge Spriggs dismissed the jury and castigated the prosecutors. They had just spent 45 minutes introducing negative evidence which had no relevance to the case. Mr. Sims responded that he and Mr. Buckley did not want to be accused of withholding evidence, or rather, their non-evidence against King.

Or so the prosecution claimed. Actually, it was trying to plant the suspicion in the jury's mind that the gloves might explain why there was no fingerprint evidence against King. During his rebuttal argument at the preliminary hearing, Mr. Buckley had talked about the gloves at great length, claiming that they were the reason that the gunman had left no prints. Apparently, while the eyewitnesses' dubious identifications of King were not to be doubted, somehow their consistent and unchanging accounts that the gunman had not worn gloves was to be totally discounted. Seemingly, the robber had totally befogged all six tellers who could not see that he was wearing these magical gloves. This, I told the court, was the prosecution's "tactical brilliance."

The gloves were only the beginning of the prosecution's phantom case. It frequently appeared that it was trying to make preemptive strikes among the police witnesses. The two deputy district attorneys knew that if they did not call many of the police witnesses, the defense would. We were prepared to have them testify that they had found no specific physical evidence linking King to the murders.

For example, an FBI agent noted the shoeprints found at the crime scenes. Three pairs of King's shoes were introduced, as were the results of the FBI tests which showed that King's shoes were *not* the ones worn by the robber. Despite this, Mr. Buckley continued to insist that it was more than coincidence that a pair of shoes with sole markings somewhat like the Stacy Adams markings at the murder scene were found in King's house. Most likely, the prosecutor claimed, King had disposed of the shoes he had worn that day, but had kept this other pair which indicated his guilt.

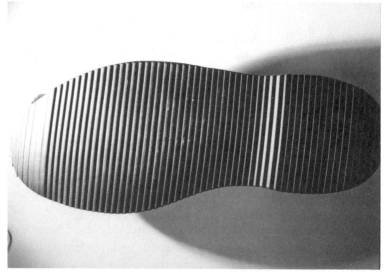

A print from a Stacy Adams shoe was found at the murder scene. The police bought a pair of the shoes. Without success, they desperately tried to make them match the assorted pairs of shoes they had seized from Jim and David King.

Detailed testimony was heard about the ballistic evidence. The prosecution focused on the +P bullets used to kill two of the guards—bullets which it claimed were identical to the ammunition issued to King during his last year on the department. Other projectiles at the murder scene were manufactured by Federal and Winchester. Some of the latter, Western .38 158-grain lead luballoy bullets, had been used by the Denver Police Department in the 1970s. Retired police officers, who had kept a few of these cartridges, had provided samples of them for the prosecution.

The bullets used to murder Scott McCarthy and Phillip Mankoff had copper jackets, very unlike the lead +Ps King carried as a police officer. Also present were +P+ bullets, +P projectiles only issued to police departments. The prosecution generally called the +Ps "Peters."

The evidence showed that at least 17 or 18 shots had been fired from a Colt revolver. The deputy district attorneys insisted that the 18 bullets equaled the bullets from King's six-shooter and the two speed loaders he had carried as a police officer. The mixture of police-related ammunition, they claimed, showed that a former policeman must have committed the outrage.

Detective Frank Kerber took the stand. A balding, powerfully built man whom fellow officers sometimes called the "meatcutter," referring to the time he had worked in a packinghouse after graduating from high school, Kerber was the department's firearms expert. He had been a detective for eight years and had spent the last six years specializing in firearms identification for the police lab. He had taken many classes on the subject and had frequently testified as an expert witness on firearms identification.

On direct examination, Detective Kerber talked in great detail about the nature of King's .38 Colt Trooper and the bullets found at the scene of the murders. To help the jury understand precisely what he was talking about, the prosecution introduced exhibits that included various bullets and revolvers, including a .38 Colt Trooper. The guns were secured with trigger locks when they were not being discussed as evidence.

Detective Kerber also talked about speed loaders. These were vital to the prosecution's theory of the case. They were to explain why 18 and only 18 bullets were fired during the crime. The police expert was insistent that the speed loaders for a .38 Smith & Wesson revolver found at Paul Yocum's apartment could not have been used on a .38 Colt revolver. Speed loaders for the different pistols, he swore, were quite different.

During cross-examination, I asked for more information about speed loaders. So the jury could see exactly what the witness was talking about, I had Detective Kerber stand, with a .38 Smith & Wesson revolver and the appropriate speed loader in hand, and asked him to demonstrate for the jury exactly how the speed loader worked. As he tried to use it, he dropped the speed loader. "I'm not familiar with it," he told the court as he continued to fumble with the speed loader. "Let me look at the directions first." "It's not too speedy," I noted, as it took the police expert quite a while to get the speed loader to work.

This allowed me to elaborate on another point. The prosecution was fixated on speed loaders. Actually, there was no evidence that a speed loader had been employed during the murders. In using a speed loader, a police officer is taught to throw the spent cartridges to the ground as he reloads his weapon. The shooter loses valuable time by putting the spent cartridges in his hand at the same time he is trying to reload the revolver.

While police officers are also taught to "pick up the brass" and leave no spent cartridges behind, it was dubious that a calculating murderer would have thrown any cartridges to the ground. One or two could have easily been lost in the dusty incinerator room or beneath the equipment in the guard shack. The fact that no spent cartridges were found at the United Bank likely indicated that the gunman had pulled out the spent shells by hand and did not use a speed loader.

Nor could Detective Kerber categorically confirm that 18 and only 18 bullets had been fired during the murders. There were numerous bullet fragments found at the scene of the crime. Many were of no value—they were either too small or too misshaped to be analyzed. Nor could he state that a Colt revolver had undoubtedly been used in the murders.

While the markings and grooves on the hollow points showed that they were not fired from a Smith & Wesson revolver, this did not necessarily mean that they had been shot from a Colt revolver.

Other weapon manufacturers made revolvers which would have produced similar markings. Indeed, Detective Kerber could not conclusively state that only one pistol had been used in the killings.

Detective Kerber had issued the original police ballistic report stating that "many different firearms could have fired these bullets." He conceded that a .38 Colt Trooper was not included in his initial list of the suspect weapons. That, he insisted, was merely an oversight. All the while, a big chart was in the courtroom that outlined the nebulous ballistic findings.

I also cross-examined Detective Kerber about surgical gloves. Members of the police lab used them all the time. There was no such thing as special police surgical gloves. The department bought them commercially. In other words, the only evidence of anybody bringing gloves to the scene of the murders was that such gloves were used by both the police department and the coroner's office. Nothing tied the gloves on the seventh floor of the parking garage to the crime.

Tom Butler followed Detective Kerber to the stand. He had served on the Denver Police Department from 1957 to 1982. His last ten years on the force had been in the police lab. The witness had worked on firearms for 25 years, including during his days as a police officer. Since retiring from the department, he had operated a gunsmith's business out of his suburban home. He frequently worked on the weapons of police officers.

Butler had known King while the two men had served together on the department. One point of similarity was that both had carried .38 Colt Troopers. The gunsmith recalled that, on October 12, 1989, he had fixed the timing on King's revolver. The cylinder, he explained, did not quite lock into place when a person cocked the pistol's hammer. That was a common problem with Colts. In the course of his examination of the Trooper, he looked at the cylinder to make sure nothing else was wrong with the revolver. While the firearm had normal holster wear, everything else was "just fine." He charged King $20 for the repair.

On cross-examination, the witness admitted that cylinders of Colt revolvers crack. Such damage is frequently caused by firing the wrong type of ammunition in the pistol. Under such circum-

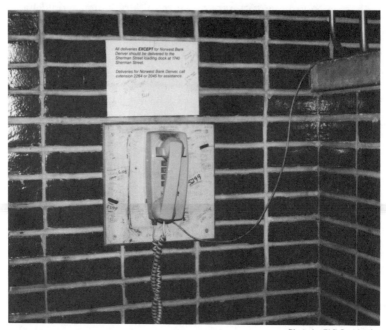

The phone next to the elevator used by the man identifying himself as Bob Bardwell.

stances, often the cylinder will fragment into two or three pieces. To demonstrate the dangerous nature of using the wrong type of ammunition, Butler kept both a Smith & Wesson and a Colt revolver that had broken cylinders in his shop. When the cylinder fractured, people rarely brought the gun to him. By the time the cylinder cracked, usually the gun was worn out and needed to be discarded.

Butler further noted that he did not fix revolvers with cracked cylinders. The manufacturer would not sell him that part. He had never sent such a gun back to Colt headquarters in Connecticut to be repaired. He had no idea how much it would cost to replace the cylinder of a Colt Trooper.

When he insisted on this last point, I produced a police report of July 5, 1991. That day a detective and FBI agent had interviewed Butler when they had obtained the receipt for his repair of King's revolver. They noted that he had stated that it would cost $70 to send the gun to Colt for the replacement of a cracked cylinder. The witness swore that he had no idea of where the police had gotten that figure. During the defense, we put on an expert witness who noted that the cost of repairs would be far more than $70, including the costs of two hours of labor and shipping charges.

Among those who subsequently testified was FBI visual information specialist George Nobel. He told precisely how he had drawn the composite sketch between June 28 and July 1. Scott Robinson asked him on cross-examination why no Band-Aid was on the robber. Nobel pointed to a smudge, claiming it was the bandage. Since, he explained, the tellers claimed that the robber had on a transparent adhesive strip, he had not highlighted it.

Why were there no moles on the drawing? Scott continued. Nobel was startled. What moles? Nobody had ever mentioned any moles to him. This was the first time he had heard about them. In other words, despite his intensive interviews with all six eyewitnesses during which he had questioned them about the robber's features, nobody had mentioned any moles on the robber. So did the eyewitnesses see King?

Prior to the trial, the prosecution had endorsed 22 FBI agents in addition to 37 police officers as witnesses. Many of them took the stand during this part of the trial. These law enforcement personnel provided further information about the precise nature of the robbery and murders. Once more we objected to the district attorney's tactics. We repeatedly noted that the defense did not dispute that the murders and robbery had been committed, but nothing in this testimony linked the crimes to King. Witness after witness conceded as much during cross-examination.

Bank employees also testified. Among them was the 35-year-old Robert F. Bardwell Jr. Supposedly, his name was used by the intruder when he called for admission to the bank. The blond, mustached, fully bearded Bardwell, a vice president of the bank, stated that he had been in the mountains during Father's Day. He also noted that he had lost his bank access card nearly a year before the robbery, reporting it lost on August 13, 1990. King, coincidentally had quit the bank on August 12. (King's service was ostensibly through August 31, 1990. However, he did not work after August 12. He was credited with time off and vacation days through the last weekend of the month. He had requested as much in his formal letter of resignation to Risk and Security Manager Thomas A. Tatalaski, which he submitted on July 29, 1990.)

Bardwell conceded that he might have lost the card prior to August 13. Not only did he not recall ever seeing King at the bank, but it was not at all unusual for someone to identify himself as a vice president at the bank. There were at least 78 people who held the post of vice president at the downtown United Bank in addition to numerous vice presidents at other branches of United Banks of Colorado. Yes, guards patrolled by his office, but guards patrolled by the offices of all the vice presidents. Finally, Bardwell admitted that he had not worked weekends at the bank since 1989. He denied he had ever contacted the guards when accessing the bank during weekends.

The Other Eyewitnesses

After 22 police, FBI, bank, and other people knowledgeable about the crimes had been called, the prosecution returned to the eyewitnesses. The 32-year-old Chong Choe was Korean born and the only non-Denver native of the six vault employees. Her last name was pronounced "cheh."

The five-toot-tall, 100-pound woman had begun her job at the United Bank on February 25, 1991. Choe explained that she had had a slight problem getting to work on Father's Day. The gate to the parking garage would not accept her pass card, forcing her to park on the street a couple of blocks from the bank. As she walked to the bank, she observed that the gate to the parking garage was improperly in the up position.

Things like that were not unusual at the United Bank. Often the pass cards did not function as they were supposed to. Choe learned to be quite adept at jiggling her card in various locks in order to get doors to open as needed. Other workers likewise reported that their cards did not work ideally. Sometimes, they would have to call the guards for admission when their cards did not work. Nobody checked their claims that they were bank employees and they had no trouble being buzzed into the bank under such circumstances.

Around 8:30, Choe had taken a break to use the restroom. As she reentered the vault, she saw that two men were attempting to get out

Chong Choe

of a mantrap. One was in a guard's uniform. She did not pay much attention to this as she went back to work.

She was diligently counting money and food stamps in station ten, letting nothing distract her when she suddenly found herself staring at the robber's gun. She admitted that she did not get a good look at the intruder, but rather only focused on his weapon with its long, black barrel. The witness was emphatic that the gunman asked "Who is the manager?" not "Who is the cashier?" The robber had ordered her and her fellow employees into the "cage," not the "mantrap." Initially, she thought the stickup was a joke, a practice run by the bank. When she realized it was for real, she became extremely frightened.

Choe told Mr. Sims that she did not really see the robber, but primarily focused on the gun. It had at least a six-inch-long black barrel. The little she remembered was that the robber could not have been older than 40. He was, she guessed, about five-foot-eight. He was not nearly as tall as her brother-in-law who was six-foot-two. Yet, she also insisted the gunman was about the same height as the six-foot-two David Barranco. The robber did not have any visible pimples, scars, or moles. He had on "hard shoes" and an "England-style" hat. The composite drawing looked just like the robber. She had not been able to identify King's photo as that of the robber at any stage of the investigation and was unable to pick out the suspect in court.

Kenetha Whisler followed Choe to the stand. Born in May 1956, the robbed teller was neatly dressed in a white blouse with a visible cross on her necklace. She repeated for the jury her previous description that the robber had been "perfectly groomed," was about six-foot-two, weighed from 240 to 250 pounds, and had on a black derby. The robber had a potbelly and was in his late 30s or early 40s.

Like Choe, when Whisler initially saw the gunman she thought it was a joke, that the intruder was Greg, a supervisor in disguise. She also echoed Christian's claim that she might have previously encountered the robber while working at the bank. But she had taken her job at the United Bank after King had quit as a guard. She further conceded that she did not recognize the robber's hair, sideburns, eyes, nose, lips, or mouth. But she did see his mustache and cheeks. The mustache, she admitted, might have been a fake.

Whisler had arrived for work at about 7:45 that Sunday. She worked full-time and rotated on Sundays. She first noticed the gunman when he was cautiously walking toward her. The witness did not initially see anything in his hand. Whisler only perceived the gun when she left her station as the intruder ordered her to "Get out and go lie with the others." By this time, the robber was only one foot from her. She clearly saw both his gun and face. His voice was also quite distinctive. She would never forget it.

Once she was down on the floor, she and her fellow workers were forced to crawl into "the doorway," i.e., the robber did not use the term "mantrap." After they had been in the little room for about a half an hour and had gotten up, they feared that they would not be able to get out. Looking around, she noticed something on the ledge of a doorsill. She asked David Barranco to hand it to her, discovering that it was a metal spoon. After monkeying with both the doors, she was able to pop open the lock to the door leading to the area where the armored car couriers brought in the money. She had heard that a plastic card could be used to force the locks to the mantrap doors in an emergency.

Whisler admitted that she had experienced severe trauma from the crime. When the police called her in for a gun lineup to see if she could pick out a Colt .38 from three Smith & Wesson revolvers, she was very nervous when she saw the Colt. Still, she had no doubts about whom she had seen and what she had heard on Father's Day. King was the man who had robbed her. He had spoken out during the stickup and the preliminary hearing in a quiet, calm voice.

I began my cross-examination by discussing Whisler's fixation on King's voice. During the March 2 motions hearing, she had identified the gunman as having a "deeper low voice." This was in contrast with what she had just told Mr. Sims about the perpetrator's voice. What had changed? She stated she did not remember testifying previously that the robber had a "deeper low voice."

The question of King's voice was crucial to Whisler's veracity. Not only did she insist she could identify the intruder by voice, but at the motions hearing in March, she swore that she had clearly heard King ask "Where did that come from?" during the preliminary hearing. The voice at the preliminary hearing was identical with that of the gunman when he barked "Get out and go lie with the others."

Photo by Phil Goodstein

The loading area where armored cars made their deliveries at the United Bank. A surveillance camera is visible just above the van.

When she insisted on this point, I pondered producing another testing device we had prepared for the trial: a recording of King's voice and several others on a high-quality digital tape. My client and five other people were recorded stating in varying sequences: "Get down on the floor and cover your eyes!" "Who is the cashier?" and "Don't look at me!" These were statements which the eyewitnesses had sworn that the robber had used.

Shortly before the trial, we filed a motion for a voice lineup. To test the tape, we sent out investigators to ask the eyewitnesses to listen to the tape and tell us which voice they thought was that of the robber. But the vault employees would not cooperate. Judge Spriggs, in turn, ruled that the police would conduct any voice lineup. In face of this, we withdrew the motion for the voice lineup on May 8, fearing that the police would taint such a lineup in the same manner that they had polluted the photo lineup.

As I continued my cross-examination, I decided against producing the tape recording. Most likely, the district attorney would have challenged it as an unendorsed exhibit and Judge Spriggs would have prohibited me from using it. But so what? The prosecution's move would make the jury think that the district attorney had something to hide.

I did not use the recording because it was a needless roll of the dice. We had lined up an excellent defense to Whisler's claim about hearing King's voice. To dispute her statement that he had spoken out during the preliminary hearing, when we put on our case, we called the court reporter, people who had been at the defense table, and spectators at the preliminary hearing to tell that King had said nothing at that time. We even had Judge Campbell, who had presided at the preliminary hearing, testify that King never made such a remark.

I spent a good deal of time during my cross-examination on Whisler's identification of King. She recalled going through the photo books with FBI agent Kirk on June 20. At that time, she had stated that photos one, eight, and ten looked somewhat like the robber, but their features did not match.

"You didn't remember King's face in there [the photo books]?" I asked. That was because "he wasn't there," Whisler firmly responded. She was convinced that she had only been first shown the photo of King on July 5. Number 16 in the guard books, according to her, was a different man.

The robbed teller was also insistent that she clearly viewed the gunman when he was one foot from her. The gun was also one foot from her. But the robber was holding the gun in front of him. The intruder was not wearing gloves.

I inquired about King's moles. To emphasize them, I had him get up and approach Whisler. She was told to state when he was about as close to her as the assailant had been. At her command, King stopped about three feet from the witness stand. With him standing close to the witness, I asked: "Can you see the defendant?" She admitted that she could. Pointing to his moles, I asked, "Can you see the moles?" "Yes," she replied. I reminded her that she had never described the robber as having moles in any previous statement. Alas, if only a legitimate live lineup of King had been held, we all would have been spared the aggravation of the trial. All the while, Whisler was extremely nervous. She had visibly cringed when King approached her.

Despite her inability to identify the defendant prior to the July 5 lineup and her admission about his moles, she was convinced that King was the gunman. When I inquired what made her so sure, she noted that a "cowboy psychic" had told her so.

In early January, Whisler explained, she had contacted Jerry Ochs of Manitou Springs, Colorado, via her citizens band radio. She met him at a truck stop. A cowboy who claimed to be a psychic, Ochs discussed the robbery of the United Bank with her. When Whisler asked him if he knew where the gun was, he stated that the robber lived in a house that faced east, close to a barn. Nearby was a well that was surrounded by about three feet of water. The well was between 30 and 50 feet deep. The gun was wrapped in a plastic bag at the bottom of the well.

The psychic continued that the gunman had a collaborator who still worked at the bank. He described the accomplice as a woman who was about five-foot-five with light-colored, shoulder-length hair and a slender build. Whisler admitted that the woman the psychic's sketch most reminded her of was the bank's general investigator Danell M. Taylor!

Whisler had informed the district attorney's office of her consultation with Ochs. While King's house faced east, no well was by it. Nonetheless, on the basis of discussing the case with the psychic, Whisler had no doubt that King was the gunman. (Some relatives of Carol King had a psychic perform a card-reading to determine King's guilt. They reported to me that it showed that King was innocent.) In this manner, mysticism and fortunetelling passed in and out of the case.

Nina McGinty was the teller who had hidden from the gunman. She told how she had been working on Father's Day morning. Maria Christian, she remembered, was saying something. Sud-

Nina McGinty

denly, Christian quit speaking in mid-sentence. In response, McGinty looked up and saw the gunman.

At first, McGinty tried to get the attention of Chong Choe, who was working in an adjacent station. But Choe paid her no heed and McGinty was afraid to raise her voice. Almost instinctively, the five-foot-six, 155-pound, 34-year-old woman ducked under a counter, curling up in a corner of her cage behind a wastepaper basket, afraid to make a noise. The gunman briefly came into her station, saw that only food stamps were there, and immediately left. An open door to the cage had blocked the sight of her legs from the robber.

After hiding for 20 to 30 minutes, McGinty realized how silent the vault had become. Eventually, after what she thought must have been an hour, she felt she either had to get out and seek help or feared that she would go crazy. By the time that the police got to her, she was shaking "ferociously," according to another witness, crying, and barely able to walk. She continued to be near tears during her testimony. McGinty lamented that she had to "relive the robbery" at every court hearing.

The witness readily conceded she had been badly scared by the encounter; nonetheless, she insisted she had a "very good look" at the gunman. Stating that "I remember exactly how he looked," McGinty described him as having "silver sideburns." He did not have really fat cheeks, but noticeable cheeks and "maybe a mustache." She did not recall any moles or facial scars. McGinty recollected hearing the robber work a zipper several times.

The intruder was wearing a "dark chocolate brown hat with a woven or beaded headband and a yellow feather." Her description was quite elaborate—she was the only witness to focus on the yellow feather. Others had described the gunman as wearing a derby or cowboy hat. The police had questioned the eyewitnesses in great detail to bring out that the hat was a fedora. As had Maria Christian, the authorities preferred to describe it as a "gangster" hat. The other witnesses, consequently, at police inducement, came to refer to the headgear as a "Bogart-style" or "Dick Tracy" hat.

McGinty was forced to modify how good a look she had at the robber when Scott cross-examined her. She conceded that she only saw the culprit in profile from the left side. The robber was "incredibly tall," six-foot, two-inches or even taller. Unlike the others, who testified that the robber's gun was in his right hand, she was sure the weapon was in his left hand. No profile picture of King had been shown to her during the photo lineup.

During her videotaped statement to the police on Father's Day, McGinty noted that when she first saw the gunman she thought this might be a bank test. The bank had conducted special operations in the vault previously. Perhaps the intruder was a manager. His voice sounded vaguely familiar. She had begun her job at the United Bank on February 11, 1991, about six months *after* King had quit.

After hiding under the desk, she cautiously ventured out, looking for her fellow employees. They were nowhere to be found. She called the guard station, but got no answer. When she phoned 911, she stayed on the line with the police until officers discovered her cowering in the vault.

The robbery had been so severe a trauma that McGinty was briefly hospitalized after it. She was not shown the photos of the 35 past and 15 present guards and bank employees until June 25. The supervising FBI agent had told her to take her time and look at each of the pictures for at least 30 to 45 seconds. She picked out three men who vaguely looked like the robber from the 50 pictures she was shown. None of the men she identified was King.

But, McGinty insisted on the witness stand, she had not the slightest doubt that King was the man. In hushed tones, she swore that when she saw King's picture on July 5, "I got terrified all over again." Holding back her tears and sometimes having to pause to compose herself, she asserted that if she had been shown his face during the initial photo lineup, she would have doubtlessly pinpointed him. The reason she failed to do so during the June 25 lineup was because his photo was not among the pictures before her. When Scott pointed out that not only was the photo in the books shown her, but that it was virtually the same photo of King she had picked out

David Twist

in the July 5 photo lineup, she insisted that the latter was not at all the same. We later called the FBI agent who supervised the lineup. He testified that, on June 25, King's photo had been shown to McGinty when she had *not* identified King as the robber.

Eyewitness David Twist had worked at the bank for a little more than a year at the time of the robbery. The 25-year-old, 150-pound Denver native was six feet tall and believed that the gunman was the same height. The robber, according to Twist, was heavyset, pudgy, and had gray hair and a well-trimmed salt-and-pepper mustache. The culprit had curly hair on the sides, but no moles or scars. He was not sure whether the robber had used the term "mantrap" or simply told him and his fellow tellers to crawl into the "little room."

On July 3, when the police had decided that King was the culprit, they visited Twist at his suburban home. There Denver Police Detective James A. Rock and FBI Special Agent Rene Vonder Haar showed him the six-man photo lineup that included King's doctored picture. They told him to visualize the photos as if the men in the lineup were wearing a hat and sunglasses. None of the previous authorities had told him as much. Obviously, there was something different about this lineup.

Twist picked out King's photo, but he immediately qualified his identification when he told the authorities: "The hair color is not quite right, but I can't tell because of the way the picture is. It doesn't show enough hair. The expression on his face almost exactly matches the face that I saw the day of the robbery. The serious appearance, [and] the features are almost exactly identical." He was drawn by the intent look of King's eyes. But he had not seen the robber's eyes. Like all the other tellers, he had described the gunman as wearing dark sunglasses.

Initially, Twist claimed that he had had a good look at the intruder for at least 30 seconds. He later reduced this to having seen the gunman for 15 seconds at the most. "It was pretty fast," he conceded. The robber had a clear complexion. He could see about one inch above the gunman's glasses. Twist did not observe any moles on the robber, including the one that is just above King's eyebrow. Similarly, he admitted the fact that he had seen King's photo before July 3 might have induced him to identify King again. He specifically answered Mr. Buckley's question about whether he had identified photo number two based on the events of Father's Day by stating: "Yeah, it's based on that and the picture I picked out."

As had the other eyewitnesses, Twist had been badly traumatized by the robbery. He quit the job at the bank shortly after the events of Father's Day. The young man subsequently underwent counseling to help him adjust to what had occurred. All told, his testimony only confirmed that plenty of reasonable doubt could be detected in the eyewitness identifications of King.

After the state had completed calling the eyewitnesses, more detectives and FBI agents took the stand. These were the men who had interviewed Jim King. They told of their initial discussions with King and his claim that he had been looking for a chess game at the time of the robbery. The witnesses noted how King's story changed during different interviews and did not precisely correlate with what Carol King had stated. The law enforcement personnel further told the jury about how they had discovered a map of the bank concourse at King's house, that King's service revolver had disappeared, and that he had lost his driver's license.

When cross-examining the numerous police officers and FBI agents, we reviewed some of the minor details. Why, for example, did one claim he had done something at 10:00 when his report listed him as having done it at 10:30? Or why did the FBI report state that they spent five minutes at one place when the police officer's report stated he and the FBI agent had spent ten minutes there? The purpose was to show that professional law enforcement agents can forget and obscure minor points. This illustrated how easy it was for King to have told slightly different stories to the police during his different interrogations when he was told he was not a suspect. It also demonstrated that it was natural that King's story did not precisely jibe with the alibi provided by his wife.

The dubious nature of the prosecution's case came out further in the testimony of police artist Paige Lida. He admitted that he was instructed to touch up King's driver's license photo to make the picture look as much as possible like the composite sketch of the robber. Other witnesses only repeated hearsay stories about King. Judge Spriggs sustained our objections against allowing some of this into evidence.

Carol King Testifies

The state also called Carol King. A few years before the trial, the legislature had abolished the long-standing rule that a spouse cannot testify against her partner in court. Previously, a husband or wife could only be called in a crime against one of the spouses or their children. On the basis of the new law, the prosecution took the initiative when it put Carol on the stand as a hostile witness. Its goal was to poke holes in the alibi she provided for King before the defense had the chance to put on its case—a bold and brave move.

A few minor discrepancies appeared between Carol's story and what her husband had previously told the authorities. But there was nothing in her testimony that impinged on Jim's essential claim to have been looking for a chess game before visiting the cemetery with her on Father's Day. Her husband, she noted, had once unsuccessfully sought to grow a beard and had worn a mustache on-and-off for the last ten years.

She did not know what had happened to the Colt revolver. While her husband was a police officer and a bank guard, he hung the gun in the holster and belt in the closet or placed the revolver in a locked box. After he quit the bank, the gun was no longer there. Her

Carol King

husband did not worship his service revolver. While he had a display case in his den which showed his sergeant's badge, handcuffs, and other police memorabilia, Jim had never been fixated by his gun.

Carol also noted how she and her husband had talked about the need for a larger safe-deposit box for at least a month before Father's Day. At the most, Mr. Buckley got her to admit that she had not accessed the larger new box. She had been with Jim when he went to the bank to get the larger box on June 17, but had not entered the bank, waiting for him in the car while she smoked a cigarette.

Prosecutor Buckley demanded to know why King shaved off his mustache about a week after Father's Day. Carol noted that he had complained about pimples under it. Thereupon, Mr. Buckley showed her the driver's license photo which had been taken on June 28. As late as June 24, King still had his mustache when he had first talked to the FBI. The June 28 photo did not show any pimples. If he had them, the photo would clearly show them, wouldn't it? Carol calmly replied that pimples can go away in a few days. Even at that, she was able to point to a blemish on the driver's license photo under Jim's nose. She could see the scar because "I knew where they [the sores] were."

During my cross-examination of Carol, I established that King had not left their suburban house until around 9:15-9:30 on Father's Day. I further brought out that King did not have any formal clothing and suits. He was a casual dresser who had few sports coats and ties. The former police officer had never been one for fancy affairs.

To accentuate this, I specifically asked, "You mean he doesn't have one [a suit] like mine, that matches?" Then, glancing down at my pants, I added, "At least I hope it matches." I used this levity to try to lighten up the courtroom. I hoped to show that the prosecution was grasping at phantom clues in its vindictive desire to get King. The point was to establish that King was not the "extremely well-dressed" man described by two of the eyewitnesses. I brought this out further by what King wore during the trial. He was usually attired in a respectable, but not flashy tan corduroy jacket and brown pants. Occasionally, he wore a dark sports coat. These were his "dress" clothes.

(King was encumbered by concealed ankle restraints in court. During breaks, he was taken to a holding cell. To vary his bleak jail diet, I arranged for a member of my staff to deliver lunch to him there during the trial.)

After Carol King had spent the better part of two days on the witness stand, her youngest son, David, was called as a hostile witness. Known as Dave, the young man was a skilled mechanic who loved to dabble with automobiles and other machinery. At any one time, he had four to eight cars around the house. He had his father store the vehicles' titles in the family safe-deposit box.

In court, Dave talked about his father's service revolver. The 26-year-old had been fascinated by it as a boy and had, on occasion, fired it at a local shooting range. King had once promised to give the pistol to his son when he retired. Dave was quite interested in weapons. His gun collection was far better than his father's.

A quiet young man with a high voice, Dave was informally dressed on the stand. He faithfully accompanied his mother to the trial. Under oath, Dave recalled that, about nine months before the bank robbery, a couple of months after his father had quit as a bank guard, in October 1990, he was working on a car in the King family garage. His father approached him, inquiring if he would like his Sam Browne gun belt. "He brought out the gun belt he had as a policeman and asked if I wanted it," Dave told the jury. "I asked if it came with the gun. He said, no, he got rid of it." That was when King told his son that he had disposed of the gun. "It would blow up in your face," his father explained about what would happen should one fire a revolver with a cracked cylinder. Dave did not want the belt if it did not include the gun.

Dave was not enthusiastic about revolvers. He preferred semi-automatic handguns to revolvers and was more interested in having the Colt Trooper for target practice than as a sentimental keepsake. Even at that, King's youngest son was emphatic that his father no longer had the .38 revolver by this time. Dave stated that, prior to quitting the bank, his father had said that the gun was defective, old, and in need of costly repairs. The son had not seen the Colt Trooper or speed loaders after his father quit the United Bank.

Mr. Buckley spent an inordinate amount of time trying to turn the witness's words around. He asked Dave why he had not told the police this story about the pistol. Dave explained what had happened. He was discussing the case with the police and was about to mention the fate of his father's revolver when the police officer was paged. The latter immediately asked to use the phone. After he made the call, the police officer did not return to the subject of the gun. According to Mr. Buckley, the police officer's failure to pursue this topic was actually David King's fault.

The district attorney scored during his redirect examination of Dave when the youth stated that his father had never told him precisely what was wrong with the pistol. This contrasted with his earlier statement that the revolver had a cracked cylinder. But since his father had already chucked the gun, Dave realized it would be beating a dead horse to discuss how to fix the discarded revolver. This led Mr. Buckley to fulminate against his own witness. It was obvious that the testimony of Carol and Dave King, far from impinging on the defendant's alibi, had supported our case.

The prosecution sought to rebut King's story that he was looking for a chess game by calling witnesses from the Capitol Hill Community Center. They did not add anything new. At the most, they merely demonstrated the difficulty of proving a negative: that because they did not see King at the community center did not mean that he had not briefly been there looking for a chess game. The center, the witnesses conceded, still got occasional inquiries about the location of the chess club.

In what the law calls a "view of the premises," at the prosecution's request, the jury took a field trip when it visited the bank to get a first-hand glance at the crime scenes. Judge Spriggs ordered everybody on the tour be completely silent. The jurors were closely under the control of the bailiff. They were not to ask any questions or speak to anyone. King waived his right to accompany the jury on the tour, but Scott and I tagged along with the prosecutors. In an eerie pantomime, Mr. Buckley was permitted silently to point at what he believed were key items at the bank. Escorted by bank and court personnel, we entered the bank by the freight elevator, walked down the hall into the control room, saw the mantrap, and entered the vault. I thought the trip was quite useful. Previously, the prosecution had wanted to show the jury a highly selective video about its version of the murders and robbery. Judge Spriggs had quashed the introduction of that evidence.

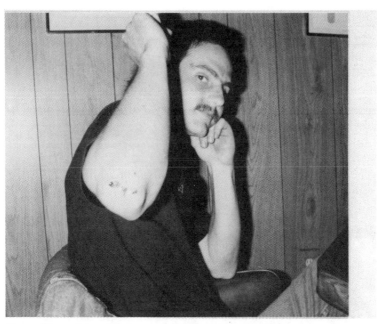

Dave King shows scabs on his elbow. He had cut it the weekend before his father's arrest. A tissue he had used to stop the bleeding was initially cited by the police as evidence of the blood on Jim King's hands.

The 5:04 Alarm

After the jury returned from the bank tour, Jim Prado took the stand. The tall, lanky, cleanly shaven man was the staff coordinator of uniformed security guards at the bank. Far and away the most knowledgeable person on the bank's security system, Prado had been with the United Bank since 1977. He had left his job in the wake of the Father's Day Massacre after protesting that new security measures demeaned and depersonalized the guards. As one of the people investigating the crime, Prado was sure it was an inside job, but thought it was quite possible that more than one person had been involved.

The witness conceded that there were a lot of lapses in the bank's security system. Many of the faults had been corrected in late August 1990, just *after* King had left the bank. Among the changes was that a pass card was necessary to access the armored vault. Prior to that time, guards entered it with what was known as an MK-1, a master key.

There had been problems with the surveillance cameras, Prado admitted. A camera monitoring the guards in the control room had been turned on and off in the years before the robbery. It was initially installed after a guard had badly damaged a VCR when he spilled a drink on the machine in late 1988 or early 1989. This was well before King had been hired by the bank. In other words, the camera was installed to protect bank property, not bank employees. The camera had only been made permanent on April 1, 1991, when Norwest Banks took over the United Bank. Now and then, guards turned the camera away from the central console in the monitor room.

Prado identified Doug Bagley, as the guard who had spilled the drink on the VCR. Another time, Prado reported, Bagley had improperly sought to leave the monitor room to get a snack, leaving the security center unattended. So this would not be noticed, Bagley had propped open the mantrap door to the guard shack with a pop can. In the process, he locked himself out of the monitor room. He had pulled off the hinges to the door to get back in. Bagley was fired for violating bank rules. His actions were amazingly similar to what had happened on Father's Day.

Sometimes, Prado continued, rules were relaxed on weekends. The camera observing the security center had been periodically moved. One guard had discovered its whereabouts and had tampered with it. The VCR for the camera had been placed in various spots around the monitor room, including the supervisor's office. On the day of the murders, the machine recording the surveillance camera's images was on the top shelf of a bank of VCRs in the guard shack.

Mr. Buckley got Prado to state that King knew about this surveillance camera. The defendant had once pointed to it, asking Prado what it was for. "To keep you guys in line," was the supervisor's response.

Not all of the guards knew about the camera. The witness doubted that Mankoff or McCullom were aware of it. As recently hired guards, Wilson and McCarthy certainly did not know it was spying on them. The implication was that there was something sinister about King's knowledge of the camera. In a June 19, 1991, statement to the FBI, Prado had reported that all the guards knew that the camera was in the control center, watching them.

Prado also noted that alarm 206 went off at 5:04 AM on Father's Day. It was located in a records tunnel near the security center and armored vault. Sometimes also referred to as a storage room or a storage tunnel, the area was used for the temporary storage of bank records. This part of the concourse level was originally designated the "security vault tunnel," designed to link the armored vault with the security vault. The idea was that employees with valuables in hand could go from one vault to the other without encountering any outside personnel or having to pass through mantraps. This never worked out. For a few years, the room was simply an empty tunnel. It was later set aside as a place to store records which needed to be retrieved or sent to an archival collection outside of the bank complex. Once inside the records tunnel, a person could access virtually any part of the concourse level, including the armored vault, with only a master key.

Microwave alarms were at both doors of the tunnel, designed to go off if there were motion in the room. They had been installed in

Jim Prado's testimony was valuable in exposing the United Bank's shoddy security system.

about 1983 or 1984, right after this section of the bank had been completed. During 1988 and 1989, the bank had considerable trouble with the alarms. The motion detectors would go off in the middle of the night and apparently for no reason. Prado observed that one was too close to a fluorescent light. When the light was removed, there was no more trouble with that alarm.

Moths would not trigger the alarms, Prado noted, but sometimes mice would. The motion detectors would also sound if something fell off the shelves or the fan blew the wrong way. Nine days after the robbery, on June 25, 1991, an alarm had sounded in the tunnel caused by a water leak. None of these factors had caused a false alarm in the month prior to the murders.

Often the witness's answers undercut the prosecution's case. Prado, for example, conceded that things were not normal on Father's Day morning. Phillip Mankoff was violating bank rules when he took Scott McCarthy into the armored vault while money was being counted there. Under such circumstances, Prado informed the jury, guards had been told to "stay out." Nor was much to be made of some of the security cameras. The one watching the loading dock was a "dummy camera." No tape recording system was attached to it and no one monitored its images. The camera observing the freight elevator, where the man identifying himself as Bob Bardwell phoned for admission, was of such poor quality that a guard could not really see the caller. The company which had installed the camera had ordered a replacement for it prior to Father's Day, but the new camera had yet to be procured.

On subject after subject, Prado's answers aided rather than hurt King. There was, for example, the question of Bob Bardwell's lost access card. As soon as a card was reported lost, Prado explained, the guards canceled it in the computer system so it would not work. They then issued and delivered a new card. Only regular weekday guards processed such cards. A weekend guard like King was not assigned this operation.

Mr. Buckley sought to make a lot about the fact that King had wandered through all parts of the bank. Was this part of his duty as a guard? Yes, was Prado's answer. The entire complex was the responsibility of the guards. "No place was off limits" to them. He was not suspicious, but rather pleased that King patrolled the bank so thoroughly. Indeed, he gave King a warm, friendly smile when he had identified him for Mr. Buckley.

Scott Robinson subjected Prado to a long and revealing cross-examination. Rather than asking leading questions and probing the witness's statements in order to trap him and show the inconsistency of his previous testimony, Scott asked Prado to tell the jury more about the operations of the security system at the United Bank. In the process, the witness cited other lapses in the bank's security system and why he doubted that the robbery and murders were a one-man job.

Among the aspects of the crime that Prado could not explain was the missing VCR tapes. Ten of the machines were empty. One, however, was still loaded. This was the one for the camera that surveyed motor bank two. That facility, at 1760 Grant Street, was not at all involved in the murders and the intruder would have had no reason to take the tape of the camera monitoring it. But most of the other surveillance tapes similarly had no connection with the crimes. So why did the intruder only fail to make off with this tape? Did he simply miss it? Or had he deliberately left it there hoping to implicate Bill McCullom who had been patrolling near that area in the hours before the robbery? Similarly, there appeared to be no reason why the murderer stole some keys and left others behind.

This was only the beginning. In great detail, Scott took Prado through the nature of the bank's alarm system. So the jury would understand exactly what had happened at the bank in the hours before the murders, he had Prado get up and write the times of the different alarms and guard reports in big red letters on a chart. Most of all, Scott thoroughly explored what had happened with the 5:04 alarm.

Prado observed that after the alarm went off at 5:04 AM, it was not reset until 9:33 AM, right in the middle of the crime, probably after the four guards had been slain. Why? What did this indicate? Moreover, the bank's computerized records of doors opening and closing on the concourse level had a crucial 22 minute gap between 9:26, when Todd Wilson entered the control room, to 9:48, when the door to the vault opened. Prado did not know what had happened here.

Other mysteries unfolded on Father's Day. Prado could not explain why there was no record of Mankoff being on the job between 12:42 and 6:33. Records showed McCullom had left the monitor room at 12:50 to make a routine tour of the bank. But if Mankoff was not in the monitor room, something was wrong. One guard was always supposed to be there. Mankoff and McCullom had worked together previously on Sundays. Sometimes they had violated bank rules by both leaving the monitor room.

Records further showed that McCullom was outside the bank at the Sherman Street entrance at 2:26 AM. This was not part of his normal rounds. McCullom's card was subsequently used to access the cash vault at 3:54. There was no record of where McCullom was for the next hour or so when the 5:04 alarm sounded.

While escorting the Metro SWAT team around the crime scene after the murders, Prado found a plastic coffee cup, partially crushed Seven-Up can, and cigarette butts in the storage area where the 5:04 alarm had gone off. He and the police did not pay much attention to them. Prado did not then know that the alarm had sounded that morning. Rather than taking this vital evidence to the police lab where it could be examined, the investigating officers had left the cup, can, and cigarette butts where they found them.

There were immediate suspicions that the storage tunnel could have been linked to the crime. During the initial efforts of the Metro SWAT team to search the bank, one officer had been stymied in trying to gain entrance to the tunnel. He asked Prado for a key to it. The policeman, with a shotgun in hand, told Prado to be careful. Prado was to unlock the door, but not to open it. He was instructed to stand back while the officer, with his shotgun ready for action and fearing that an intruder might be hiding within, burst into the tunnel. Silence!

As the policeman secured the door, he flicked on the light switch. He did not see anybody lurking in the tunnel, but did not want to take any chances. The officer left to get reinforcements to search this area of the bank. About this time, Prado noticed the coffee cup, cigarette butts, and Seven-Up can right inside the doorway. Nothing was done with them, he explained, because of what happened next. The police officer returned with reinforcements who searched the tunnel, looking for a gunman or McCullom. About the same

Photo by Joe Mahoney, courtesy Scott Robinson

Scott Robinson, left, cross-examines Jim Prado.

time, a detective, who needed Prado's help elsewhere, called the guard supervisor away. The coffee cup, cigarette butts, and pop can remained in place for almost a month.

They only again came to light when Prado was discussing the crime with an off-duty policewoman, Sue Scott. She was among the officers who had responded to the United Bank on Father's Day. Shortly thereafter, she had taken a part-time job as a guard at the bank. As she was going through the innards of the financial institution with Prado on a shift from 11:00 PM to 7:00 AM on July 13-14, he mentioned the items in the records tunnel. When she observed they were still there, untouched since the time of the crime, she took out an evidence bag and turned the coffee cup, cigarette butts, and pop can over to the authorities.

These items could be evidence that the intruder and a possible inside accomplice had been waiting around in the bank since the 5:04 alarm. But the police did not do much with them. While they dusted the cup and pop can for King's prints—the examinations were negative—no efforts were made to test the coffee cup or cigarettes for DNA which might have shown who had committed the crime. (King did not smoke.) By the time this material was produced as exhibits in court, the cigarette butts had disappeared. Nobody was sure what had happened to them. Was this the meticulous, step-by-step investigation of which the FBI and police had boasted? Was somebody trying to hide something?

Once the alarm to the records tunnel had sounded, Prado explained, it automatically reset itself. A guard, in turn, was expected to "access" it. This meant he was supposed to acknowledge the alarm by pushing the appropriate button on the central console and filing a report. He should then investigate the alarm. If he was alone in the control room, he was to radio his partner and have him survey the area. If nobody was available to check the source of the alarm, a supervisor should be contacted. The witness was not sure of precisely what had happened since the pages from the log book, which would have recorded the guards' response to the 5:04 alarm, were taken by the killer.

Another curiosity was the Mosler system. This was the brand name of the bank's security alarm system. It recorded on a computer the opening and closing of all alarmed doors. The terminal for the computer, which printed out its records, was in the monitor room, close to where the guards were killed. If the murderer was such an intimate insider who knew all about the security system, why did he not try to destroy or steal these records? Prado noted that the computer could generate them anew. But, he conceded, no effort had been made to damage or destroy the computer.

The Mosler records were crucial. They allowed Prado and the police to trace the exact time when doors had been opened, markey cards were used, and alarms had gone off on Father's Day. The system further noted that the records tunnel alarm had been accessed. It also showed that the alarm had not been reset by the guards as it should have been. Not until 9:33, apparently right after the guards had been murdered, was it "secured," i.e., turned off on the central control panel so that no one looking at the monitor would have been able to tell that it had sounded that morning. In other words, no alarm guarded the tunnel, right off the cash vault, from 5:04 until 9:33. Therefore, Prado did not know how many people could have come and gone from the storage area during that period. Criminals could well have been hiding there in preparation for the robbery and murders. Maybe someone was searching for compromising bank records there and had betrayed accomplices afterwards.

Prado did not discover that the 5:04 alarm had gone off until one or two days after the murders when he reviewed the Mosler records. But, he stated, when he first entered the monitor room after the murders and examined the console table, he immediately noticed a green light on—an indication that the alarm to stairwell C, the path taken by the intruder from the subbasement to the concourse level, had been tripped. If the murderer had deliberately reset the alarm to the records tunnel, why did he not do the same to the other alarm? Prado had no answer to this question.

Courtesy United Bank

The Denver-U.S. National Bank was renamed the United Bank in 1970. Shown are officers of the corporation hoisting its flag near the bank at East 17th Avenue and Broadway.

Alarms had also gone off at 8:15 and 8:17 on staircase C, an hour before the intruder had gone up this flight of stairs. Prado could not explain why the culprit would have taken the stairs from the subbasement to the concourse level, setting off the alarm. No such alarm would have sounded had the gunman taken the freight elevator. A former guard like King would have known this.

Could it be, Scott asked, that maybe the intruder deliberately used the door? Might he have wanted the alarm to sound to draw a guard out of the monitor room? Prado admitted there would be no other reason for the guards to have gone to the subbasement that morning. Once more, the missing pages from the log book meant that the security supervisor could not explain precisely what had happened in response to the 8:15 and 8:17 alarms.

Between 9:05 and 9:07, McCarthy, Mankoff, and McCullom each separately used their markey cards to enter the guard shack. Todd Wilson was also in the room. It was highly unusual to have four guards on duty during the weekend, much less all of them together in the security headquarters. Shortly thereafter, Wilson had left to patrol other parts of the bank. This was the situation when the man identifying himself as Bob Bardwell called for admission at 9:14. It was possible that McCullom was then out of the guard center and was ordered by radio to let Bardwell into the bank. Prado did not know for sure. Mankoff's writing was in the recreated page of the log book that described this event.

There were no signs of struggle in the freight elevator. This could show, Prado conceded, that McCullom knew the intruder. He might not have been immediately overpowered by the gunman as the police had hypothesized. The more Scott took Prado through the details of the security system and the specifics of the morning of June 16, the more questions arose about precisely what had happened.

Another curiosity was that the killer or killers had not taken McCullom's radio. If the next goal of the murderer or murderers was the guard shack, it would seem natural to have taken it. That way he/they could have listened to the guards' conversations to hear if anything appeared amiss.

The security supervisor further noted that there had been major changes in the United Bank security system after King had left the bank. King would not have known about them. Nor did the prosecution present any evidence that King had any connections with the bank after he had quit as a bank guard in August 1990.

The prosecution witness was dubious of the claim that King or any one man had committed the crime. He noted that King was a competent guard who reported faulty doors, burnt-out light bulbs, and similar faults which other guards missed. Nor was there anything unusual about King having a map of the bank concourse. Such plans were issued to all guards. It usually took a weekday guard one to three months to get a grasp of the topography of the United Bank. Weekend guards, naturally, needed even more time to learn the layout of the institution.

King, Prado stated, showed his commitment to the job by seeking to master the complicated system of corridors in the interior of the complex. The witness also observed that King had worked the shift between noon and midnight. He would not have known the precise procedures of what went on at the bank on Sunday mornings when the money was counted. By the time Prado left the stand, it was obvious that the prosecution's theory of the case did not come close to explaining what had happened on Father's Day.

Mr. Buckley sensed this. To rebut his own witness, he again called Detective Priest. Now he was an expert on the bank's security system. Detective Priest swore that power fluctuations sometimes caused false alarms in the storage tunnel. It was possible that a fan in the storage area had moved light fixtures, setting off the motion detector. But he could establish that this had happened. Nor did it explain why the coffee cup, pop can, and cigarette butts were in the records tunnel. The prosecution dismissed them as litter, possibly left there by the employee supervising the storage area.

Thomas A. Tatalaski Sr. was the next witness. As the bank risk and security manager, he was the official in charge of hiring and firing all guards. The 51-year-old executive came off as pompous on the stand. Rather than answering "yes" and "no" to questions, every response was a formal declarative sentence. Typical was his reply to the question of whether he noticed King in the courtroom. He hesitated for a while before saying that he could identify James King. Even at that, the James King he knew had a mustache and long sideburns. Tatalaski was the only man who had ever seen King with such long sideburns. Similarly, despite all the evidence and bank records to the contrary, Tatalaski declared that floor L-7, where the secured elevator had been found, was the place where weekend and evening employees were assigned to park.

On cross-examination, Tatalaski admitted that he believed that the composite drawing most closely resembled Mike McKown. He likewise stated that he was initially sure that Paul Yocum was involved. The risk and security manager was insistent that Yocum was the man who had stolen the money from the automated teller. Besides, he had told the police during the initial phases of the investigation that Yocum was a lot smarter than he appears or acts. If protruding ears were added to the composite drawing, he confessed, he would have identified it as a sketch of Paul Yocum.

The Mind of a Police Officer

In its effort to attack King's character, the prosecution relied heavily on psychology. Dr. John Nicoletti was a clinical psychologist who had received his Ph.D. from Colorado State University in 1972, writing his dissertation on "Use of Anxiety Management Training in the Treatment of Generalized and Specific Anxieties." His résumé noted that he had spent 19 of the 19.7 years he had had his doctorate working with law enforcement agencies. After he had requested a $540 fee for his testimony in this case, the court granted him a payment of $240.

Dr. Nicoletti insisted that police officers have a deep attachment to their guns. The only times he had found when a former officer had disposed of his weapon was if he had had a very negative encounter during a shooting or had left the police department in disgrace. The probability was low, he told the court, that a retired officer would throw away both his badge and pistol. In other words, King's junking of his revolver indicated he might have committed the crimes.

There was no evidence, Dr. Nicoletti conceded on cross-examination, that King had thrown away his badge. He likewise stated that his studies did not address the question of defective weapons. On the contrary, in the instances where police officers had gotten rid of their weapons, he had assumed that the firearms were safe and in working order.

I confer with Jim King during the trial.

Dr. Nicoletti also admitted that he had not had the opportunity to make a direct clinical examination of King. To accentuate the dubious nature of his testimony and psychological portrait of the retired police sergeant, I showed Dr. Nicoletti the trophy case the police had seized during their search of King's house. Here was King's sergeant's badge, handcuffs, stripes, whistle, identification card, and other evidence that showed that the defendant took pride in his years as a police officer. All he was testifying to, the psychologist replied, was about what a "typical cop" would keep. King, Dr. Nicoletti concluded, was not a "typical" police officer.

Mike McKown

Central to the prosecution's case was the testimony of Mike McKown. He was a former guard who had worked closely with King when the two were at the bank. Not only was McKown a suspect since he wore a mustache and had been vaguely identified as the possible killer, but a chess set belonging to McKown was found at the site of the crime. The evidence against him seemed so ominous that, after King had been arrested, the authorities brought McKown to Denver from Seattle on August 1, 1991. They intensively grilled him for seven hours during the next two days, videotaping his statement. They further took him to a storage locker he rented in the area, examining it. Nothing connected to the bank robbery was found. By the time of the trial, McKown had relocated to Butte, Montana.

Born on April 14, 1947, McKown explained that he had retired from the Air Force in February 1988 after a 20-year hitch. During his years in the military he had been an intelligence expert. After getting out of the service, he had sought to get a teacher's certificate by attending school at the University of Colorado at Denver while he worked weekend shifts at the United Bank from February 1988 until June 1990. Before long, he was the senior weekend guard. In that capacity, he was charged with training new guards. He showed them how to patrol the bank and perform minor maintenance tasks. There was a high turnover in the guard ranks and he usually trained one to two new workers a month. All told, he figured he must have trained about two dozen guards. Among them was King.

After King had been on the weekend job for about six months, he and McKown were assigned to work together. They became close buddies. Typical was how McKown explained to King the

Mike McKown as viewed with the overlay of the robber's disguise.

necessity of having good walking shoes on the job. A couple of weeks after McKown had shown King the superior qualities of his particular pair of Reebok shoes, the former guard noted King wearing a comparable pair of shoes.

Much of the guard's work was extremely boring. The guards overcame this by watching videos and playing video games on the television monitors. King, in turn, let McKown and the other guards know that he was an avid chess player, always ready for a game. He kept after McKown to play chess when they were on duty together. Responding to King's suggestions, McKown brought a gold and silver chess set, which he had owned for some years, to the bank for games. Before long, one of the bishops broke. They usually played on King's much more durable traveling set.

McKown readily conceded he was not much of a chess player and that King always beat him. Even when the retired police sergeant gave him a heavy advantage, McKown lost to Jim. The witness thought so little of chess that he left his set behind after he quit the bank.

When first interviewed on June 17, McKown informed the authorities that the bank's security system was atrocious. Doors which the guards had locked would be left unlocked by cleaning crews and other employees. Frequently the keys did not perform as they should. It was to King's credit that he had discovered some blank master keys in a maintenance station where there was a key-making machine. He had made better master keys for himself and his fellow guards.

Unauthorized people were always in secured areas of the bank. On more than one occasion, McKown had encountered tourists within the bowels of the bank. They had wandered into the public bank atrium, taken a wrong turn, and had suddenly found themselves lost in limited-access areas. There were somewhere between 15 and 20 places where unauthorized persons could enter the bank on weekends. McKown dismissed the security cameras and locks as "window dressing." All told, "there was no security in the bank."

After resigning as a guard, McKown had to undergo surgery. King acted as his personal chauffeur upon his release from the hospital. McKown then considered King his best friend. The health problems made McKown's black hair start to turn gray. To cloak this fact, he dyed his hair. Meanwhile, McKown's marriage collapsed and he moved in with his sister in Kent, Washington, working part-time in an elementary school in Federal Way, Washington.

The former guard still kept in touch with King. To attend his daughter's graduation, he visited Denver in early June 1991. While in town, he had lunch with King on June 1. McKown learned of the Father's Day Massacre when his former wife called him at his suburban Seattle home on the night of June 16. A few days later, King sent McKown a handwritten note, dated June 21, which McKown received on June 24:

> I thought you might want to hear about the United Bank murders and robbery? Have you been getting the news of it up there in the far northwest? Of course they are blaming the guards and ex-guards. The police and FBI have not yet questioned me, but I guess they'll get around to it soon. I'm going to Las Vegas and Phoenix, Ariz. next month for a short vacation.
>
> Have you found a full-time job yet? United Bank will be hiring more guards since several have just quit.

McKown's uncle, a practical joker who was visiting, saw the letter. He figured it was written in a light-hearted vein and suggested that McKown spook King. This seemed like a good idea to McKown. He decided to call King in the middle of the day while the uncle would play the role of an FBI agent. Telling his uncle: "This is my old partner. Watch this, I'm going to really pull his chain," he placed the call.

King usually screened his calls via an answering machine. When he heard McKown call in the middle of the day, he figured it must be important and picked up the phone. McKown, in a deadpan voice, told him that the FBI had been to see him and had found King's letter. The feds wanted to know where King got the money for his trip to Las Vegas. While McKown was expecting King to laugh at this, he found King unnerved.

The call came about 30 minutes after the FBI had first visited King. "The FBI was just here, but I don't have an alibi," he told his buddy in Washington state. McKown initially thought that King was responding to the joke in kind, saying that he would let his FBI agent talk to those in Denver. Only then did he realize that King was deadly serious and afraid. "Why do they want to know?" King asked about the Las Vegas connection. "I explained that to them already." Realizing that the call was, in McKown's words, "the classic example of a joke gone flat," he tried immediately to end the conversation. He spent the next few minutes discussing with the former police sergeant what had happened.

District Attorney Sims sought to make a lot out of McKown's phone conversation with King. According to the prosecutor, King's remarks were evidence of his guilty conscience. Rather than expressing his sorrow about what had happened to the murdered guards, King had told McKown that "he was kind of stuck." He only cared about himself. An innocent man, the prosecutor implied, would not need to worry about an alibi or bemoan that he was stuck.

Finally, Mr. Sims showed McKown the composite drawing. Who, he demanded, does it look the most like? McKown, after a brief pause, admitted that it reminded him of Jim King.

During cross-examination, McKown conceded that, as someone wearing a mustache, he could easily have been tabbed as a suspect if he had not been living in Washington state at the time of the murders. "I would have been looking for me," he stated. The former guard also affirmed his earlier statements that he thought that the bank had shoddy security.

The witness testified that he and King had discussed the deficiencies of the bank's security system. So did other guards. Frequently the guards played "war games" about how to rob the bank. All agreed that they would gain access via the freight elevator since the surveillance cameras were of such poor quality that guards could not tell who was requesting admission.

McKown also thought that a robbery would be most likely to succeed where the perpetrator had an inside accomplice in the vault. Such a collaborator would call the police in case an alarm was tripped, telling the authorities it was an accident. It would be necessary that the robber lock up the tellers and guards in a mantrap or a closet. The robber, he and other guards agreed, would best succeed if he only took as much money as he could easily carry.

A further problem of bank security was that the guards were badly treated and poorly paid. There was a "lot of ineptitude, a lot of silly things" at the bank. Despite receiving little more than the minimum wage and getting virtually no benefits, McKown told how the guards were called upon to fill in reams of paperwork and had to undergo long, condescending review procedures. All this added up to a high turnover among the guards. As he had in his videotaped statement to the police, McKown concluded that security "leaks like a sieve" at the United Bank. Indeed, there was no security. "I didn't feel safe. I made suggestions on improvements and they were ignored." The bank's poor security and lack of respect for the guards had been the motivating factors in leading him to resign as a guard a couple of months before Jim King likewise quit that post.

Lastly, McKown praised King to the heavens. He was insistent that King could not have committed the crimes. "This man's probably the most honest person I have ever encountered." During redirect examination, the most that Mr. Sims got out of McKown was that none of the guards had talked about killing anyone during a proposed bank robbery. As he left the stand, in a gesture of

III. **Performance Rating**   Indicate the overall performance rating which best reflects your achievements for the review period. The rating should be based on your performance in all major areas of responsibility and on performance improvement or decline since the last review.

☐ Rating 1 Results achieved consistently far exceeded the requirements of the job.	☐ Rating 4 Results achieved met minimum requirements of the job
☐ Rating 2 Results achieved consistently exceeded the requirements of the job.	☐ Does not meet minimum requirements of the job
☒ Rating 3 Results achieved consistently met the requirements of the job.	

Comments on the overall level chosen: Considering my short time with United Bank and since I only work part-time (when the bank is closed) and my contact with customers and bank employees is limited, a rating of 3 is appropriate. I would not expect my rating to change working in a part time position.

IV. **Performance Strengths**   Comment on your talents, both specifically relating to current job responsibilities and those that may enhance your performance of future responsibilities. If your strengths and expertise could be better utilized, explain how.

My major strength would be that I wish to learn as much as possible concerning private security operations. Also I have a strong back ground of knowledge of criminal law and criminal behavior.

V. **Factors Limiting Performance**   Comment on characteristics of yours that may limit your job performance and therefore need improvement, and those circumstantial, external factors that have inhibited your performance. Both types of factors should be included in the assessment, if appropriate.

Factors limiting my performance would be a lack of motivation or initiative to advance to other areas within United Bank. An external factor that tends to inhibit my performance would be a general lack of concern for real security by most bank employees that I come into contact with.

Jim King was called upon to fill out long self-evaluations as part of his duties as a guard at the United Bank.

solidarity, McKown went over to King and briefly grasped the defendant's shoulder.

Harry Glass testified next. He was the guard whose fingerprint was found on the can of Mountain Dew. The witness was among many former and current guards called by the prosecution. As with McKown, Glass helped rather than hindered King's case.

A stocky young man, Glass explained that he was working part-time at the bank, hoping to be taken on full-time while he studied music at Metropolitan State College of Denver. He had been on duty with guard Richard Rosenberg on the evening shift on June 15. During that time, Rosenberg had been called away from the bank to check on a power outage at a branch bank about a mile away. Upon returning, around 6:15-6:30 PM, he brought Glass a snack from a local fast-food restaurant. To wash it down, Glass had bought the can of pop from a machine near the bank cafeteria, taking it to the guard shack. While he knew it was against regulations for guards to eat in the monitor room, he figured that the rules were relaxed on weekends and eating in the security headquarters was okay as long as the guards kept it under control. He had placed the partially filled can in the trash.

One reason that he ate on duty, Glass explained, was because guards were not given true lunch breaks. The working conditions for the guards were very poor. Compared to other security posts he had taken, the guards were not properly trained. Parking gates were periodically left open, not all guards checked identifications, and unauthorized personnel were often allowed into secured areas of the bank. Among them were members of outside maintenance crews. Sometimes, maintenance workers were not only given free rein in the monitor room, but they even signed the log book for the guards.

On the verge of tears, the long-haired young man explained that he had quit the day after the robbery because "I was emotionally upset over the loss of my friends." The guard also conceded he could have easily been implicated in the crime because his finger-print had been found on the can of Mountain Dew.

Glass further observed that Tom Tatalaski, the director of security for the United Bank, was widely hated by the guards. If anyone was suspect, according to Glass, it was Tatalaski. He had refused to listen to the guards' complaints about the poor security system. Glass had told the police and FBI, when they interviewed him on June 18, that he thought it was curious that Tatalaski happened to be out of town at the time of the robbery.

Next, District Attorney Buckley sought support from the testimony of former guard Dana Pappas. The curlyheaded 29-year-old had only worked at the bank three or four months, from approximately August until October 1990. Jim King had helped train him and had been his mentor. But Pappas was immediately suspicious of King. The retired police sergeant had prowled through the bank's tunnels while on duty and had talked about how a skilled robber could beat the system. King had an "intimate" knowledge of the bank and would go to "irrelevant" places, spots which Pappas could not imagine a guard checking out.

In addition, the defendant was always armed and was insistent that all the guards should be armed. One time, King brought in a newspaper clipping about the shooting of an unarmed guard in a bank robbery. Pappas conceded he had no knowledge that King had actually tried to rob the bank.

On cross-examination, Pappas confessed that he did not have the best record as a bank guard. He had been terminated for unauthorized absences and failure to patrol the bank in the same manner that King did. Other guards described Pappas as strange, anti-social, and deceitful. We noted how Jim Prado, the guard supervisor, had originally suggested that Pappas might be a suspect. This did not make Pappas guilty of the crime, but how was it any more or any less damning than what Pappas told against King? Similarly, what about Pappas' statement, two days after the robbery, that he was sure that Paul Yocum committed the crimes? Did he have any more evidence against King than he did against Yocum? Or was he simply venting his personal hunches?

The prosecution, which had put Pappas on the stand to discredit King and show that the defendant was cynical—as if that were a crime—had problems with Pappas' statements. He insisted that the guards had been disarmed by the bank while he worked there. He had left by October 1990 while the disarming of the guards only occurred in April 1991. The witness claimed that King knew both Bill McCullom and Scott McCarthy. Neither of them had ever worked with the defendant. In fact, Pappas admitted that his entire bank robbery conversation with King had lasted only two minutes and he did not have a very clear memory of it.

Roger Gottschalk was another former guard. He had worked in the weekend post for about four or five months in late 1989/early 1990. Mike McKown had trained him and he had worked shifts with King. Gottschalk recalled that the defendant spent little time in the monitor room, preferring to patrol the bank. During a 12-hour shift, it was not unusual for King to undertake five or six separate patrols. King explained that he needed the exercise provided by walking all around the bank.

When they were in the guard shack together, King informed Gottschalk about his days on the police department. He also spoke about his weapon. The witness specifically remembered King showing him his hollow-point bullets, explaining their superior stopping power.

During cross-examination, Gottschalk conceded that he did not notice anything strange or suspicious about King's work as a bank guard. He was shocked when he initially learned of the arrest of his former partner. Moreover, guards were treated poorly. He also reported that sometimes former guards would visit the monitor room during weekends. Usually, their presence was not recorded in the log book.

The Missing Money

FBI Special Agent Lloyd Cubbison testified on the way in which the bank had determined that $197,080 was missing. He had worked closely on this aspect of the investigation with Craig Suazo of the bank. Craig's brother, George, was a laid-off United Bank guard whom the FBI had investigated as a possible suspect in the robbery.

Craig Suazo told how he had collaborated with the FBI agent in calculating the amount of money that was stolen. They had first added up the total of money listed as having come into the bank that morning. They next reviewed the records in the teller cages prior to the robbery. Finally, the remaining money was physically counted. On this basis, the authorities determined that $38,900 in $100 dollar bills, $33,500 in fifties, $117,880 in twenties, $2,000 in

Examples of the sizes of safe-deposit boxes available at the 1stBank of Westland. King exchanged a box the size of the one on the right for a larger one like that at the left on June 17, 1991, the day after the Father's Day Massacre.

tens, $4,500 in fives, and $300 in ones had been stolen. Altogether, this came to 17,884 separate bills.

The bank provided the FBI with an equivalent amount of cash so the authorities could weigh and measure it. The pile was 1,009 cubic inches, just a bit more than the 1,000-cubic inch capacity of King's new safe-deposit box. The implication was that King had deliberately and knowingly only stolen enough money to fit into the newly rented, larger safe-deposit box.

I objected to this testimony as "ridiculous." It "was wishful thinking, a facade." Besides, Agent Cubbison admitted that he had not been present at the opening of the safe-deposit box. The figure he cited about the bulk of the money did not include room for the other materials King had in the safe-deposit box. Nor did the dimensions of the cash equal the dimensions of the box. The result of the testimony was again to emphasize how nebulous and reaching the prosecution's evidence was.

Nevertheless, the state focused on the safe-deposit box. It called Elizabeth Peralez, the manager of safe-deposit boxes at the bank where King had his box, the 1stBank of Westland. The witness remembered King. She had picked him out of the six-man photo lineup when the police had asked her whether she had ever dealt with King at the bank. She observed that King's eyes were extremely intent in the picture.

The witness stated that King had requested a new, larger box on June 17, the day after the murders. He had spent 12 minutes at the bank at that time. He returned later the same day to visit the box, spending three minutes there. Peralez recalled that one time King carried a green plastic accordion-type folder with him as he went to the safe-deposit box. The container, she informed the jury, seemed ideal for transporting materials to a safe-deposit box and she had wanted to ask King where she could get a comparable folder. According to her records, Peralez told the court that King had visited his new box six times between June 17 and July 1.

Peralez never saw King carrying any bulky packages from the safe-deposit box. At the most, the green folder appeared to be "lumpy in the middle" when he was delivering something to the box. The defendant was always calm and relaxed. She also testified to the size of King's previous box and how it would not have easily contained the box of floppy disks which King wished to store in the safe-deposit box.

Still, the prosecution sought to make the multiple visits to the safe-deposit box a link with criminal intent. Detective Priest testified to the materials taken from the box. He swore that they could easily fit into the smaller box. During cross-examination, Scott Robinson asked him to demonstrate, giving the detective the storage box for floppy disks. Detective Priest was not enough of a magician to be able to get it to fit in the old, narrow safe-deposit box.

Surprise Witnesses

Finally, the district attorney sought to call a couple of unendorsed witnesses who would rebut King's alibi. Mr. Buckley told the court that he had found two men who would testify that they had seen King at the West Ninth Avenue and Bannock Street VFW hall which had been the meeting place of the Denver Chess Club after it left the Capitol Hill Community Center. This would prove that King would not have been looking for a chess game at the community center on Father's Day.

I objected. Mr. Buckley has a notorious reputation for last-minute surprise witnesses at murder trials. Before someone is allowed to testify, the prosecution must tell the defense about that witness. This allows us to investigate and try to question the witness.

In seeking to learn more about these surprise witnesses and the whole issue of King's involvement with the Denver Chess Club, my chess ties were crucial. Officers of the chess club, when interviewed by the police and FBI, kept referring the authorities to me as the person most knowledgeable about the Denver Chess Club. The district attorney even subpoenaed some of the club's rather scanty records from me. I, in turn, was able to use my links with people around the Denver Chess Club, the Colorado State Chess Association, and the United States Chess Federation to produce King's chess records and information about the surprise witnesses.

Despite my objections, Judge Spriggs permitted two men to testify for the prosecution about the Denver Chess Club. Larry Duke had been active at the club when it was at the Capitol Hill Community Center. He had also played at the West Ninth Avenue and Bannock Street VFW hall, but had not gone to the West Colfax location in recent months. It was "well over a year ago" or "one or two years ago" that he had last seen King at the chess club. Perhaps, it was the evening when I was playing King on July 2, just before the arrest.

"I'm just guessing" the witness told Mr. Buckley about the assertion that he might have seen King at the Bannock Street location. He did not know King personally and never recalled playing chess with him. It was quite possible that the defendant would not have known that the chess club had moved from the community center. Neither the chess club nor the Capitol Hill Community Center could produce specific records showing exactly when the club had vacated the center.

The other prosecution chess player was Al Skarie, a post office employee, who came into court wearing his summer carrier's uniform. I did not know him from my days at the chess club. Neither did most of the other active members of the club. His abode was not the Denver Chess Club, but the Aurora Chess Club. Somehow, the authorities had dredged him up in their desperate efforts to get King. On cross-examination, he readily admitted that he was not 100-percent sure about his memory about where he had played chess with King, whether at the Bannock Street VFW or at the Capitol Hill Community Center. The VFW hall never had the kind of 24-hour-a-day informal games which were part and parcel of the chess club at the community center. No one would go there on a Sunday morning looking for an informal chess game.

After Skarie stepped down from the witness stand, the prosecution rested its case at noon, Tuesday, June 2. It had called 64 witnesses and presented 248 exhibits, mostly photos of the crime scene and evidence that four men had been murdered. Upon the conclusion of its case, I naturally moved for a verdict of acquittal. Judge Spriggs, as I expected, denied it.

Though the prosecution had failed to produce any physical or scientific evidence against King, it had put on an extremely impressive case. While we had done our most to raise doubts about the accuracy of the eyewitness identifications, the district attorney could still point to the fact that five of the tellers had specifically stated that King had robbed them. The prosecutors had done an excellent job of bringing out all the suspicious coincidences that implicated my client. They had likewise well illustrated the weakness of his alibi. I knew we had some hard work before us in putting on the defense.

11

Dewey Baker:
Do We Believe Him?

Right about the time the prosecution was calling its final witnesses, we received new communications from convicted bank robber Dewey Baker. He watched the case on Court TV. This led him to write Scott Robinson three times during the trial on May 13, May 29, and June 4. Typical was his letter of May 13. After stating that he was being framed for the California bank robberies, Baker wanted to make sure that Scott knew he hated lawyers:

> You're the enemy. Cops, lawyers, prosecutors, judges, & politicians, are all the enemy insofar as I'm concerned. I wouldn't piss down a one of your throats if your lungs were on fire. You all of you fall into the classification of "cops," & my feelings are that the only good cop is a dead cop. You & whoever reads that can label me as you will, just remember: it's war & you're the enemy. . . . As little communication as we have, the better I like it. Speaking to you, writing you, going to your courts of injustice—all of it makes me ill. So regardless of how you receive this missive, be it with joy, askance glance, disbelief or without caring one way or another, let's freeze on communicating further. Just leave me be as much as possible, or, as much as circumstances will allow.
>
> Now, what I'm writing at all for—your client, James King, is innocent. I know this because it is I who am responsible for the crimes

224

he's charged with. I don't admit that lightly, & admit it only for my own peace of mind. I'm not trying to imprison innocent persons for my crimes, &, to keep regrets, should'ves, etc., to a minimum, I tell you now I'm guilty for the crimes James King is charged, & he is indeed an innocent man.

The letter had been sent to 149 Court Place—a non-existent address. My office is at 1439 Court Place. Consequently, the post office was delayed in delivering Baker's note. Since Scott did not immediately receive this message, he could not get back to Baker. Meanwhile, on May 29, while the jury was retired, we again asked Judge Spriggs to permit us to point to Baker as an alternate suspect during the defense. Scott outlined the evidence against Baker.

The California suspect was a thoroughly shadowy character. He had stated that he had flown from Denver to California on May 13, 1991. After great efforts, we managed to get the passenger manifests for Continental and United airlines, the two non-stop carriers from Denver to California. None of their flights showed Dewey Baker to have been a passenger on May 13. If he had indeed gone to California on May 13, he must therefore have flown under an alias or by a round-about route.

Otherwise, Baker left a trail of his whereabouts. He continually used the phone calling card of his girlfriend, Linda Johnson, to make long-distance calls. It recorded that he had made calls to or from Berthoud, Longmont, Fort Collins, Pueblo, and Canon City, Colorado, during May. He last used the card in Denver at 11:34 AM on May 13. The next call charged to it was at 2:27 that afternoon from San Francisco.

The calling card showed Baker in California through June. There was, however, about a 24-hour gap between Baker's use of the card at 4:46 PM on June 15 and 6:10 PM on June 16. This was enough time for him to have flown to Denver, commit the robbery, and return to California. It was significant that Baker looked a good deal like the strange man seen at Stapleton Airport shortly after noon on Father's Day. That individual, after all, had been trying to rent a car in California. It was possible that someone other than Baker had been using Linda Johnson's calling card in California as an alibi for the bank robber.

To be sure, a lot of this was no more than sheer conjecture, suspicion and guessing—just like a good part of the state's case against King. Prior to his letter of May 13, 1992, which we had yet to receive when we raised the issue of Baker as an alternate suspect with Judge Spriggs during the trial, Baker had yet to make a direct confession. He had previously stated that his attorney had told him to take the Fifth Amendment if asked about any involvement in the United Bank robbery. A lawyer cannot call a witness whom he knows will invoke his right against self-incrimination.

Mr. Buckley opposed allowing us to mention Baker as an alternate suspect. He was ready to produce another Baker letter where the California prisoner stated that the accusations against him were "a crock. I never even knew about the job until the PI [private investigator] interviewed me." Some "punk," Baker continued, had made up the charges to get out of a 30-day sentence by foisting the murders on him.

Judge Spriggs was similarly skeptical of Baker as an alternate suspect. He noted that our evidence against him was extremely scanty. "You'd never get this case to a jury." Only if we had a clear confession coupled with the evidence of Baker's presence in Denver at the time of the robbery would he allow us to present him as an alternate suspect. Besides, all the evidence indicated that the murders were committed by someone with an intimate knowledge of the inside workings of the United Bank. Nothing showed that Baker had ever visited the bank. Therefore, Judge Spriggs ruled, we could not mention Baker as an alternate suspect.

One man viewing this hearing on Court TV was Dewey Baker. He called my office at 1:55 PM that afternoon, right after Judge Spriggs' ruling. My secretary, Annette Calvert, took the call, letting Baker do all the talking. He told her about his previous letter in which he confessed the crime. "As someone who had spent 14 years in prison, he had no love of the police," she explained. Still, he stated that "your guy is as innocent as the day is long." King is a "poor, innocent son of a bitch." He noted he might be willing to come to Colorado to implicate himself in the murders, but would most likely plead the Fifth Amendment if he was called to court.

When the jury was again retired, I had my secretary testify before Judge Spriggs about the nature of the call. He thoughtfully listened,

Dewey Baker as disguised with the overlay.

but he did not change his decision. Meanwhile, the next day, a collect call from Baker was inadvertently refused in my office. In response, Baker wrote King, lamenting that we had not replied to his confession:

> Listen, I dunno what da fuck is going on, but whilst trying to take the beef off your (innocent) shoulders, I can't seem to be heard. And to top it off, your attorney is now refusing to accept a collect call from myself. I call "collect" because being in county jail, I *have* to. I talked to your attorney's secretary once, & when next I called, my call was refused. I bring this to your attention only because it's been my experience in the past that attorneys work hand-in-hand with prosecutors, feds, judges & such. And if "The Powers that Be" *want* you to be guilty, you by damn sure will be so adjudged, *with* your attorney's compliance. . . . It seems to me that you're gonna be guilty, innocent or not. But that's our judiciary for ya.

We had sought to endorse Baker and his girlfriend, Linda Johnson, as witnesses prior to the trial. Toward this end, we brought Johnson and her adult son, Michael Mathe, from Ann Arbor,

Michigan, to town to testify. She was ready to state that Baker boasted to her of "the big job in Denver" and "dusting four bank guards." His intent, she informed us, was to use the money from the robbery to buy the couple a new recreational vehicle.

Scott Robinson informed the court how Johnson would testify that Baker told her, after he was paroled from a federal prison in early May, that he "would come back for her in a brand-new RV just as soon as he had done a big job in Denver." A May 17, 1991, letter from Baker to the 44-year-old Johnson read: "Okay, baby, I'm gonna do something big, and then I'm gonna buy us a big old brand-new recreational vehicle." Baker had promised Johnson that he would return to her home in Michigan for the wedding of Mathe on June 24, but he had missed the ceremony. Something had gone wrong, he explained, with the Denver job.

Johnson had met Baker through a personal ad. The California suspect had been serving time for four bank robberies when she responded to his plea for friendship. The two shared an interest in

The United Bank was previously known as the Denver-U.S. National Bank. Before it changed its name, its logo was an outline map of the United States. A bronze model of the bank symbol has been turned into a flower bed.

target shooting. While he was in prison, he frequently wrote and called her. She had picked him up when he was released from a federal prison in Oxford, Wisconsin, on May 2, 1991. As soon as he got in her car, he ripped up his parole papers. Shortly thereafter, he left for Denver. In addition to her story, we also told the court we had uncovered evidence about Baker trying to enlist an ex-con in Pueblo, Colorado, to borrow a pistol.

One person who did not like Baker, and who thought he might well have committed the Father's Day Massacre, was the 25-year-old Michael Mathe. He was displeased by his mother's involvement with Baker. When he had first heard her reflecting that she thought her boyfriend might be involved in the murders, he contacted the FBI on December 3, 1991. He was ready to voice his suspicions about Baker in court.

Given this and Baker's letters, which appeared to be confessions, Judge Spriggs set up a conference call during the noon recess on June 1, between himself, the prosecutors, the defense, Baker, and Baker's attorney, California public defender David Greenbaum. Baker immediately announced that he would not talk to the judge over the phone. He would only speak out in court. Mr. Greenbaum similarly advised his client of his right not to testify. Judge Spriggs thereupon dismissed Baker's claim as "jailhouse chatter." He once more ruled we were not to be allowed to show that Baker was an alternate suspect as the bank robber.

In some ways, Judge Spriggs' ruling helped us. By this time, Scott was jokingly calling Baker "Dewey believe him?" Baker's statements to the press kept changing. In one missive, for example, he claimed he was only coming to King's defense because the defendant was an ordinary fellow and not a cop. Shortly thereafter, he claimed to be shocked to learn that King was a former police officer.

The alternate suspect and his girlfriend were both inherently unbelievable. We feared we might lose credibility with the jury by calling them. After all, the person responsible for the massacre showed extreme sophistication and intelligence. Nobody who had ever talked to Baker would attribute those traits to him. He came across as a simple over-the-counter bank robber, not someone with the discipline and inside knowledge needed to stage the crime.

The prosecution would mock Baker's testimony as a sign of our desperation to get King acquitted. It was ready to produce another Baker letter in which he asserted "I never claimed to have done NOTHING. . . . It takes a weird sumbitch to do that. That isn't my style." Therefore, it was probably best that we did not call Baker or his girlfriend as witnesses. Nonetheless, we insisted that the record show we had pointed to Baker as an alternate suspect—that would help us in case of an appeal.

Other Developments

During the trial, we and Judge Spriggs also received communications from anonymous sources claiming to have special knowledge about the case. Invariably, it was nothing more than fascinated viewers of Court TV who were caught up in the world of Perry Mason. For instance, on May 28, the court received three garbled messages from a man described as having a thick Slavic accent. He promised that he would send the court the sunglasses worn by the robber to show that King was innocent and that the money had been "transferred from your state." Nothing came of this. Numerous other individuals called the court with advice, criticism, and questions. Court personnel reported receiving upwards of a dozen extra calls a day with requests for special favors concerning the case. Court TV, in turn, had the best ratings of any cable station in the area for the 9:00 AM-9:00 PM slot during the trial.

Usually, the courtroom was packed. The demand for a seat at the trial was as great as that for a popular play or sporting event. People lined up for admission and sometimes had to draw lots to get into the courtroom. Local newspapers continually featured the trial on the front page. Reports about it were frequently the lead-off item on local newscasts. The *New York Times* chimed in with a story about the trial.

Shortly before putting on defense reputation witnesses for King, Judge Spriggs held an evidentiary hearing about some of King's writings. We had announced that we would call King as a defense witness. Mr. Buckley insisted that he have the right to introduce to the jury sections of the defendant's unpublished novel which the authorities had discovered on the King's personal computer. Once more, the prosecution sought to tarnish my client before the jury by citing irrelevant materials.

The fictional work was little more than an outline and was as much a possible movie script as it was a novel. The book was something of an eclectic mix of action-adventure scenes, science fiction, detective work, philosophy, and creation myths. Characters represented such figures as Satan, Pandora, Eve, Hercules, the Archangel Michael, Pluto, and Hebrew, Islamic, Chinese, and Hindu versions of God. The theme of the book sought to depict good versus evil and a gathering of the souls as embodied by the horrendous life of the child of a rape victim.

Like most action-adventure works, there was a good deal of sex and violence in the extremely rough draft of the uncompleted book.

CHARACTERS

Major Characters

Satan **(DIANA NATAS)**, The Prince of Darkness, AKA- Daphne (the goddess of the earth), AKA-Dictynna (Greek name of Diana. Greek meaning "hunting-net, refers to Diana as "Huntress", AKA-Alecto (one of furies) She is represented with her head covered with serpents, and breathing vengeance, war and pestilence.
Physical characteristics- Red hair and Green eyes, 5'6" tall, slim build, approx. 125 pounds,
Family back ground- Ancient Greeks believed their gods were the same as them, but far greater in beauty, strenth and dignity. Were immortal, but might be wounded or otherwise injured. Could make them selves visible or invisible to men and assume the forms of men or of animals. Gods needed food and sleep. The meat of the gods was called "Ambrosia", and the drink was "nectar".
Emotional needs-Souls and power, escape to heaven.
Mannerisms-What ever is needed to meet her needs. Mother of Lies.
Speech patterns-What ever she feels like
Where characters live-Earths center, and important buildings in major cities, and likes castles.

ANNE SMITH, AKA-(Eve) and Pandora.
Physical characteristics- Brown hair and brown eyes, large protruding nipples, 5'3" tall, slim build, approx. 110 pounds. The gods made presents to her, Venus gave her beauty and the art of pleasing, Graces gave her the power of captivating, Apollo taught her how to sing, and Mercury instructed her in eloquence and brought her to   epimetheus   ????
Family back ground- Small farm in Colorado, near Grand Junction.
Emotional needs-True love
Mannerisms-
Speech patterns-
Where characters live-Colorado

FATHER JIMMY DeANGELO, AKA- Michael (Angel of God), Hercules (son of Jupiter).
Physical characteristics-6'1" tall, slim build, 180 pounds, brown hair, brown eyes.
Family back ground-Son of God.
Emotional needs-Love
Mannerisms-strong determined movements.
Speech patterns-
Where characters live- Al Si-Rat ??? (A narrow bridge extending from this world to the next over the abyss of HELL, which must be passed by every one who would enter paradise.

Jim King sought to define the characters in the draft of his science fiction novel.

Many of the scenes took place in Denver and Delta, Colorado, and the novel included details of police investigations. In one chapter, the heroine becomes a *Playboy* centerfold who works as a female wrestler. During a televised bout, her bra is pulled off before the cameras. Another scene involved torture and sexual bondage. A third focused on rape.

According to the district attorney, the unpublished writings were evidence of King's psychopathic personality. The book, the prosecutor told the court, was a "pornographic novel and properly exposes the author's fantasies" of wishing to engage in vicious gang rapes. To prove the point, rather than submitting the whole novel, the district attorney's office had prepared a brief synopsis of it, selecting highly inflammatory parts as representative of the totality of the work.

We objected. In response to Mr. Buckley's accusation, Scott Robinson noted that "lots of people write things without acting them out. Fiction is fiction. It's not what you do with your life." If one were to be convicted of murder on the basis of fiction, no crime writer was safe. Jim King's namesake, Stephen King, could easily be a suspect if the district attorney used an author's fictional writings as a criterion of guilt. To move from an unpublished, uncirculated manuscript which King had written on his personal computer to actual criminal action was a ridiculous "quantum leap." This effort to gain a conviction based on unpublished writings "spits in the face of hundreds of years of authors."

Judge Spriggs glanced at the manuscript, noting "well, Shakespeare's place in history seems safe." King thought this a clever remark, laughing at it. Meanwhile, the sparring on this point went on quite a while. It impacted the nature of our defense. The prosecution's assertion was that if we wanted to call witnesses who would testify that they knew King to be a peaceful, law-abiding man, it had the full right to impeach them by disclosing any violent activities associated with King, including this work of fiction.

Judge Spriggs sided with the prosecution. He agreed that the writing was "sadomasochistic." "They have very crystal clear evidence that inwardly things may not be what they seem. Their evidence clearly shows his exterior demeanor and interior thoughts may be two entirely different things. . . .

"You want to say that just because he's not firing off his six-gun on the streets of downtown Golden, he's a calm, peaceful, law-abiding citizen. If one inference can be drawn, why can't the other?" Therefore, if we called character witnesses for King, the prosecution would be able to cite the novel in its efforts to show that there was a violent side to King's personality.

Finally, at the end of the day, after Judge Spriggs had left the courtroom, a reporter from the *Rocky Mountain News* was snooping at a copy of the district attorney's biased account of the book. I snatched it away from her. The journalist thereupon wrote a sensational account of King as a sadomasochistic novelist. She also cited Mr. Buckley's assertion that there were 21 separate incidents of ambush and the shooting of police officers in the back or the back of the head in King's draft of his police manual. This, the newspaper and the prosecution argued, was even more conclusive evidence of King's criminal mind and premeditation to pull the Father's Day Massacre.

The next morning, I complained in court that the *News'* story, with its heavy reliance on Mr. Buckley's comments, was an effort to bias the case. The prosecutor was "corrupting the reportage for his own purposes." To prevent a mistrial, it was necessary to "muzzle this orgy by the press and make them become ethical and responsible" instead of callously filling their papers with the most outlandish of the prosecution's charges so that their newspapers would sell like hotcakes.

Judge Spriggs questioned the jurors about whether any of them had seen the *News'* article. None admitted reading it. He noted that the press had the full right to publish the melodramatic smear on King and chastised me for denouncing this libelous action. Nor was Judge Spriggs happy about my statement that a mistrial might result if such irresponsible coverage continued. The trial was already in its fourth week. Anybody deliberately causing a mistrial, Judge Spriggs noted, would be in trouble and answerable to him. By the time all this happened, we were in the third day of putting on our defense of Jim King.

12

Defense

We began our case by placing former guard Paul Yocum on trial. Law enforcement officials involved in investigating him and searching his Denver apartment and mother's house were called. They told about the numerous guns and rounds of ammunition they had discovered. To accentuate this point, we introduced photos of the arsenals seized from Yocum in Denver and Flagler. FBI Special Agent Charles Evans read excerpts of Yocum's diary into the record.

JoDeen Lang was active in a neighborhood watch on the 1200 block of Pearl Street where Yocum lived. She had frequently observed him on the street, though she did not personally know the man. In the wake of the murders, she informed the police that she had seen Yocum walking toward the bank shortly before 9:00 AM on Father's Day, carrying a dark bag, and dressed somewhat like the man described by the eyewitnesses. The purpose of all this testimony was not to convict Yocum, but to raise considerable doubts about whether the state had much of a case against King compared to the prima facie case it could have easily made against Yocum.

Mr. Buckley continually objected to our evidence implicating Yocum. He sounded as if he had suddenly become a criminal defense attorney who was vehemently protesting that we were using improper materials to accuse Yocum of the murders. The prosecu-

*Paul Yocum as he looked with the
disguise described by the tellers.*

tor wanted to keep from the jury information about all of the police
suspicions which pointed to Yocum as a possible defendant. The
district attorney seemingly feared that, compared to the case that
could be made against Yocum, the jury would see that there was
even less connecting King to the crimes.

In presenting evidence about Yocum, we noted that the police
had seized numerous speed loaders from him. This allowed the
defense to elaborate on another point. The prosecution was fixated
on speed loaders. Actually, there was no evidence that a speed
loader had been employed during the murders. In using a speed
loader, a police officer is taught to throw the spent cartridges to the
ground as he reloads his weapon. The shooter loses valuable time
by putting them in his hand at the same time he is trying to reload
the revolver. But no spent cartridges were found at the site of the
crime. Mr. Buckley claimed that a speed loader must have been
used since apparently only 18 bullets were fired and King had
carried two speed loaders while a police officer.

We also pointed out that another prosecution claim was dubious:
that a speed loader designed for a Smith & Wesson revolver would
not easily work on a Colt revolver. During the prosecution's case,
detectives Priest and Kerber had been insistent that Yocum could
not have committed the crime because his speed loaders were only
for Smith & Wesson revolvers. Detective Priest noted, for example,

that some of the speed loaders seized from Yocum clearly stated on them "Not for a Colt." While the detective admitted that it might be possible to use such a speed loader on a Colt, it would not be a very swift operation. By showing that this assertion was not true, we could create reasonable doubt about the prosecution's entire theory of the crime.

Compared to Detective Kerber, who had dropped the speed loader when he tried to use it, we called our expert on guns and speed loaders, private detective Tony DiVirgilio, our lead investigator and consulting expert in the case. DiVirgilio testified that neither Colt nor Smith & Wesson specifically manufactured speed loaders; rather, these devices were made by third parties. For example, among the speed loaders seized from Yocum were ones produced by HKS and Dade Screw Machine. Often the same speed loader would work on both Colt and Smith & Wesson revolvers even if the manufacturer specifically stated that the speed loader was only for a Smith & Wesson. During a break in the proceedings shortly before he testified, DiVirgilio had been allowed to experiment with the prosecution's Smith & Wesson speed loader and a Colt revolver in the presence of the court clerk. He confirmed his belief that the Smith & Wesson speed loader could be used with the Colt.

When DiVirgilio took the stand, he demonstrated that the speed loader designed for a .38 Smith & Wesson revolver would work on the prosecution's .38 Colt Trooper as he reloaded the revolver in a snap with the speed loader. This gave him a chance to inform the jury all about speed loaders and how Yocum's speed loaders could have been used in the murder weapon. We also established that speed loaders are quite common. Our witness related that upwards of 80 percent of the people who own revolvers have speed loaders. One can see people using speed loaders at firing ranges all the time. Virtually all armed guards who carry revolvers also carry speed loaders.

Nor was the evidence concrete that 18, and only 18, bullets had been fired. To develop this point, the defense consulted Dr. Charles Wilber. An emeritus professor of zoology at Colorado State University in Fort Collins, he was also the director of the school's forensic science laboratory and had immense knowledge of physiology. Dr. Wilber had worked with the FBI and other law enforce-

Guard Todd Wilson was slain in the control room. NASCAR and Wolfpack video games are on the top of the counter at the far left.

ment agencies in studying ballistics and had served as deputy coroner for Larimer County, Colorado. Our expert had published five books on forensics and had testified in court over the years, usually for the prosecution.

The defense can never blindly trust the results of tests by the police and FBI labs. On the contrary, it must have its own experts. I knew all too well from past experience that the prosecution's evidence and scientific examinations cannot always be relied upon. Sometimes the police engage in shortcuts or conduct tests with the predetermined goal of finding evidence against the defendant. Other times, their conclusions are blind leaps of faith. Therefore, I want my own experts to review the physical evidence.

Dr. Wilber had assisted me in a couple of my previous successful defenses of men facing murder charges. One was the high-profile case of heavyweight boxing contender Ron Lyle in 1978. The fighter was accused of first-degree murder after he killed an ex-con in self-defense who had been shaking Lyle down for money and threatening the boxer with a semi-automatic pistol. In the other case, Dr. Wilber discussed the strange way bullets ricochet when the defendant was accused of killing a bystander after firing a revolver into the lawn of a neighbor who was continually harassing, threatening, and insulting his family in a racist tirade.

The forensics expert thoroughly reviewed the autopsies of the murdered guards. He noted that McCullom had been wounded seven times, Wilson six times, Mankoff four times, and McCarthy three times. This was a total of 20 wounds in the bodies of the four dead guards, suggesting that 20 different shots could have been fired. Nor were all of the bullets alike. That was further evidence, Dr. Wilber observed in his report, that more than one gunman could have committed the murders. We had used Dr. Wilber's research to cross-examine the prosecution's ballistic experts.

We also wanted the jury to know about the unusual happenings at the airport on the day the bank was robbed. Lloyd Quintana was a city employee charged with assisting passengers with problems at the airport. The bearded, mustached witness steadily answered questions "affirmative" and "negative." He insisted that, as an airport troubleshooter, he usually had a feel for people who needed help. Around 12:30 PM on Father's Day, he spotted a man who looked somewhat like the gunman described by the tellers.

The man in question, according to Quintana, was between 45 and 50, had salt-and-pepper hair, and a bushy mustache. Six-foot or six-foot-one, the individual had a kind of bald spot on the top of his head, buck teeth, and a round, reddish mark on his left cheek that was about the size of a quarter. He was carrying a black satchel and told Quintana that, despite having plenty of cash on him, he was having severe difficulties renting a car. All the rental car companies would only rent him a vehicle if he presented a credit card.

Four rental car agents, representing National, Avis, Superior, and USA-Rent-a-Car, verified Quintana's story, describing the man. The police had initially interviewed all five of them in the wake of the robbery. But they did not pursue this lead, especially when none of the airport witnesses pointed to King. All denied the former police officer was the man who had been seeking to rent the car right after the murders. This was significant when we recalled that, upon the arrest of King, the biased media accounts insisted that

King was the man who had been seen trying to rent the car at the airport. If anybody, the man at the airport looked like Dewey Baker.

During cross-examination, the prosecution brought out that the airport witnesses widely differed in their precise descriptions of the man seeking to rent the car. Some reported that he had a full head of hair and was at least six-feet, two-inches tall. He was variously described as "red-eyed" or red complexioned. None remembered him with a hat. The district attorney implied that these diverse accounts showed that the man was of no import. Actually, all he did was to accentuate our claim that eyewitness testimony should be treated with extreme caution. What Mr. Buckley said about the unreliability of the airport witnesses was far more apropos concerning the statements of the robbed tellers.

King's Neighbors

Our alibi witnesses took the stand. Roberta Jo Trujillo had been the Kings' neighbor since they had moved to 665 Juniper Street in 1985. She recalled that she had seen Jim and Carol working in their yard shortly after 8:00 AM on Father's Day while walking her dog and pet potbellied Vietnamese pig. Then, around 9:00, as she was getting into her car to drive to her mother's house, she again noticed Jim King in his yard. He was wearing a straw hat, shorts, and a T-shirt, as he worked in his yard with a weed eater. Carol was nearby. Trujillo called to him: "Happy Father's Day, you old fart." King waved to her as she drove away.

"Old fart" was Trujillo's fond name for King. Born in 1960, she was young enough to be his daughter and teased her older neighbor, sometimes giving him wolf whistles. She also referred to Jim as "Pa" or "Pops." Carol King was "Ma." Trujillo was quite close to Carol. Like King's wife, she had suffered from breast cancer and the two women shared their health concerns.

The FBI had been the first to talk with Trujillo on July 5, 1991. When the FBI initially interviewed King on June 24, he could not recall any witnesses who might have seen him coming and going from his house at around 9:00 and 10:00 on Father's Day. Not having done anything wrong, he had no reason to remember what neighbors had been about that day. He had not arranged for anybody to confirm his alibi. I only learned about Trujillo's

Roberta Trujillo testifies that she greeted Jim King around 9:00 AM on June 16 by calling out, "Happy Father's Day, you old fart."

statement from discovery materials supplied by the prosecution. I thereupon spoke with her and brought out that she definitely recalled seeing the "old fart" on Father's Day.

To confirm the witness' story, we called Trujillo's mother, Joy Ann Reher. She testified that her daughter had driven up at her home, about four blocks from the King house, shortly after 9:00 AM on Father's Day to take her to a weekly coffee klatsch/card game. She attended it "religiously" on Sunday mornings. That circumstantially strengthened Trujillo's claim that she had seen King around 9:00.

The prosecution was unhappy about Trujillo's testimony. Not only did Mr. Buckley and Mr. Sims send out an investigator to talk with her right before she testified, but they both individually visited her at her home. They tried to turn her words around and get her to change her story. Their officious visits were to no avail.

The FBI had also been the first to learn about our other alibi witness, David Lee Bell. He lived at 675 Juniper Street, directly north of the Kings, and had been the Kings' neighbor for about six years. His home was flanked by two large lawns. It was quite a chore mowing them. Bell spent about an hour to an hour and a half cutting each of them, riding about on a small tractor. He usually tackled the north lawn before mowing the south lawn that separated his house from the Kings. During the summer, he mowed the grass once a week, frequently on Sunday mornings.

Bell recalled he had been cutting his lawn on Father's Day because his young nephew was riding on the lawn mower with him. He had insisted that his nephew call his father—that was how he remembered these events occurred on Father's Day. The witness told the jury that he recollected seeing King work in his yard sometime between eight and nine o'clock on Father's Day before he started cutting the grass at about 9:00. Bell had just finished the north side an hour later when he noticed King, dressed in a T-shirt and shorts, drive up—it must have been about ten o'clock. Bell did not see anything unusual about King on Father's Day. King was not carrying a black satchel nor did he appear to be upset or nervous as would be expected from someone who had just murdered four bank guards and committed the bank robbery of the century. Shortly after King had pulled up, Bell had a brief verbal exchange with Carol King when his dog, which recently had puppies and was defensive of them, got into a slight scrap with the Kings' dog.

During cross-examination, the district attorney got our alibi witnesses to admit that they were not sure of the exact time they saw King. By coincidence, none were wearing watches and could not state at precisely what time they had seen King. Despite this, the alibi witnesses showed that King's documented activities on Father's Day meant he could not have been the robber.

Ballistics

FBI metals expert John Riley came to Denver from Washington for the trial, reporting his ballistic tests on the bullets recovered from the bodies of the slain guards. He had been with the FBI since 1966 and in the FBI lab since 1968. His specialty was trace elemental composition. The G-man had worked with numerous law enforcement agencies in trying to determine the precise composition of bullets found at crime scenes.

The Denver branch of the FBI had asked Riley to come to Denver in July 1991 at the behest of the Denver Police Department. The authorities had removed four bullets from McCullom's body. They not only wanted them analyzed by the Washington specialist, but also compared to police department +P bullets that were used in 1985-86. The department happened to have four extra boxes of +P bullets dating from the time King had retired. The four boxes of 50 bullets each were all that were left of an order of 40,000 bullets.

There had been a lawsuit over the quality of these projectiles. The plaintiff claimed that a police officer had been killed because his +Ps lacked sufficient stopping power when he shot an insane, elderly man who had fired a shotgun at him. The suit had forced the department to save samples of this ammunition. As a result of the litigation, Remington had *modified* the composition of the +Ps.

The goal of Special Agent Riley's test was to prove the prosecution's contention that the +P bullets used in the murders were identical with those issued to King by the Denver Police Department. King, after all, had told fellow guards that he retained the bullets he had been issued when he retired. By linking the bullets at the murder scene to King, the prosecution would have damning evidence against my client.

Agent Riley, however, was not able to provide it. But he did not want to help the defense. When I first saw Agent Riley's report during discovery, it was extremely cryptic. At the most, Agent Riley conceded he had made an "unusual" finding in his study of the bullets. He provided no details.

The report immediately raised my suspicions. My investigator, Tony DiVirgilio, called Agent Riley. He got the G-man to admit that the antimony levels in the bullets recovered at the murder scene were quite different from those issued to King as a police officer. Agent Riley testified about this during the preliminary hearing.

In court, Agent Riley stated that he had randomly selected ten bullets from each of the four boxes of the ammunition used by the police during 1985-86. He tested them for various metals and compared them with the bullets taken from McCullom. The latter four bullets did not match. Two of them, the law enforcement expert discovered, had a .65 percent antimony content. Two others had an .85 percent antimony content.

Antimony, Agent Riley explained, is a hardening agent used in bullets. Opposed to King's bullets, which were pure lead, bullets laced with antimony were harder and passed through flesh faster. Compared to the "purposeful" amount of antimony found in the four bullets taken from the dead guards, all the other +P bullets he tested, i.e., those taken from the police ammunition samples of 1985-86, had *no* antimony. He concluded in his report that the bullets from McCullom were "significantly different" than the +Ps provided to King by the Denver Police Department at the time he retired from the force.

The weakness of the prosecution's ballistic evidence was confirmed when I introduced a letter from an official of the Remington Arms Company, the manufacturer of the +P bullets the police department had used. Since the late 1970s, the document reported, such bullets were easily available to the general public. Both Agent Riley and Detective Kerber conceded that, in addition to Remington bullets, Winchester and Federal projectiles were found in the bodies of the murdered guards. Therefore, the prosecution had no case when it claimed that King must have committed the murders because only a former Denver police officer would have had access to +P bullets. More poignant, there was no antimony in the rounds issued to King just before he left the police force, i.e., they were not the antimony-laced bullets taken from McCullom's body.

Chess Moves

I called several members of the Denver Chess Club. My goal was to establish that King's alibi of seeking a game at the Capitol Hill Community Center on a Sunday morning was believable. In the process, I frequently shared with them the aphorism that "he who plays chess should have a hobby."

The testimony of Steve Jared was convincing. He, coincidentally, lived in an apartment house right across the alley from Paul Yocum. A balding man in his mid-40s with a graying beard and mustache, he had been a chess fanatic for years. A member of the chess club since 1975, he had previously lived in a Capitol Hill apartment right above where the chess club had gathered before it had relocated to the Capitol Hill Community Center.

The United Bank Tower is visible in the distance from VFW Post No. 1 where the Denver Chess Club gathered after it had left the Capitol Hill Community Center.

Jared had once been a close chess buddy of George Oross. The two frequently met at the chess club at the Capitol Hill Community Center for hours of speed chess. When the Denver Broncos were playing, they gathered there on Sunday mornings. After numerous games of speed chess, they would go to Oross's house to watch the Broncos on television.

When King's arrest was announced, Jared, whom I knew from the chess club, wrote me. He recalled a distinctive incident about King. During the late 1970s and early 1980s, he had played three or four tournament games against King. He did not, however, know anything personally about the man. Then, one Sunday morning before a Broncos game—he guessed it was just after nine o'clock in 1984—he was playing Oross at the community center. Shortly after they had started, King came in, looking for a game. Jared asked King what he did. When King told him he was a police officer, Jared did a doubletake, responding, "I'll be sure not to steal any pawns." The point was that King had previously played chess at the Capitol Hill Community Center on a Sunday morning—there was nothing inherently implausible about his alibi that he was seeking a chess game at the community center on Father's Day morning. (We were not able to locate Oross, who had since moved to Long Island, to confirm Jared's story.)

Michael Presutti was another regular at the chess club. He fondly recalled the days at the Capitol Hill Community Center. All-night sessions of chess were common there while the players frequently joked while playing both five-minute chess and relaxed games. Presutti did not recall ever encountering Al Skarie, the prosecution's expert on the Denver Chess Club, during his years around the organization.

Presutti and other chess witnesses frequently mentioned "skittle" games. They referred to informal matches of which no records were kept. Participants in the club played them for the sheer enjoyment of the game. Along with speed chess, skittle games were the stock-in-trade of the Denver Chess Club at the Capitol Hill Community Center. They are drastically different from tournament chess. There a player is given two hours to make 40 moves. If he touches a piece, he must move it. All moves are recorded by both players. Such games can often last four or five hours.

While the Denver Chess Club hosted tournament games at the Capitol Hill Community Center, it was also a site for skittle games any hour of the day or night. Opposed to the quarters of the chess club at the old mansion, the situation at the VFW at West Ninth Avenue and Bannock Street was time-limited. The club gathered there only once a week for sanctioned, rated games. It was not the place where anybody would go seeking a skittle game on a Sunday morning. The prosecution never attempted to rebut this point; rather, it continually claimed that if King had been looking for a chess game on Father's Day he would have naturally gone to the VFW post.

Richard Buchanan, a teacher from Manitou Springs, a suburb of Colorado Springs, was the head of the Colorado State Chess Association and editor of the *Colorado Chess Informant*, a local chess magazine. In a scholarly tone, he told about the records of King's rated games and information about tournament games that the defendant had played. Prior to his July 2, 1991, encounter with me at the Denver Chess Club, King's last over-the-board tournament game was on August 26, 1981. Buchanan also noted the records about King's postal games. The witness did not know the prosecution's star chess player Al Skarie. There were no records of Skarie playing rated games at the Denver Chess Club.

On cross-examination, Mr. Buckley established the obvious: that because King had not been playing rated, tournament games, that did not mean that King might not have been playing informal chess since 1981. Mr. Buckley also made a great deal about a "club director" card which King had received from the United States Chess Federation. It expired on August 31, 1989. Nothing indicated when the card had been issued. It authorized King to conduct small chess tournaments. No records showed that King had ever conducted any sanctioned tournaments.

Mr. Buckley inquired of the club director card from other chess witnesses. However, he never contacted the United States Chess Federation. He made no effort to produce documentary evidence which would contradict my chess experts. Nor did he attempt to subpoena any official chess records. Instead, he concentrated on trying to discredit my chess witnesses.

Then came Rodney Eric Cruz. A newcomer to the Denver Chess Club, Cruz had joined it in December 1989, when it met at the West Ninth Avenue and Bannock Street VFW post. Quickly rising in the small organization, he had become president of the club and helped oversee its relocation to the VFW hall at 4747 West Colfax Avenue in September 1990. During his tenure as president of the club, former members had contacted him, seeking information about where the club was currently meeting. Cruz was emphatic that he had not seen King around the club prior to July 2, 1991, when I had introduced the defendant to him.

Cruz knew Al Skarie as a member of the Aurora Chess Club. Skarie was not an active participant at the Denver Chess Club. At

I am on the left in a chess game at VFW Post 501, the site where I played Jim King the evening before his arrest.

the most, Skarie had played in simultaneous exhibitions against chess masters at the West Colfax hall. Cruz had never seen Skarie playing King in chess at the Ninth Avenue meeting place of the club.

Richard Garcia was the current president of the Denver Chess Club. He was a chess expert, a ranking just below that of chess master. During the 1980s, he spent a great deal of time at the chess club's headquarters at the Capitol Hill Community Center. Opposed to the 24-hour-a-day activities at the community center, it only met on Tuesday evenings at the West Ninth Avenue and Bannock Street VFW. As had Steve Jared and Michael Presutti, he testified that nobody would go to the VFW hall for a skittle game on a Sunday morning.

As one who hung out regularly at the chess club and helped arrange its tournaments, Garcia knew all the regulars. He was familiar with Larry Duke, Steve Jared, and Rodney Eric Cruz. But he did not recall Al Skarie playing rated or informal games at the Denver Chess Club.

During cross-examination, Mr. Buckley insisted that King had been a director of the chess club, producing the club director card.

The witness explained that nothing was to be made of the card. Anybody who was a member of the United States Chess Federation could get such a card. King had never directed any tournaments at the Denver Chess Club.

Typical of the lax administration of the chess club was that the precise date it exited from the community center could not be established. Word of mouth, not a documented mailing to past and present members, was how the club informed chess players that the meeting place had been moved.

Reflecting the theme of the entire case, a coincidence marked Garcia's testimony. He lived on King Street, about a mile away from the West Colfax meeting place of the chess club. By the time Garcia, the last chess witness, had left the stand, I was sure that the jury had learned all it would ever wish to know about skittle games, chess tournaments, and why a former member of the Denver Chess Club might well have looked for a chess game at the Capitol Hill Community Center on a Sunday morning in June 1991.

Jim King's shoes were thoroughly examined to see if they matched the prints of the sole marks found at the scene of the murders. All tests proved negative.

Expert Witnesses

Denver Police Technician Jeanne E. Kilmer followed Richard Garcia to the stand. A forensic serologist—a blood expert—she had examined King's shoes. They were dirty when they were given to her, i.e., there was no sign that they had recently been washed in an effort to remove blood or other incriminating evidence from them. She rigorously tested the shoes for traces of blood. Her procedures were so precise that they could detect one particle of blood amidst 250,000 other particles. But there was no trace of blood on the shoes. The copious amounts of blood from the murdered bodies would have left minute traces of the blood on the killer's shoes regardless of how well he had cleaned them. The robber, she concluded, could not have worn these shoes.

Then I called gunsmith Ikey Starks. A former machinist with United States Steel, he had been fascinated with guns since he was a boy. Over the years, he had been a competitive shooter in the Army reserves. The witness had been a full-time gunsmith since 1967. After working as a gunsmith in San Francisco for eight years, he had been a sales and service representative for Remington Arms in Colorado from 1974 until 1976 when he established his own gun store. It was located about five blocks from police headquarters and he had many police officers as customers. Police officers, he affirmed, were no different from other customers in continually buying, selling, and swapping firearms.

In great detail, Starks explained the workings of revolvers to the jury. With the prosecution's Colt Trooper in hand, he stood a few feet from the jury, explaining how excessive use, pressure, and wear all cause a revolver's cylinder to crack. A misalignment of the chamber with the firing pin or other timing problems can also cause a cylinder to crack. A gun with a cracked cylinder might explode when it is fired. Starks knew this quite well since he had once been hit with debris from the exploding cylinder of a fellow participant's revolver at a shooting competition.

Once he had finished his explanation to the jury, Starks asked whether its members had any questions. Judge Spriggs cut him off, telling him he was only to answer the lawyers' questions. About the same time, Starks noted that the gun the prosecution had submitted into evidence as a sample of King's revolver had a timing problem which he would be glad to fix. "This is how I make a living."

There were at least 29 types of Colt revolvers which could have fired the .38 bullets found at the scene of the crime. The Trooper had been discontinued by Colt in 1969. Starks was not sure whether Colt sold its cylinders or not. He estimated the cost of such a cylinder would be $100 to $120. It would take a skilled gunsmith about two hours to replace it. The total charge for such repairs would be about $200 to $220. It was usually not worth getting a revolver fixed once the cylinder had cracked. By that time, the gun was usually worn out and it was best to dispose of the weapon.

On cross-examination, Mr. Buckley sought to make a big deal about Starks' knowledge of Remington ammunition. Among the bullets found at the murder scene were +P+ projectiles. These were +Ps that were specially manufactured and only sold to police departments. Their only difference from +Ps, the gunsmith explained, was an additional plus sign. Otherwise, they were identical with the +Ps that Remington sold to the general public.

John Kirk, the 27-year-old FBI agent who had conducted the June 20 photo lineup, testified next. A couple of staffers at the local FBI office had put together the two photo books of past and present guards. They had used pictures which had been reproduced from microfilm files of the Colorado Division of Motor Vehicles. Agent Kirk not only asked the witnesses to tell him if any of the faces looked familiar, but also whether something about the features of any of the photos reminded them of the robber.

The bank vault employees spent anywhere from ten minutes to 45 minutes with him. They turned the pages of the photo books at their own speed. They only glanced at a number of the pictures, which included photos of about eight women guards. None of the eyewitnesses had pinpointed King as the robber when they were first shown his picture. Agent Kirk also told the court about the extremely diverse descriptions of the robber which the eyewitnesses had given him. This reminded the jury that it was more than two weeks after the robbery when the eyewitnesses decided that they "remembered" King was the person they had encountered at the bank.

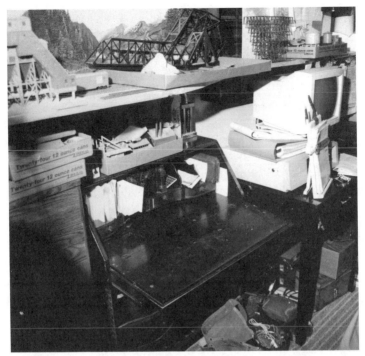

Jim King's study shows both his computer and some of the model bridges he liked to build. We stressed that the police had discovered nothing in their two thorough searches of King's house that linked him with the bank robbery.

During Mr. Sims' cross-examination, Agent Kirk conceded that some of the witnesses had problems with the photos. They asked if they could draw a hat and sunglasses on some of the faces. The G-man advised against that. There was no hat or sunglasses on the July 3-5 photo lineup of King.

Neilus Rome was King's barber. He had known the defendant for 25 years. King's hair and mustache had always been ash blond and he had always worn a flattop. The defendant usually came in every three weeks, often early in the week, to get his hair cut.

Rome had last seen King the Tuesday after Father's Day or the Tuesday a week after Father's Day. At that time, to the best of his recollection, King did not have a mustache. But there was nothing unusual in this. He had seen King a number of times without a mustache. His customer, who always neatly trimmed his own mustache, frequently cut it off in the summer when he was bothered by the heat.

King, the barber explained, had straight hair. He had never seen King with hair curling to the back of the neck or the long, silvery sideburns described by some of the eyewitnesses. King's sideburns were usually only an eighth-of-an-inch long, going at the most to the middle of the ear. They never approached the bottom of the ear lobe. King's hair and mustache were brownish-blond, not the salt and pepper or gray described by the eyewitnesses.

I also wanted to turn the initial massive prejudicial publicity against King slightly to our account. I notably wished to introduce into evidence some of the police smears against King, such as the mendacious article that his two "brothers" were notorious robbers. Toward this end, I requested that I be allowed to call former Police Chief Ari Zavaras. I not only desired to show the false nature of that accusation, but also use it to illustrate how the police had failed to check and double-check their facts in this instance. They rushed to justice, or rather, to injustice. If they did so here, it indicated that they might have done the same in other areas of their investigation. Judge Spriggs, however, ruled that since everybody conceded that the story about King's "brothers" was a lie, the former chief's testimony would be "as irrelevant as anything I can imagine."

Photo by Phil Goodstein

Jim King worked at Pierson Graphics/Maps Unlimited, at West Ninth Avenue and Broadway, after retiring from the Denver Police Department.

During the defense, we also educated the jury about the shoddy security at the bank by introducing a photo showing video games on the control room counter. Witnesses told how the guards sometimes played games on the bank's television monitors when they were supposed to be watching the surveillance cameras. A tape of *The Trials of Rosie O'Neill* was discovered in the VCR that was set aside to review surveillance tapes. The police found two chairs facing this television when they first entered the security headquarters on Father's Day. It seemed that the guards might have been watching it at the time the intruder burst into the monitor room. Bank documents revealing past concerns about the security system were shown to the jury.

We further presented numerous photos of the police search of King's house and safe-deposit box. Our point was clear. We wanted to make sure the jury knew exactly what the authorities found in their searches of King's home, computer, and safe-deposit box: nothing that incriminated King in the crimes.

Police and Guard Witnesses

Because of Judge Spriggs' double-edged ruling about King's novel, we did not call any character witnesses for King. Still, we placed selected individuals on the stand who had served with King as a police officer or bank guard. They testified that, on those jobs, the defendant was a calm, easy-going, cool-headed man.

Strong evidence was provided by Tony Pierson. A 19-year veteran of the Denver Police Department, he had served under King on the graveyard shift at Stapleton Airport. While on patrol with King, Pierson noted, they prowled through the airport. King would walk on the roofs and check the doors everyplace and anyplace in the facility. In the airport police office, the sergeant spoke of the way terrorists could attack the airport and the police need to prepare against this contingency. In other words, he was acting as a good police officer, prepared for any problems: precisely the same kind of planning and study of the security system which King employed while a guard at the United Bank.

Pierson also noted that King had not thought much of his "old beat-up Colt." He had heard King call it "that old piece of garbage" and a "piece of junk" which he planned to discard as soon as he no

John Perpetua masked by the overlay.

longer needed it. Pierson stated that he too might well dispose of his pistol after he retired from the force. "My personal feeling was I was going to take a torch, cut the thing up, and throw it in the river." In other words, he had no qualms about getting rid of his gun when his days as a police officer were over. His remarks impeached the testimony of Dr. Nicoletti, the police psychologist who had testified about officers' attitudes to their weapons.

John Perpetua, a guard whom some of the eyewitnesses had tentatively identified as the gunman during the photo lineup of June 20, took the stand. The heavyset, soft-spoken, 47-year-old man had worked as a regular guard at the United Bank for 16 years. Wearing a salt-and-pepper mustache in court, Perpetua noted that, on occasion, when there was a shortage of weekend guards, he volunteered to cover for them. In the process, he had worked with King one or two times. King seemed to be a diligent bank guard as the witness swore to King's integrity. Perpetua confirmed that the guards were poorly paid and badly treated.

Other guards similarly testified in King's behalf. Among them were other heavyset men with mustaches, i.e., individuals who looked somewhat like the man described by the robbed tellers. These witnesses noted it was natural for guards to prowl about during their runs. They had to know where everything was in the bank. Otherwise, they would not be able to respond to calls for assistance.

The guards also brought out the ineptitude of the bank's management. Former guard Dwayne Borski noted that he did not believe that bank Security and Risk Manager Tom Tatalaski knew what he was doing in his job. Borski had quit because of the poor pay, rotten treatment, and the disarming of the guards.

Nicholas Joseph Trujillo had worked as a guard from September 1988 until May 1989. Despite receiving excellent ratings, the bank insulted him by offering him a five-cent raise after his first six months on the job. He figured it was not worth it and resigned.

During his tenure at the bank, the 270-pound, 29-year-old Trujillo, had worked many shifts with Mike McKown. The two guards discussed how easy it would be to rob the bank. They differed over whether a robber should murder any witnesses or simply tie them up. McKown insisted that any witnesses—including guards—be killed. This contrasted with McKown's testimony that he had never talked about killing guards in his scenarios of bank robberies.

Such talk about robbing the bank was not unusual. All the guards discussed it. This point was so well established that, halfway through our guard witnesses, Judge Spriggs ordered that we were not to have any further witnesses testify about this subject. Similarly, in response to Mr. Buckley's fixation on the gloves, we had so many people inform the jury how easy it was to obtain surgical gloves that Judge Spriggs prohibited any more testimony on this point. This limiting of evidence, in legal parlance, is that "it is cumulative."

None of the guards thought that King was stupid. If the retired police sergeant was going to pull the robbery, he would never have used his own weapon. On the contrary, he would have gotten a special gun for the job and had his .38 Colt Trooper ready for inspection when the authorities called. Nor would King have worn a disguise which did not cover up his moles. Yet none of the eyewitnesses had described the gunman having a mask over his chin where King's moles were most visible.

Then there was the question of why, if the crime was committed by only one man who was a maniacal killer, the robber did not murder the tellers in the same manner that he had killed the guards. Could it be that the robber executed the guards because they could identify him as a fellow guard? But no evidence had been presented to show that King knew or had worked with any of the four dead victims.

Eyewitness Expert Edith Greene

Dr. Edith Greene was a crucial expert witness for the defense. She had helped me test the overlays of the disguise and testified as a specialist on eyewitness identification. Dr. Greene informed the jury about the assorted studies that had been done of this matter. While many of the traits of eyewitness identification are common sense, others are myths. For example, nothing substantiates the belief expressed by David Barranco that the more traumatic an event is, the more clearly the victim remembers it.

Frequently standing in front of a big writing pad that was on an easel, she put figures on it in the way that an instructor writes down numbers for a class on the blackboard. The numbers helped Dr. Greene explain how, under stress, eyewitnesses are notoriously unreliable. There were nine specific factors which led her to doubt the identifications during the photo lineup. She spelled them out. Foremost was what she termed "weapon focus" or "gun focus." This is how a victim of an armed robbery concentrates on the weapon rather than on the face. Dr. Greene further talked about the vastly different nature of the eyewitnesses' original descriptions of the robber, the character of facial details, and the impact of a disguise.

Carefully, Dr. Greene noted the percentage of eyewitnesses who make false identifications based on disguises, on fear, on gun focus, and other specifics. Of particular import was that in 66 percent of the cases where eyewitnesses were shown a target-absent lineup, i.e., a lineup where the suspect is not included, the victims still make identifications. This false identification is compounded by the other factors.

In a bold counterthrust to Judge Spriggs' ruling that we could not use the overlays to cross-examine the eyewitnesses after we had employed them when questioning David Barranco, we had Dr. Greene resurrect these testing devices. We wanted the jury to know

Dr. Edith Greene illustrated how difficult it was to identify a man in a disguise by showing her students four well-known people cloaked by an overlay comparable to the disguise worn by the man who robbed the United Bank. See p. 259 *for who the men are beneath the overlays.*

more about them and the problematic nature of identifying someone in a disguise. Dr. Greene discussed the overlays. She reported that, in a psychology class, she had had 44 subjects try to identify the persons behind them. Unlike David Barranco and the jury, the participants in her study had not been told that famous faces were behind the disguises.

One by one, we showed the overlays of six well-known faces to the jury, letting its members guess for themselves who was behind the disguises. Judge Spriggs was fascinated by this, asking that Scott Robinson clearly hold up the pictures for him. Sometimes, the judge quipped about the identifications.

Dr. Greene told how all the subjects in her experiment had failed to recognize Harrison Ford under the overlay. Eighty-nine percent had been able to identify him without the disguise. One hundred percent could identify President Bush without the overlay. However, once the mask was added, only 28 percent could tell that the president was behind the disguise.

Subject number three in her test was Robert Duvall. Nobody had recognized him under the overlay. Only 17 percent had recognized him without it. Eleven percent of her study participants, Dr. Greene continued, had identified Jack Nicholson behind the mask as opposed to 73 percent without the disguise. A similar contrast was found in the six-percent recognition factor of Lee Iacocca behind the overlay as opposed to 81 percent without it. Finally, seeking to show how sometimes youthful appearances become etched in the public mind, Dr. Greene used a photo of the mature Marlon Brando. Only six percent identified it without the mask. Three percent could tell who the famous actor was behind the hat, sunglasses, and mustache.

Having established how well disguises work, Dr. Greene turned to other problems of eyewitness identification. There was, for example, what she labeled "photo-biased" identifications. She cited studies where those who had already been shown a picture might pick it out of a subsequent lineup even if it was the wrong person who was accused of committing the crime. Those who had seen such prior photos were far more likely to make misidentifications than were those who had not previously viewed any mug shots.

Lee Iacocca   Marlon Brando

Robert Duvall   Jack Nicholson

The men lurking beneath the overlays. To be sure, the quality of these photos is not ideal. But neither were the pictures shown to the vault employees by the FBI.

Only in 25 percent of the cases where eyewitness identification was of paramount importance were eyewitnesses completely accurate. "The most important consideration for jurors is how confident the eyewitness seems," she continued. However, "highly confident witnesses are not necessarily accurate." There is only a "very minor" correlation between the confidence of a witness and his accuracy. Often the more confident a witness is, the less accurate his testimony. Under the trauma of a crime, a victim wants *someone* convicted, and is susceptible to suggestions made by the authorities. The result is that sometimes an innocent person is convicted on the basis of erroneous eyewitness testimony.

On cross-examination, Mr. Sims got Dr. Greene to admit that most of her studies were only based on experiments with students and other volunteers. It was unethical, she explained, to subject people to violent crimes as part of psychological research studies. The prosecutor further emphasized her admission that eyewitnesses are correct 25 percent of the time. Therefore, since five eyewitnesses had identified King, at least one of them must be telling the truth. He made it sound as if this was a virtual confession on King's part. Actually, the result of Dr. Greene's testimony and Mr. Sims' cross-examination was to increase doubt about the reliability of the tainted eyewitness identifications of King.

Family Members Testify for King

I called King's eldest son, James Jr., known as Jim Jr. or Jimmy. A computer whiz, he worked for an oil exploration company that did business in Mexico. Tall, thin, and handsome, the 29-year-old Denver native testified with a quiet demeanor about how he had been after his father for some months prior to Father's Day to get a larger safe-deposit box. His father needed it to store the car titles of Jim Jr.'s brothers. He had given his father a Packard Bell computer in 1990. When his father started writing the three books on the computer, he insisted that his father make backups of his writings and place the floppy disks in a secure place-such as the safe-deposit box. Many corporations, Jimmy told his father and the court, used bank vaults to store vital backup information. He recalled that his father had complained that he could not fit the computer disks into his existing small safe-deposit box.

The need for a bigger family safe-deposit box came home to Jim Jr. when, on June 17, 1991, he asked his father for his birth certificate. The son was preparing to work in Mexico. To get a passport, he needed his birth certificate. His father drove to the bank to find Jimmy's birth certificate which he stored in his safe-deposit box. While looking for it, Jim King realized that his existing box was too small and hopelessly cluttered. That, according to Jimmy King, was the specific incident that spurred his father to get a larger box that day. His father had procured the birth certificate for him the next day. A day or two later, Jim King needed to get a car title for Dave King. Jim Jr. picked up the passport from his father around June 24.

Carol King followed her son to the stand, finally testifying directly for her spouse. She swore to Jim's dedication as a police officer and a loving husband. Carol noted she was mowing the lawn when he returned home around 10:00 AM on Father's Day. She was surprised to see him since she remembered, that in earlier years, he was usually gone for about four hours at a time when he left to play chess. He was disappointed he had not found a chess game at the Capitol Hill Community Center. After he helped her complete cutting the grass, the two sat on the patio a bit before going to Mount Olivet Cemetery.

The witness told about her and Jim's travel plans. They had visited King's mother in Mesa, Arizona, annually for the last ten years. In the process, they often stopped off in Las Vegas. They had been planning to do so at the time of the Father's Day killings.

An early riser, Carol had gone to bed about the time the fireworks display had started on the evening of July 3, 1991. Shortly before retiring, she had looked out on the street. At least 25 spectators were on the road near her house. When the police ordered her out on the porch, the street was packed with neighbors watching the eerie scene at her home. In addition, police cars were everyplace. Her house was in shambles after the police left it. They had thoroughly searched every nook and cranny.

Carol testified that Jim had first been diagnosed with a high cholesterol problem in 1976. He then gave up his beloved regular Pepsis. He could only have diet soft drinks. He did not smoke and never drank tea or coffee. In other words, his personal habits proved

James King Jr. stands in front of his father's home.

he would not have left a coffee cup, cigarette butts, or a Seven-Up can in the records tunnel where the 5:04 alarm had sounded.

Returning to her husband's cholesterol problem, Carol noted that Jim tried to deal with it by exercising regularly as the doctor had ordered. A preferred means of getting this exercise was by walking. She assisted her husband by giving him the pedometer he wore at the United Bank and by walking with him. Since his retirement, the two tried to go out for a walk at least three times a week. When inclement weather prevented them from walking outside, they would walk through a local shopping mall.

Carol also noted that, in the year before the bank robbery, she and Jim had frequently had small children visiting the house. Jim was concerned that one of them might accidentally discover his revolver. Consequently, he took it down from the regular storage place in the holster in the closet and placed it in the locked box. That was the last time she had seen the Colt Trooper.

On cross-examination, Mr. Buckley tried to get her to help him build his case of conjecture. Didn't Carol know that Pierson Graphics, where her husband had worked, was near the Ninth and Bannock VFW? Didn't this prove that King obviously knew that the chess club met at the VFW? But his questions missed their mark. Carol stated that she did not visit Jim at Pierson Graphics and knew little about the specific locations of the chess club.

Jim King Takes the Stand

On Friday, June 5, King took the stand. I was initially a bit nervous about having him testify. I feared that the prosecution would try him on his unpublished writings, attempting to bias the jury against him. Prior to having King sworn in, I sought to have Judge Spriggs rule that the defendant could not be cross-examined on his unpublished novel and autobiography. Judge Spriggs refused to announce whether this would be permitted before King was sworn in, noting that such a pre-testimony ruling would be an advantage to either the prosecution or the defense. I figured that this meant Judge Spriggs would allow the prosecution to raise these issues. Such was the case with his autobiography.

I carefully discussed with Jim the problems he would face on the stand. He was insistent that he testify. Jim had testified in court while he was a police officer. He fully understood the workings of the court system and knew that he should not engage in any arguments with the district attorney during cross-examination. King, a likable guy, has a wry sense of humor and is anything but a violent, psychopathic killer. I was sure his personality would come through during his testimony, strongly influencing the jury in his favor.

A defendant need not testify. In such circumstances, the judge will instruct the jury that nothing is to be made of the fact that the defendant did not take the stand and no inference of guilt can be made from his failure to testify. But juries seemingly consider the defendant's failure to testify during their deliberations. They hold it against the accused if he does not speak out for himself. Therefore, I usually call my client as the last witness for the defense. If nothing else, by testifying he has a chance to show the jury that he is human, sweats, is nervous, and is impacted by the same concerns and aspirations as anybody else.

Shortly before King took the stand, I met with him in his holding cell in the sheriff's office. Jury consultant Richard Crawford was with me as I reviewed Jim's direct testimony and conducted a mock cross-examination. I had not done the latter at great length previously, fearing that the authorities might be spying on King in jail.

Jim started out as a witness with a bang. When I asked him if he had robbed the bank and killed the guards, looking directly at the jury, he emphatically replied: "I did not."

"Did you have any involvement in these crimes?" I continued.

In an even more insistent voice: "No, I have never killed anyone or robbed anyone."

After going through his childhood and how he came to join the Denver Police Department, I inquired if he had ever fired his gun while on duty. He noted there was only one instance. It was when he was a rookie and had fired a warning shot at a fleeing suspect.

"Then what happened?" I wanted to know.

"He ran faster."

King eventually caught the fleeing suspect. Firing the gun had done him no good. It was in violation of police regulations and he was reprimanded for having discharged the warning shot. He never again had to shoot his revolver during his police career. "I never fired my pistol at any human being," he trenchantly explained.

I had Jim trace his career on the police department and his various assignments. On this basis, I asked him about his gun. He had not always carried the .38 Colt Trooper as an officer. When he had worked in the identification and communication bureaus, he was armed with a .38 Colt Cobra Airweight. It was a small, light gun with a two-inch-long barrel. He frequently wore it in an ankle holster since he did not wear a uniform as part of these jobs. After he was sent back out to patrol the streets, he sold that weapon, which he had owned for 12 or 13 years, to a fellow police officer.

About the time he had joined the department, King had purchased a .25 Browning semi-automatic pistol. He had carried it when not on duty. He had later sold it to another officer. A few years before the United Bank murders, he had purchased a five-shot .22 North American Arms revolver. It was a tiny gun which he kept in a case in a drawer of his nightstand. His weapons, he explained, were simply tools of the trade. He appreciated the protection they afforded him, but he was not married to any of his guns.

When King had first joined the force, officers were required to practice with their weapons once a month at the police firing range.

This had later been modified to four times a year. If an officer failed to shoot, he was reprimanded. On occasion, King had been so reprimanded.

At the range, the police officer was expected to use up all of the ammunition which had been previously issued to him. Each time, he was given new bullets. Officers were only to use the cartridges handed out by the department. King had never kept up closely with what he termed the "+P stuff."

As a father of three growing boys during his police career, King sometimes moonlighted. He reviewed his job at the Bank of Denver, where he had stopped a bank robbery. King also mentioned his employment at Beth Israel Hospital and KLZ-FM.

In great detail, I took King through his doings on Father's Day. He explained that his usual summer attire was a T-shirt and shorts. His shoes were likewise informal. He had one pair of what he called his "yard shoes." They were a set of shoes which he did not mind if they got dirty and which he usually wore while puttering around his lawn. When he had returned from the Capitol Hill Community Center, he went into the house to put on this pair of shoes before resuming his work in the yard. Shortly thereafter, he again changed his shoes when he left for the cemetery with Carol.

I talk with Jim King during a break in the proceedings.

During my examination, I asked King about his glasses. Throughout the trial, he had occasionally worn them, but he mostly watched the proceedings without them. King did not have his glasses on when he took the stand.

He needed the glasses, the retired police sergeant explained, both to read and to see better in the distance. His driver's license required that he wear glasses while behind the wheel. So "why aren't you wearing your glasses now to see me better?" I inquired. "I don't really need to see you," was King's clever reply.

Despite this witty answer, it was obvious that King was a police officer during his testimony. He replied to my questions with concise "yes, sir," and "no, sir," answers. If anything, I had a bit of a problem with him because he sometimes answered the questions too literally. For example, when I had him relate his activities on Father's Day, I had reached the point where he had returned home from the cemetery. I next asked him he if had again left home on Father's Day. Thinking the question was that had he left home on Father's Day, he surprised me by saying yes. I quickly established, however, that upon returning from the graveyard, he had spent the rest of the day at home.

King was also quite literal when I examined him about the safe-deposit box. Carol had been with him when he first rented the box several years before. He therefore said yes when I asked him if Carol was with him when he got the larger box on June 17, thinking I was asking him about the time when he originally got the box.

I cleared up this confusion as King explained that Carol had been with him when he went to the bank to get the larger box on June 17. By the time they arrived at the bank, Carol had desperately wanted a smoke and so stayed outside the bank while he went in to get the larger box. Knowing that she was waiting outside, he did not bring anything to or remove any items from the box at that time. During the next few days, he had made several trips to the box, trying to get things organized in it, obtain a car title for Dave, and find Jim Jr.'s birth certificate.

In accessing the box, King explained, he had to show the bank supervisor his driver's license as identification. During one of his visits to the bank, he discovered that his driver's license was missing. He feared he had dropped it during a previous visit to the box. He immediately got the license replaced.

The former sergeant reviewed his work at the United Bank. He was expected to complete patrols throughout the bank complex. Guards checked in at various key points during their runs. To help the guards find their way around the bank, numerous different charts, maps, and plans of the complex were readily available in the control headquarters. Generally, he liked the job.

King admitted that he was insistent that the guards be armed. Not all the guards who had requested to be allowed to carry a weapon were permitted to do so by the bank. To carry the gun at the bank, he had to have it reviewed by the police department and fire it once every six months. He followed the regulations to the letter. It was when he had the gun reviewed by the police that he discovered the timing problem which he had Tom Butler fix.

The defendant explained that "I had no need for a revolver after I left the bank." He had originally paid about $62 for the gun and did not believe he should spend more than that for repairs to a beat-up old weapon for which he had no further use. He therefore dismantled it and put it in the trash. So no one would find the whole of the gun, he placed the cylinder in the trash one week and the main part of the gun in the trash the next week.

There were problems with his job at the bank. Security was poor. He and other guards discussed this. He had made several suggestions to change and improve the security system, but no one listened

*I hold Jim King's trophy case, which had been on the wall of his
study, while I examine him.*

to them. Consequently, right after the theft from the automated
teller on Memorial Day weekend 1990, he was ready to resign. As
he wrote in the outline of his autobiography, the investigation of the
robbery was extremely poor and he thought that the bank's Risk and
Security Manager, Tom Tatalaski, had bungled the job. But, he
explained, he did not immediately resign because he feared that that
would call attention to himself—the guards were blamed for everything that went wrong with security at the United Bank. The
institution was looking for a scapegoat to excuse its own failures.
King further explained he wanted out of the bank because "the
treatment of the guards was so poor."

I also had King review his career as a chess player. He had first
become fascinated by the game as a teenager. While on the police
department, he regularly played Tom Coogan, the man who served
as chief of the department between 1983 and 1987. He also played
other cops who had become senior officers.

He had first begun playing at the Denver Chess Club in the late
1970s, before the organization had moved to the Capitol Hill

Community Center. Over the years, he had played both tournament and informal games. He had never enjoyed speed chess that much, but preferred relaxed games for their fun and intellectual stimulation. His last rated over-the-board game was in 1981. He had continued to come to the chess club for skittle games until about 1984 or 1985.

Discussing his many correspondence games, King noted he had given up on postal chess when he realized that he was actually playing other people's computers. Since he had a computer of his own, he might as well play it. He had played chess informally at the United Bank with Mike McKown and a couple of other guards.

The defendant discussed his activities on Father's Day. He brought out how he did not know that the chess club had moved. After all, if he was aware that the club had long vacated the Capitol Hill Community Center, that would have been the last place he would have cited in an alibi if he were consciously out to deceive the police about his whereabouts during the robbery. They were easily able to prove that the chess club was no longer at the Capitol Hill Community Center, an institution which is not that far from the United Bank.

King also explained how he came to shave off his mustache. To establish that he had periodically shaved off his mustache, I showed him the trophy case with his police memorabilia. It included three picture identification cards. One was with the mustache. Two were without the mustache. He was aware that the FBI had seen him with the mustache when the two agents had first called on June 24. But he did not care. The mustache was bothering him. Sometimes he could live with the heat rash under the mustache; other times, especially in the summer, he shaved it off. "I'd like to say I felt like it," was his specific explanation of why he had shaved off his mustache about ten days after the Father's Day Massacre.

By the time I had finished with the witness, I was sure King had come across to the jury as the victim of a terrible set of coincidences. He had answered all my questions directly, but he had not volunteered any information. Maybe he should have. That would have allowed him to cover any points I might have missed when I questioned him. Now, he needed to hold up under Mr. Buckley's withering cross-examination.

The Cross-Examination of King

I had prepared King for the cross-examination. Remember, I advised him time and again, do not go off on tangents. Just stick with an account that is consistent with all your previous statements to the newspaper reporter, FBI agents, and the police. The prosecution has nothing that ties you to the robbery or murders.

The district attorney knew this. Since no physical evidence implicated King, Mr. Buckley sought to prove that King must have a guilty conscience. He began by trying to establish that King was an expert detective. Hadn't he sought to write a book on police procedures? Didn't he know that a criminal should not leave behind any clues? Wasn't he a member of the International Association for

```
                        A Life! What for?

                            OUTLINE

Chapter 1- The Begining
          The Early years
        James William Ette was born on July 10, 1936 in San Francisco,
California. My birth certificate was recorded on July 14, 1936 in
San Francisco, California.
        I lived at ?# on Roosevelt Way, San Francisco, Calif. from
Jan. 1939 to Sept. 1939.
        Then I lived ?# on 48th Ave., San Francisco, Calif., from Sept
1939 to March 1940.
        58 Laura St., San Francisco was my next home from March 1940
to Feb. 1941.
        ?# Bush St., San Francisco, Calif. from Feb. 1941 to May 1941.

Chapter -The School years
        2270 133rd Ave., W. San Leandro, CA May 1941 to May 1942.
        512 Oakland Ave., CA May 1942 to July 1943. Grandparents
house.
        At some point during these years my mother remarried and my
step father (Harold Scott King) adopted me and my name was changed
to James William King.
        7# North Dr. Naval Housing , Pearl Harbor, HI. July 1943 to
Feb. 1944.
        My sister and my future wife where born in July of 1944.
        120 Florence Ave., Sunnyvale, CA. Feb. 1944 to Feb. 1946.
        Dad tried the repair business "King's Appliance Repair" during
these years, I helped !, but the business failed to make a go.
        129 Aqana Vista, Aqana, Guam M.I., Nov. 1948 to Nov 1949.
        512 Oakland Ave. , Oakland, CA. ,Nov. 1949 to Feb. 1950.
        THE OAKLAND TRIBUNE, Oakland, California, part time, Nov. 1949
to Feb. 1950.supervisor-Mr. Sernand Albert
        7# West F St., Oakdale, CA., Feb. 1950 to Dec. 1950.
        6826 Lucille St., Oakland, CA., Dec. 1950 to Feb. 1952.
        THE OAKLAND TRIBUNE. Oakland, California, part time Dec.1950
to Dec. 1951. Supervisor- Mr. Vigor
        546 Empire St., San Lorenzo, CA., Feb. 1952 to Aug. 1954.
        Louis Stores, San Lorenzo, California, Part time, Jun. 1953 to
Jun. 1954. Supervisor- Mr. Henry Gonzales

Chapter -The military years
        U.S.Army, Military Police Corp., Aug.1954 to July. 1957

Chapter -The college years
        2036 Shipway Ave., LongBeach, CA., July 1957 to June 1959.
        Los Angeles Police Dept. Los Angeles, California Sept. 1958
Training Division.
        Phyllis Rice
Chapter -The University years
        1053 15th St., Boulder, CO., June 1959 to Dec. 1959.
        Retail Credit Co., 620 Sherman, Denver, Co. Dec 1959 to Jan.
1960 Supervisor- Mr. Myers
```

King's autobiography was more a brief outline than it was a detailed work. Nonetheless, the district attorney sought to impeach King's life by referring to the draft of the book.

Identification? Didn't it deal with ways of identifying fingerprints? Didn't this show that King, the criminal mastermind, would know better than to leave any incriminating evidence behind? Wasn't this the reason why King had left no fingerprints or shells or other incriminating evidence at the murder sites?

I objected to this line of questioning. King had not been qualified as an expert on police work. He was never a detective. This was nothing more than trial by innuendo. Judge Spriggs overruled my objection, but Mr. Buckley did little more than establish that King knew the ABCs of police procedure. None of this linked King to the crimes.

Having failed in his first thrust—the implication that the *lack* of evidence made King guilty—Mr. Buckley shifted gears. If he could not portray King as a genius, maybe he could transform him into a coward. On this basis, the prosecutor probed King's police career.

Isn't it true, he asked, that after only three years on the force, King had been transferred to the radio room? Didn't officers usually spend their first five years on the streets? Hadn't King been moved to the communications department because no other officer wanted to work with him on patrol? King denied it. Well, what about the time when King and his partner had been involved in a barroom brawl and King had run away to the squad car, calling for help?

In an angry tone, King denied any knowledge of such an incident. Could Mr. Buckley, perchance, give him a specific date and place when and where this event occurred? "I don't have it," the district attorney conceded. He was forced to retreat because he could not substantiate this occurrence.

There was nothing in the police records of this alleged incident. The rumor stemmed from Dallas Ted Fuller, a former police officer living in Yuma, Arizona. Though he was unable to provide the prosecution with details of this encounter and was not called to testify about it, the district attorney had listed Fuller as a possible witness in the punishment phase of the trial should King be found guilty. But even if this event had occurred, it had absolutely no connection with the killings on Father's Day. It was simply typical of the prosecution's relentless effort to besmirch my client with irrelevant collateral material.

This did not deter Mr. Buckley from trying to connect King with every suspicious circumstance on Father's Day. Once more, he hit a dead end when he asked King about what kind of training he had in using surgical gloves as a police officer. "None," was the defendant's reply. They were not widely issued to the police back in the early 1960s when he joined the force. Only with the rise of AIDS did the gloves become standard issue. King had never used them during his police career.

In a sarcastic tone, the district attorney again reviewed King's story of his locations on Father's Day. Isn't it strange, Mr. Buckley asked, that you just happened to shave your mustache, dispose of your gun, lose your driver's license, and get a new safe-deposit box right at the time the bank was robbed? "And it's also a coincidence, is it not, that you just happened to be in downtown Denver at the time these four guards were murdered?"

"It was my misfortune, yes, sir," King replied.

The prosecutor proceeded to take King through his different statements to the FBI, police, and what he had testified during direct examination. He stressed the inconsistencies. In one account, for example, King stated he had seen no one at the community center. In another statement, King noted that he had encountered a well-dressed man at the center. Why the contrasting statements? Wasn't this evidence that King was lying?

Unflappable on the stand, King easily explained these seeming contradictions: they were due to misunderstanding by the police or FBI or were outright fabrications by the authorities. He had not seen any fellow chess players at the community center, though he had encountered a well-dressed man.

Mr. Buckley next turned to King's family. He sought to make much of the fact that King had said nothing about his biological father and had referred to his stepfather as his real father. He also tried to establish that King did not like his middle son, Greg. Hadn't he referred to him as the "tattooed one"? Didn't this show he hated both his son and his father? The implication was that King was the kind of man who would commit these gruesome murders on Father's Day. I objected to these cheap shots. Once more, Judge Spriggs overruled me.

Turning to King's supposed autobiography, Mr. Buckley asked why he called it *A Life! What For?* Didn't that show that he was

Photo by Phil Goodstein

The basement entrance to the Capitol Hill Community Center led to the meeting room of the Denver Chess Club.

a failure? Why did his sons so fete Carol on Mother's Day but virtually ignore him on Father's Day? Didn't that prove that his sons disliked him? Wasn't that because he was ready to kill guards who were young enough to be his sons?

The undaunted defendant answered Mr. Buckley in short, concise, logical responses. His so-called autobiography was nothing more than a three-page outline. He had simply jotted it down as a very rough draft of ideas he would like to develop sometime. Just because someone or something was missing from it, that did not mean it was unimportant. King further emphasized that the family was informal. It had few organized sit-down affairs.

"I love all my sons," was the defendant's pithy response to the prosecutor's implication that he did not like his middle son. Anyone who had ever seen Greg King would immediately notice all the tattoos on his arms. The "tattooed one" was simply a fond description for him. King had referred to his stepfather as his real father because he was. His mother had divorced his blood father when Jim was three years old. King had no memories about his biological father.

Still, Mr. Buckley would not let go of his psychological inquisition of King. What about the statement that, after finishing first in the police class of 1961, he had wanted to become chief of police? Why hadn't he? Wasn't it true that he had failed in his efforts to advance beyond the rank of sergeant? Didn't this show he was a failure who was at war with the police and the world and had struck back on Father's Day?

> Police Officers Guide/Page 234
>
> be formed which could cause a riot. Peaceful crowds sometimes panic when danger becomes apparent.
>
> An unplanned assembly is a gathering of which the police have not advance knowledge. Any unusual event will draw a crowd. People flock to automobile accidents, fires, or disaster scenes. Groups will stop before interesting advertisements, on-the-street radio or television broadcasts, or similar events. The Police Officer have no way of knowing when these events will occur. Police action in these situations is often advisable.
>
> If you come upon this type of gathering you should take a few minutes to size up the situation to determine whether any action is necessary. If the crowd is small and the personnel changes as they lose interest, no action may be necessary. People tend to lose patience with you, if you try to take action when they are keenly interested in some event. They want to see what happens next, and don't want a policeman telling them to move on.
>
> Circumstances may occur where you will have to move the crowd on, or out of the street, etc. For example, people may be obstructing traffic or be too close to a fire. Even when it is difficult to move the crowd, you must retain your own self-control. Try not to display anger or excitement either by expressions or actions. Try to avoid using force or threat of force, unless it is absolutely necessary. If you believe that the crowd is in danger, or that they are hampering rescue

A page from King's Police Officers Guide.

When he again failed to make any headway, the prosecutor finally shifted to King's work at the bank. Why was King always prowling about while working as a bank guard? Wasn't he trying to learn the exact layout of the basements and secured areas so he could pull the crime? King replied he was doing what any good security guard would do: know the property he was defending. Besides, he observed that the tunnels beneath the bank were a virtual labyrinth. "I worked there about a year, or a little over, and I hadn't mastered" the system of tunnels and vaults.

"I made suggestions on changes" of security at the United Bank, King stated, when Mr. Buckley grilled him about why he thought the bank had an inadequate security system. Mr. Buckley continued, noting that King had mentioned the heist from the automated teller in the draft of his autobiography. Why had he noted that he feared he might be accused? Why was he so concerned that he did not have a good alibi? "You wouldn't need an alibi, would you, if you did not do anything wrong?" he asked. "That's true," King admitted.

I vehemently objected to this question. There is nothing wrong with or incriminating about somebody having an alibi. An alibi is a legitimate defense and there is nothing derogatory about the legal term. Despite my argument, Judge Spriggs overruled my objection, telling me not to make speeches when I objected. Still, I hoped the jury got the gist of my objection.

Mr. Buckley wanted to know why King did not express any regret over the fate of the murdered guards in his letter to, and conversation with, Mike McKown. Wasn't that because he was, in McKown's words, "stuck"? Didn't he only care for himself as he tried to evade responsibility for his crimes?

King denied he had told McKown he was "stuck." Yes, he was worried. He realized the suspicious set of coincidences about his disposed revolver, planned trip to Las Vegas, new safe-deposit box, and former employment at the United Bank. That was why he had taken McKown's call so literally. It was not a confession of guilt.

The cross-examination turned to the draft of the police manual King was writing. Why was there such a fascination with people being shot in the back of the head? Did this not show King's premeditation to murder four bank guards by shooting them in the back of the head? King replied by noting that professional killers frequently murdered their victims by shooting them in the back of the head. He was not a professional or any other kind of killer.

What about the statement in his police manual, Mr. Buckley continued, that "the person who commits the worst of crimes under the cover of darkness, or the one who acts without considering he might be caught and punished, may submit to arrest, often meekly, when confronted by the police"? Did not King meekly surrender to the police? Did not this prove that he was guilty? Once more, King firmly stated that there was no substance to the district attorney's charges.

The one place where Mr. Buckley scored was in the matter of the Colt Trooper. As he had during direct examination, King described his weapon as simply a "tool of the trade." He admitted that he had discovered the cracked cylinder while cleaning his pistol after firing it at a shooting range when he still worked at the United Bank. He realized that he would be in danger if he discharged the weapon with the cracked cylinder, but he also knew that the only reason he would be using the weapon was because his life would be threatened by an armed intruder.

King stumbled here. He was so wrought up that his answer was different from the previous explanation he had given me. Knowing it would be dangerous to fire the revolver, he had made sure not to load a bullet in the chamber near where the cylinder was cracked. I purposely did not develop this point during redirect examination since it would have emphasized the weakness of King's story.

"I had no need for a revolver after I left the bank," King continued, explaining his decision to dismantle and dispose of the damaged gun. King did not immediately recall what he had done with his two speed loaders. After a bit of confusion, the defendant noted he had disposed of them about the time he had gotten rid of the Sam Browne belt.

Mr. Buckley got King to admit that the speed loaders, belt, and holster all belonged to the Denver Police Department. Why didn't King give them back when he retired? Nobody asked for them was the defendant's literal reply. He had no idea of what they cost. He had no need for them and so threw them away.

What happened to the 18 rounds of +P ammunition which King still had from his days as a police officer? When the retired sergeant noted that he had also thrown them away, Mr. Buckley asked in an incredulous voice, what, you put live ammunition in the trash?

King explained that he had first pulled the projectiles apart and dumped out the gunpowder before placing them in the trash. Therefore, the cartridges were not dangerous when he disposed of them. While this did not sound like the most convincing of explanations, it was typical of King: it was his literal-minded, pragmatic solution to what to do with the bullets for which he had no use after he had disposed of his defective revolver.

I did not think that Mr. Buckley had badly damaged King during cross-examination. While his voice had cracked on a couple of occasions, he held up remarkably well. Out of a scale of ten, I figured he scored a nine and a half as an effective, most believable witness. His testimony had confirmed how the prosecution's case was nothing more than shadowy suspicions, conjectures, and a set of unfortunate coincidences.

Rebuttal Witnesses

When King stepped down after four hours on the stand, we rested our case. The prosecution called five rebuttal witnesses. One was a victim's advocate who repeated Kenetha Whisler's story about hearing King's voice at the preliminary hearing. She had not heard King's voice, she explained, but believed she had seen King moving his lips at the preliminary hearing. As she left the courtroom with Whisler at the preliminary hearing, the eyewitness had immediately informed her that she had heard and identified the robber's voice while she was on the stand. Three rebuttal witnesses were law enforcement officials who talked about speed loaders. Finally, the district attorney called Paul Yocum.

The prosecution's main goal was to let the jury view the rapidly aging former guard. It wanted the jury to see how physically Yocum drastically differed from the composite drawing of the robber. Yocum spoke in a dull, slurry voice and was unanimated. With his lips usually puckered and walking to and from the witness stand in a slouch, he denied that he was angry at the bank for falsely charging him with the theft from the automated teller.

Since I had Scott Robinson deal with the whole subject of alternate suspects, he cross-examined Yocum. Scott brought out that Yocum was in poor health, had lost 40 pounds since the Father's Day Massacre, and did not look the same as he had a year earlier. The witness complained that he was in debt from the costs he had incurred defending himself from the charge of stealing money from the automated teller.

Yocum further lamented that he had been unjustly charged with the theft. That was just what we wanted to hear. "How does it feel to be falsely charged?" Scott asked Yocum. This gave the witness a chance to tell his woes at the hands of the authorities. The message was that the jury should be doubly cautious in judging King against whom the evidence was even more scanty than that against Yocum.

We did not call any surrebuttal witnesses. By the close of testimony on Friday, June 5, it appeared that we would be ready to proceed to closing arguments on Monday morning. When court opened that day, however, we moved to reopen the case. Our investigator had finally located a missing witness.

Kenneth Couch drove a van for Smart Shuttle, a charter company that transported customers between downtown and the airport. I had wanted Couch to be our lead-off witness, but he did not show up in court in response to our subpoena. I thereupon had Judge Spriggs issue an arrest warrant for Couch to appear in court. We only found him at the very last minute. Judge Spriggs, ruling that Couch had not shown up for the trial due to a misunderstanding, allowed us to place him on the stand.

The driver had surfaced on June 17, 1991, the day after the murders, when the authorities asked that anybody who had been near the bank on the morning of the robbery contact them if they remembered anything unusual which had occurred. His testimony would immediately force the jury to think twice about the prosecution's claims. Couch frequently drove his route on early Sunday mornings, scouting out the streets for possible problems that might be caused by detours and construction. As he was nearing the United Bank, somewhere between 6:00 and 7:00 on Father's Day morning, he encountered a man in his 40s who was driving an oxidized gold or tan 1974 or 1975 Toyota or Honda Civic in an extremely erratic manner.

Couch first noticed the mysterious motorist about a block to the northwest of the United Bank, along 17th Street as it nears Broad-

The photo of Paul Yocum shown to the tellers.

way. The driver was looking about wildly, changing lanes, and not paying attention to traffic. Couch, who feared he might get into an accident with this vehicle, believed that the suspect was "out looking for a hooker."

As Couch made a right turn onto Broadway, the other driver did the same. The car continued to weave about for two blocks on Broadway as Couch made a left turn to head east on Colfax Avenue. About that time, from his right, the man in the suspect vehicle nearly cut Couch off. Couch had to slam on the brakes to keep from hitting him. The witness last saw the Toyota or Honda as it turned north on Lincoln Street, headed straight toward the freight elevator entrance of the United Bank.

What made this ominous was Couch's description of the driver: He was wearing a 1950esque plaid fedora with a yellow feather on the left side of it. The suspect had on dark sunglasses and looked a good deal like the man in the composite drawing. Given the sunlight at the time, Couch thought it unusual that the other driver then had on sunglasses. The man whom he saw, Couch swore, had a "hawk nose." He was not James King. Therefore, since the prosecution did not dispute that King had still been around his house as late as 8:00 AM on Father's Day, this was evidence that the retired sergeant was not the robber. The prosecution had offered no explanation of the presence of this driver. Maybe he was driving erratically because he was casing out the bank. Indeed, he could have been the man who had buzzed for admission as Bob Bardwell.

During cross-examination, the most that Mr. Buckley got out of Couch was that he had previously reported that this incident had occurred somewhere between 6:30 and 7:30 on Father's Day morning. Now, he insisted that it was between 6:00 and 7:00 AM. The witness was sorry, but that was the best he could do with the time line.

After Couch left the stand, Judge Spriggs read the jury 19 different instructions wherein he spelled out the law and defined the meaning of specific legal terms. (Each juror received a printed copy of the instructions.) Most of the instructions were standard for a criminal trial, such as that the jury give no more weight to direct evidence than to circumstantial evidence. The instructions also informed the jurors how they were to evaluate the credibility of the witnesses and consider each crime separately. With this done, Mr. Sims rose to make the first part of the prosecution's closing argument.

13

Closing Arguments

The testimony and exhibits had established that the case against King consisted of tainted eyewitness identifications and suspicious circumstances. The prosecution emphasized the latter as it wove an elaborate net to convict King when Mr. Sims and Mr. Buckley spoke their last words to the jury. As they had from the time of his arrest, they depended on character assassination, inferences, and conjectures rather than hard evidence or unimpeachable eyewitness identifications linking King to the murders and robbery.

As Mr. Sims started to address the jury, sirens temporarily drowned him out. He went over to where the Styrofoam heads of the murdered men had been exhibited at the clerk's desk. One by one, he placed them on the panel by the witness box. In a very powerful and dramatic gesture, he solemnly called off the names of the dead guards as he arranged the faces to stare at the jury. With that he launched his oration.

*The police believed that the killer bought his shoes
from Toth's Specialty Footwear.*

"What manner of man is this that slays four men in the prime of
their lives on a Sunday morning?" Mr. Sims asked in an angry,
shouting voice. "What manner of a man? What manner of a man?"
he repeated. The answer was obvious: "He is a coward and a killer.
He is a retired police officer who is a coward and a killer.... He is
a cold, calculating chess player and he is a murderer, . . . a
psychopath who lies easily and convincingly." He is a man who has
committed "one of the most hideous crimes that any of you could
have imagined." A newspaper account credited Mr. Sims with a
combination of Shakespearean diction and the rhythms of a gospel
preacher as he viciously denounced Jim King's life and police
career.

Mr. Sims traced the crimes. In a dramatic voice, he had us enter
the elevator with McCullom. Suddenly, the diligent bank guard was
overpowered by the greedy, vicious murderer. After the killer had

left McCullom in a pool of blood in the subbasement, Mr. Sims described how the intruder had invaded the control center, murdered the other guards, and then robbed the tellers. It made little difference whether the gunman asked for the "cashier" or "head teller." Guards did not know those terms. But this former guard knew his way around the bank, he knew it well enough to commit these awful deeds.

At times, Mr. Sims sounded like a mathematics teacher, taking out a marker and writing down on a big chart the odds of five people simultaneously misidentifying King in a six-man lineup. He peppered his speech with "ain'ts" and double negatives. The prosecutor contrasted this streetwise style with indignation as he continually pointed toward King.

There was only a one in 7,776 chance, Mr. Sims observed, that five people would coincidentally choose the wrong person in a six-man photo lineup. The eyewitness testimony proved that King was the murderer. These people, robbed at gunpoint by this ex-law enforcement officer, were not lying, but definitely pointed out that King was the man. Besides, the physical evidence proved that King was guilty.

The ballistics showed a link with police-issued ammunition fired from a .38 Colt revolver comparable to the one that King had carried. King was the only weekend guard who was armed with a Colt. All the other guards were unarmed or carried Smith & Wessons. King was a former police officer and must be guilty.

Despite our evidence to the contrary, the prosecutors insisted that no police officer would dispose of his service revolver. But King had! That indicated his guilt. Similarly, King had not told the authorities exactly the same thing every time when they questioned him. Besides, King was known to have discussed the shortcomings of the bank's security system and talked about how it was possible to rob the bank. It was also ominous that no gun belt, no service revolver, and no speed loaders were found in King's house.

The last statement was typical of the district attorney's argument. Because no incriminating evidence was found, King must be guilty by circumstances—he is a calculating criminal who destroyed this vital evidence. In Mr. Sims' hands, precisely the lack of evidence made King guilty.

Mocking King's alibi, Mr. Sims noted that there were certain people who appeared to be accident prone. Well, "the defendant tells you he's just a guy who is coincidence prone." Nonsense, the physical and direct evidence show that King committed these crimes. The prosecutor thereupon reviewed the testimony about the Capitol Hill Community Center. Wasn't it strange that a policeman and guard, who took great pride in prowling through all parts of his assigned areas, would drive for miles and miles to the community center, look around for only a couple of minutes, and leave without trying to find out more about the fate of the chess club? Besides, the community center's caretaker, Ed Huntington, would have undoubtedly seen King if the defendant had actually been at the mansion looking for a chess game. Mr. Huntington clearly told you he saw nobody looking for a chess game on Father's Day.

Equally ridiculous was King's claim that he had shaved off his mustache because pimples and sores were irritating him. That was his seemingly clever diversion, his way of seeking to avoid a lineup and identification as the killer. Hair is not an irritant, Mr. Sims the dermatologist proclaimed, but shaving irritates sores. To shave the mustache to ease the irritation "ain't no common sense." Besides, King's recently obtained driver's license photo of June 28 did not show any pimples or rashes. This is a smoke screen. Do not be fooled by it.

Mr. Sims further reviewed the eyewitness testimony. It was not to be doubted. The tellers had no reason to lie and unjustly accuse King. The July 5 lineup was a far better and more accurate test of their memories than was the June 20 photo lineup. In the second lineup, after all, the heads had been cropped so the witnesses could get a better feel of what the gunman actually looked like with his hat and sunglasses. Even Chong Choe, with her inability to identify anybody in the lineup, conceded that the FBI's composite drawing looked just like the killer. Everybody knew that the drawing was of Jim King.

Lest there be any doubt about this point, Mr. Sims continued, recall the testimony of Mike McKown. Better than anyone else, he knew all the suspects and guards and former guards. On the stand, he had tried to do his most to testify in favor of James King. But when asked whom he thought the composite drawing most closely resembled, McKown admitted that it was James King.

Nor was anything to be made of King's moles. He had on a disguise that covered some of them. The Band-Aid distracted the eyewitnesses from seeing the others. Probably, you did not even notice these moles when King was on the witness stand last Friday. They are a minor part of his description. They are literally molehills which the defense has tried to transform into mountains.

After going over the eyewitness identifications, Mr. Sims further turned to inflammatory rhetoric and character assassination. This was seen in his review of King's unpublished police manual and autobiography. He reminded the jury that King had made some rather bitter comments in them. And had not people who knew King described the former police officer as something of a loner? Was not this the classic criminal-type? Didn't it indicate that King pulled the job?

Don't acquit King, Mr. Sims warned the jury, because he does not look like a killer. No one looks like a killer, no one sounds like a killer. The belief that murderers have certain preconceived traits is a fantasy of Hollywood. You can only know a killer by his deeds. You agreed during voir dire that you cannot judge a book by its cover. So let's turn the pages of the book and get to the core of the volume. There you will find that James King is a vicious killer.

King is an "arrogant elitist," someone who thought he was so good he announced that he would become chief of police while still in his rookie class. He is a man, who having only served five years on actual street patrol during his 25-year police career, was ready to write the authoritative police manual. He is a man who was so upset by losing chess games to players whom he thought he should beat that he shunned the chess club until he found it convenient to use it as an alibi when he staged these atrocious murders. Make no mistake about it. King "can blend in and appear normal," but he is an evil man who coldly murdered the guards.

In trying to explain the crime by demeaning King's personality, the prosecution had a key advisor, Dr. Kathy Morall, a psychiatrist who sat in on much of the trial. I had previously encountered her during the Ross Carlson murder case. The defendant was a deeply troubled 19-year-old lad who killed his 36-year-old mother and 37-year-old father on August 17, 1983. When I pled him not guilty by reason of insanity, defense psychiatrists and psychologists discovered that Carlson suffered from the Multiple Personality Disorder, a dissociative mental disease whereby he was possessed by about eight or ten different personalities. (When one personality was functioning, it was amnesic to the other personalities' prior experiences. Hence, the loss of time and memory prevented Carlson from assisting counsel and himself in his defense.)

The court ruled that, on account of the disease, Carlson was incompetent to stand trial. He was ordered held at the Colorado State Hospital in Pueblo. Only once the disorder was cured could we proceed to the sanity trial. Rather than treating Carlson's mental illness, psychiatrists and psychologists at the State Hospital vehemently insisted that Carlson was a malingerer who was hiding behind the sham diagnosis of suffering from the Multiple Personality Disorder to escape the penalty of the law.

Among those who had failed to obey the court orders to treat Carlson, despite seeing him about 33 times in the course of two years, was Dr. Morall. For her services, the state paid her $12,000. She was so determined to expose Carlson as a fraud, rather than offering medical assistance, that prior to a court hearing about Carlson's competency to stand trial in September-October 1987, she secretly flew to Philadelphia where she paid half of her fees in the case to Dr. Martin Orne, a national prosecution psychiatric expert, for "consultations" and coaching about how she should testify against Carlson in court! Despite Dr. Morall's testimony, the court again ruled that Carlson was suffering from the Multiple Personality Disorder and was incompetent to stand trial. (Before the legal sanity of Carlson could be resolved, the defendant died of acute lymphoblastic leukemia at age 25 in November 1989.)

The prosecution had listed Dr. Morall as a witness to testify why King should be executed should the jury rule him guilty. To assist the district attorney, Dr. Morall had prepared a four-and-one-half-page, single-spaced "psychological profile" of King. Though she had never met the man or had the opportunity to make a clinical examination of the defendant, she thoroughly denigrated his life and career on the police department. He was, she concluded, a "passive-aggressive, narcissistic person" who had delusions of grandeur. As such, he was fully capable of committing the murders.

The psychiatrist urged the prosecutors to point to King as often as possible. Mr. Sims followed her advice, vehemently gesturing toward King more than two dozen times at the crescendos of his cascading argument. Dr. Morall had also told the prosecution that she was sure King would be a poor witness who would be unable to maintain eye contact with the jury. On the stand, the retired police sergeant had frequently spoken directly to the jury, showing the dubious validity of Dr. Morall's analysis.

On the advice of Dr. Morall, the district attorney focused on the psychology of King. The retired sergeant, it appeared, had actually committed the murders and bank robbery because he was angry with the world, because he was out to prove something, and because he had an animus against the police department and the bank. The jury was not to convict him because the prosecution had produced the loot and murder weapon along with unquestioned eyewitness identifications; on the contrary, it was to convict him because of what he had written on his word processor.

While relying on Dr. Morall's advice, Mr. Sims vigorously denounced Dr. Greene. She was nothing more than a "high-priced experimental psychologist," a "mercenary" who testified for pay. An academic, she only knew the sterile classroom, but not "real life" and the agony suffered by the victims of a brutal crime. Sarcastically, Mr. Sims made it sound like Dr. Greene had rediscovered the wheel when she testified that people have trouble identifying criminals in disguise.

Even at that, Mr. Sims enlisted Dr. Greene's testimony. He admitted that Kenetha Whisler had claimed the gunman weighed 240 to 250 pounds. But, as Dr. Greene told you, victims sometimes overestimate the height and weight of criminals. Besides, Whisler was a most perceptive witness. Just take the case of King's voice at the preliminary hearing. Amidst the controversy over this, he claimed, I had so dominated the proceedings that everybody in the courtroom turned their attention to me. The only person not fooled by my devoted defense of King, according to the prosecutor, was Whisler. That was why she alone heard King's voice at the preliminary hearing.

Whisler had quivered when King had approached her during the trial. "Her body knew, her body recognized that man." This seemingly psychic phenomenon, Mr. Sims proclaimed, was undoubted evidence that King was guilty.

True, eyewitnesses might be mistaken in their specific descriptions, but their overall recognition was accurate. While each person's mistake is different, "one person's truth is completely consistent with another person's truth." There is no doubt. King was the man who killed the four guards in cold blood.

Mr. Sims effectively used repetition in his closing argument. Pointing continually at the defendant à la Dr. Morall, he noted that King was the man who broke into the United Bank by guise, and "shot and killed William McCullom, shot and killed Phillip Mankoff, shot and killed Scott McCarthy, and shot and killed Todd Wilson." He "murdered them without mercy and without regret. He was cool and calm." You, the jury, must hold him responsible for these crimes. "I am confident you will find this defendant guilty as charged."

The prosecutor took 70 minutes to turn King into the bank robber/murderer of the century. I was glad I was about to have a chance to answer him. His summation had been dramatic and powerful. Right then, I feared, the jury might have been ready to agree with the prosecutor.

My Closing Argument

As I moved to the lectern, the sky had clouded over and the thunder was heard outside the courtroom. Was I about to be Rocky Mountain Thunder? The media claimed I was thundering when I told the jury that this was a case with no foundations. After thanking the jurors for their close attention to all the testimony and their ability to fairly, fully, and honestly weigh the evidence, I noted that sometimes during the case, I had turned to humor. This was an effort to relieve the "anxious tensions" and bear the "unbearable burden" of representing a person who is not guilty.

"Jim King has been a part of the justice system all of his life and he has believed in that system all of his life. He and his family have lived a nightmare year as they have watched the system as it has broken down. Jim King knows that system he believes in can break down. But he continues to believe in that system because he knows you, as jurors, can stop this government mistake with your verdict. You are not only his last hope; you are the last hope of the jury system in this case.

"There is no greater horror than for an innocent man to be trapped by an arm of government which has gone wrong. That's why the jury system is so precious. You are the safety net which says that without evidence beyond a reasonable doubt, nobody's freedom gets taken away. Jim King puts his faith in you and your common sense evaluation of the inadequate evidence in this case. . . .

"In one sense, this case is about a quest for a chess game. Had that chess game been played as Jim King hoped that Sunday morning, we wouldn't be here. But there is something else which would have happened if that chess game had been played as planned. You see, once the government got fixed on Jim King, the tremendous and powerful resources of the state were focused on trying to make their case. And even as they failed to find connecting evidence, they persisted in focusing on this one man.

"If that chess game had been played, the government would have continued to spend their heavy resources to find the right people who committed this unspeakable crime. They might even have found the right people by now. But the last year has been spent trying to put together some kind of case against this man. And sometimes these intensive efforts by law enforcement pay off and they find connecting evidence and prove their suspicions correct. But not here! The more they found, the more they found which pointed to some others. Their case just didn't come together despite their extraordinary efforts. The evidence just wasn't there because they had the wrong man. And if the government had kept looking and spent their time where it should have been focused, this would be a different story and a very different world for Jim King and his family. . . .

"This is a case of total exoneration." On June 20, 1991, four days after the robbery, I repeatedly reminded the jury, the eyewitnesses were asked to look at photos of Jim King and tell the authorities whether he was the robber. All failed to identify him "when the memories were fresh in their minds." Initially, the authorities, through the media, insisted that King was trying to make a getaway at the airport. We called five witnesses who reported the mysterious character at Stapleton on June 16. All agreed that he was *not* King.

"Ironically and forthrightly, this is a case where the microscopic eye of the FBI and the hard scientific evidence clear Jim King of any connection to the case." I cited the preface to an FBI manual on the need for good police work and an examination of the physical evidence. I had previously read it during the trial when I had an FBI agent identify the source of this quotation:

> Wherever he [the criminal] steps, whatever he touches, whatever he leaves, even unconsciously, will serve as silent witness against him. Not only his fingerprints or his footprints, but his hair, the fibers from his clothes, the glass he breaks, the marks he leaves, the paint he scratches, the blood he deposits or collects, all of these and much more bear mute witness against him.
>
> This is evidence that does not forget. It is not confused by the excitement of the moment. It is not absent because human witnesses are. It cannot perjure itself. It cannot be prejudiced, be influenced by suggestion, by falsely reinforced identity. It cannot be wholly absent. Only human failure to find it, study and understand it can diminish its value.

I returned to this statement throughout my closing argument, repeating sentences from it in contrast to the state's lack of any

I address the jury.

physical or scientific evidence against Jim King. There were, for example, the lack of King's fingerprints or palmprints, the shoeprints that don't match his shoes, the prosecution's inability to tie the gloves to King, the failure to investigate the mysterious 5:04 alarm, the unexplained coffee cup, pop can, and cigarette butts in the storage area. The specific evidence shows no trace to King. There is no blood, no hair, no fibers, no incriminating ballistics, no loot, no clothes. There is no evidence. The prosecution has no case.

But innocent circumstances can build up to charges. It would have been as easy to charge Paul Yocum, Harry Glass, or Mike McKown with these crimes as it has been to target Jim King. I reminded the jury of the incriminating evidence against Yocum, noted Glass' suspicious fingerprint on the Mountain Dew can, and recalled how some guards and bank officers had originally suggested that Mike McKown had done the job. But the authorities were honest and realized that this did not make these individuals guilty. King was not as lucky. The police, unable to seize the culprits, wanted a victim and had selected Jim King as the fall guy.

This resulted in "shameful acts of intimidation" by the district attorney. This case is an effort to force a number of coincidences into a pattern, so much so that it appears to be a nefarious conspiracy. From the time that the FBI first questioned Jim King on June 24 until the police arrested him on July 3, he was fully cooperative. Despite my advice not to talk to the authorities without the presence of an attorney, he still talked to the police on July 2 and 3. His thanks for his cooperation was this nightmare.

The evidence against King does not add up. The witnesses who testified about revolvers told you how Colt cylinders can crack. By the time they do, usually the gun is no good anyway. And what about the phantom speed loaders so beloved by Mr. Buckley? You saw how their witness could not make them work very speedily while Mr. DiVirgilio demonstrated how a speed loader designed for a Smith & Wesson revolver could be used on a Colt. But what did this prove anyway? Where was there any evidence of speed loaders in the murders? The same place where all the other physical and scientific evidence was—nowhere to be found!

Still the eyewitnesses claim that King was the man. They did not identify him in the photo books on June 20. They exonerated him on June 20. So "what happened to change their minds? You can use common sense to answer that." The eyewitnesses did not lie. "They are not corrupt, they are not dishonest. They are mistaken. They are not the first witnesses to accuse an innocent man and they will not be the last to do so. It is just too easy to make a mistake like this when you are terrorized with a weapon and especially when the robber is in disguise." But they were not mistaken on June 20 when they carefully examined the photo books and cleared King of the robbery. They now sincerely believe he is the man. This is the result of dubious moves by the authorities, moves that make us angry.

"We are angry because of the indefensible actions of the government in this case. They were so fixed on Jim King, they were so eager to meet the public pressure on them to find somebody, they were so zealous to back up their fixation on Jim King, that they went too far. They poisoned the photo lineup. They manipulated these honest citizens by abusing the process. In a very real sense, these victims of the robbery have again become victims, this time victims of a desperate prosecution. Jim King cannot and should not forgive these law enforcement people for that. Jim King should not be in this courtroom and, but for this abuse of the process, this abuse of the system, he would not be here."

The eyewitnesses, who have been pounded and cajoled to change their testimony, "were right, right about the first time they saw Jim King and exonerated him as a robber" on June 20. Only two weeks later, after repeatedly showing them King's photo, the authorities prodded the witnesses, and cropped and redrew the photo of King to look like the man in the composite drawing so that five of the six eyewitnesses came to remember seeing "what they never saw before" at a "photo-biased lineup." In the process, the authorities made victims of the tellers again, seeking to turn their words around so they would testify against King.

These five men and women are sincere. Not only are they victims of the robbery, but they are also victims of the authorities who induced them to identify King after they had vindicated the retired police sergeant on June 20. Take the testimony of Kenetha Whisler. She denied that she had been shown King's photo on June 20 despite the fact that FBI Special Agent Kirk confirmed she had seen it. The way the authorities cropped and redrew the photo of

King, repeatedly showing it to her, made her believe that she could not have possibly failed to identify King when she had first seen his picture.

Given this, and the prejudicially tainted eyewitness identifications of July 3, 4, and 5, it was no wonder that the police refused to permit a live lineup which would have exonerated my client. Rather, they literally framed King with the cropped photo. This becomes clear when you recall the specifics of the eyewitness identifications.

Take the story of King's mustache. Two of the eyewitnesses noted that the robber's mustache was most likely phony. Another eyewitness did not have any recollection of seeing a mustache. Yet now the prosecution, which admits that King still wore his mustache as late as June 24, when the FBI first interviewed him, charges that King deliberately shaved off his mustache to conceal his identity. Using that as an excuse, the authorities refused to have a live lineup where the tellers could have had an honest chance to identify King as opposed to the doctored photograph they were shown around the time of the defendant's arrest. If the eyewitnesses were correct in their assertions that they would never forget the face of the robber, they would have been able to identify King in a live lineup, mustache or no mustache.

This is the heart of the case: not concrete eyewitness identifications, but a malicious conspiracy by the police and FBI to frame a man who had given 25 years of his life to the Denver Police Department. Already, at 3:30 AM on July 4, right when I was awakened by the phone call telling me of King's arrest, the theme of "a police conspiracy was ringing in my ears." Time and again, I repeated to a crescendo: "June 20, June 20, June 20, June 20." I wanted to make sure the jury did not forget what had happened during the first photo lineup. "This is a case when the mighty mountain labored and did not even give forth the mouse!"

Having established this framework of a malevolent Big Brother persecuting King, I proved it. Look at the stories of the eyewitnesses. Look at how their stories kept changing. Remember Barranco's sudden revelation in court or Whisler's dependence on a psychic cowboy to convict King? I do not seek to denigrate Whisler by mentioning the psychic. She sincerely believed him.

My body language spells out my question during the closing argument: how can they charge King given their polluted eyewitness identifications and lack of any physical or scientific evidence?

Her consultation with him was a sign of how desperate she was to try to figure out who was actually responsible for these vicious crimes.

I noted the differences between the contrasting eyewitness identifications. One claimed the robber's voice was deep, another said that it was a tenor. One described his hat as black, another stated it was chocolate brown, a third identified it as dark gray. One argued the shirt was dark or black; four others said it was white. Some had him wearing black-framed sunglasses with plastic frames; others argued they were brown-tinted with metal frames or were flip-up sunglasses. Some said the gunman used the term "mantrap"; others said he referred to the "cage," the "doorway," or the "little room."

Actually, it was refreshing to note that the eyewitnesses differed on details. It showed they were human, that it was easy under stress for them to forget or fail to focus on details. Yet, when the tables were turned and Jim and Carol King were grilled on what Jim did on Father's Day, the prosecution sought to seize on minor variances and turn them into criminal intent.

The fact that there were small discrepancies between the stories of Jim and Carol King about Father's Day was natural. They proved that the couple did not sit down and deliberately seek to fabricate an alibi. Like the eyewitnesses, Jim and Carol King have memory lapses. If their stories had matched in all particulars, you should be concerned. As it was, here was an innocent couple desperately trying to remember the exact events of what they thought was going to be a most uneventful Father's Day.

"A humble public servant told the whole world where he was and what he did. They have twisted every part of normal living into a phony framework of suspicion, guesswork, and imagination. This structure won't pass your inspection. This structure has been pounded by scientific evidence and rendered with big gaping holes of reasonable doubt. . . .

"This is a case where intense and massive publicity pressured the police to poison the victims of the robbery to make them see what they never saw before. This is a case where continued publicity etched the poisoned lineup in the minds of living victims of the robbery. This is a case where multiple exposure on TV and in the press of Jim King in courtroom appearances reinforced the poisoned photo array." Consequently, not on June 20, but only in early July did the eyewitnesses come to swear King was the robber.

I next reviewed the scene of the crime and the actual physical evidence which had been found: the shoeprints which did not match King's shoes; the bullets which were not necessarily of police issue; and the fingerprints found in the control room. I reminded the jury that we had called a number of police officers and FBI agents on behalf of King. One and all agreed that the prosecution's assertions did not hold up, that the physical and scientific evidence did not implicate King in the robbery and murders. We had to extract this exonerating evidence, such as Agent Riley's testimony about the antimony-laced bullets, from the law enforcement officials.

"Doesn't this raise a reasonable doubt?" This is hard scientific evidence, not like the "mushy" psychology which Mr. Sims so cavalierly dismissed when he discussed Dr. Greene's poignant testimony in his closing argument. But the more we look at this hard scientific evidence, the more it becomes clear that Jim King was not involved in the crimes.

A very clear palmprint was found on the doorjamb to the battery room. The police compared it with a palmprint they took from Jim King. The prints did not match. Fifteen good latent fingerprints were taken from the walls, windows, VCRs, and safe. The police had only been able to identify six of them. One was of Scott McCarthy on the cellophane wrapper of a cookie. That showed how carefully the authorities sought to identify these prints. But none of the fingerprints, palmprints, or shoeprints which did not belong to the guards have yet been identified.

"What are they waiting for?" I asked. Pausing, and lowering my voice, I told the jury in a whisper: "They want to get Jim King at any cost." They have ignored the evidence as they try to send this man to the gallows based on the most dubious and contaminated of eyewitness identifications.

Typical was the prosecution's red herring, its beloved magical surgical gloves that had no connection with the robbery and murders. "When the FBI and Denver Police Department found no hard evidence versus Jim King, they should have been out looking for the vicious culprits. We all know what happened. Jim King was cleared on the 20th of June. He talked freely as to where he was and what he did. But the police refused to look elsewhere. They jumped to conclusions and would not let go. They tried to save face. They tried to turn words around. They made a mistake from the chief of police on down."

Noting that the prosecution had never explained the mysterious 5:04 alarm and how it was reset at 9:33, I continued, "We know that it was an inside job. The alarm was turned off and then, four and a half hours later, the killer or someone turns it back on . . . [amidst] all this mayhem going on and before the robbery took place."

Rather than explaining such confusion and lacking any physical or scientific evidence against King, the prosecution has grasped at straws. Take, for example, the question of the larger safe-deposit box. It had a 1,000-cubic inch capacity. "Although the prosecution has attempted to show that you could get $200,000 in such a box, which is 18,000 pieces of currency, it is astonishing to think that someone who has robbed a bank could simply look at a safe-deposit box, eyeball it, and choose a box that just conveniently happens to be large enough to take the exact amount of money stolen.

"Jim King was never seen to be bringing anything in that could possibly have passed for 18,000 pieces of currency." He did not seek to hide from the bank official the green folder in which he was carrying materials to and from the box. Besides, "when did Jim King leave with all this money? Assuming he brought it in, a little at a time, how could he possibly have gotten it all out, in one trip, without being noticed? How could all that money fit in there with the stuff that was found in the box?" So where is the loot?

The question of the safe-deposit box was indicative. It, combined with his innocent acts of disposing of his unsafe, beat-up old revolver and shaving his mustache, had become, in the eyes of a ruthless prosecution, criminal intent. The utter desperation of the state's case was illustrated by the comments of "Race Car Driver" Priest. I recalled his far-fetched testimony that King's home in the far western suburbs was but a 12-minute commute, ignoring the time the robber must have spent leaving the seventh floor of the parking garage and the numerous stoplights between the bank and the freeway. Besides, a cold, calculating killer would have never sped after committing the bank robbery of the century. He would not have taken the risk of being stopped and discovered.

Mr. Buckley, you will recall, spent an inordinate amount of time trying to rebut King's alibi about seeking a chess game at the Capitol Hill Community Center. If King had been out to construct a phony alibi for his whereabouts during the robbery of the United Bank, the community center would have been the last place the defendant would have cited. After all, if he was aware that the chess club was no longer located there, he knew that his story would be easily shredded. Besides, why would he place himself so close to the United Bank? Would not a desperate bank robber have constructed an elaborate excuse about being with friends or family miles away from the site of the murders?

Instead of accepting that Jim King, who had given up across-the-board chess for more than five years, did not know that the club had moved from the Capitol Hill Community Center, the prosecutor sought to dredge up witnesses disproving the defendant's story. Neither of Mr. Buckley's chess witnesses, however, substantiated the prosecution's claims. Couple this with Speedy Priest's testimony, and it becomes crystal clear that the prosecution's case is nothing more than unwarranted innuendo and guesswork.

Time and again, the district attorney's case has collapsed like a house of cards. All that remains are the poisoned and polluted eyewitness identifications. Therefore, the prosecution has sought to impeach King based on his personality, based on unpublished writings on his computer, and even based on his being a chess player. This is ridiculous! Opposed to this vengeful prosecution,

Photo by Phil Goodstein

Shortly after the Father's Day Massacre, fellow employees planted a tree and placed a plaque outside the bank in memory of the slain guards. See p. 323 for an enlarged view of the plaque.

note the words engraved in stone on the walls of the Department of Justice headquarters in Washington, D.C.: "It matters not who wins or loses. If justice is done, the government always wins."

The witnesses we called who know Jim King all testified that the defendant is a mild man, a law enforcement official who relied on reason and conviction, not brute force, to achieve his ends. It is also well to remember that King is a chess player. "Chess is a sublimation for a contest. A chess board is not a lethal weapon; nor are the wooden pieces. Chess is a quiet game."

Shifting gears, I reminded the men and women who were to determine Jim King's fate, that they had promised to judge the evidence. At the end of the testimony, Judge Spriggs had defined the legal meaning of reasonable doubt—a doubt with a solid foundation, a doubt produced by inconclusive evidence, by inferences and innuendoes that do not add up. This is the "wisdom of the common law and the wisdom of how we grapple with facts." It is a safety net for any person accused of a crime. Please, let reasonable doubt, not the state's tactics of defamation and slander, guide your judgment.

The prosecution's case is like a house. "The structure consists of innocent acts and faulty identification of scientific evidence exonerating the defendant. . . . This structure is . . . of sand. There is no concrete and steel. The walls are of shadowy suspicion. The halls are hunches. The floors are speculation and the roof is guesswork. . . . Would you purchase this house beyond a reasonable doubt? Or would you hesitate and pause?"

Review all the factors. Think about the evidence, or rather the non-evidence as you take your time in reaching the verdict. After all, this is a capital case. "You cannot wake up the day after your verdict and say you made a mistake because this is a matter of life and death." By ruling Jim King not guilty, you will free the police and FBI to fully pursue the true killers to vindicate these vicious murders.

After I finish speaking, Mr. Buckley will get the last word. I can't answer his rebuttal. But you can answer him in the jury room. If he again attempts to turn words around as is his wont, you can expose his tricks. "We have annihilated their case. If what is left is guilt beyond a reasonable doubt, then convict Jim King." But you promised him a fair trial and I know you will give him one. The burden of proving him guilty beyond a reasonable doubt protects us all, it protects us from the power of the state to charge, destroy, and imprison. Keep this in mind as you go to the jury room to do your democratic duty.

"On June 16, Jim King went out to finally resume his love of chess. On June 20, six victims of the robbery cleared him of the robbery. From June 24 to July 2, Jim told all he knew and you know what happened.

"On July 3,4, and 5, he was literally framed with the same photo and you know what happened. But when the state's mistakes put this innocent man on trial, thank God, we have the power of the jury to protect us from the power of the state. . . . Bring Jim King back to his beloved Carolyn and his quiet and gentle boys. Please end this ongoing nightmare.

"From June 16 to July 2, mountains of scientific evidence were analyzed and found wanting versus Jim King, exonerating Jim King. But Jim King has still stood trial." Up to last week, witnesses were "badgered and intimidated." The victim is "a man who protected our community for 25 years. He never brutalized or hurt a soul in his 25 years.

"This is a case where a quiet family man of 30 years was rooted out of retirement . . . [and] has been in the hands of the police and sheriff for 11 months, manacled and holed up like a dog. Will you bring an end to this torment? Will you treat him differently? Please free him."

Scott Robinson's Closing

Initially, I was going to deliver the complete closing argument for the defense. The Friday before the start of the summations, Judge Spriggs noted that the case had been extremely complex. He further observed how I had had Scott Robinson focus on the nature of the alarm system and the alternate suspects. The judge therefore permitted Scott to follow me in concluding our closing argument for King. Altogether, we took five hours to sum up the case.

In our concluding closing argument, my associate contrasted himself to Mr. Sims. "I am not going to shout, I am not going to pound on the table, I am not going to point to anybody," he explained. "I am going to deal with the evidence," evidence which shows that King is not guilty.

Please excuse him, Scott continued, if he was sometimes repetitious or made seemingly redundant points. If he did so, he explained, it was due to fear. The stakes in the case are enormous. It is a matter of life and death. If the state loses, the state will go on. But if Jim King loses, there will be no tomorrow.

Scott got down to the specifics of the crime. It did not begin after 9:00 when somebody drove in from the Pleasant View section of Golden and misidentified himself to the guards as Bob Bardwell, but it started much earlier. Father's Day was not a normal day at the bank. Already at 5:04, the mysterious alarm had gone off. Maybe something had happened even earlier, but we will never know. The 5:04 alarm is the earliest evidence we have that something was amiss.

My co-counsel reviewed the chronology and all the unexplained events on June 16. Here was the alarm going off in the records tunnel. It was immediately accessed and the tunnel was left unsecured for the four and a half hours before the murders. Then, right during the crime, the alarm was reset. What about this coincidence? Was the alarm a minor, unimportant accident as the prosecution asserts? Or is the fact that the alarm sounded vital scientific evidence that somebody was lurking in the bank? It could well have been the place where the murderer or murderers had been hiding prior to the arrival of their cohort at 9:14.

One could pass from the records tunnel into the armored vault without a pass card. Just think about the location where David Barranco found the robber's bag. It was quite a ways from where he first saw the intruder. Could it be that the gunman or an accomplice had previously planted the bag in the vault? Again, we will never know. But evidence like this suggests that the prosecution's theory of the case does not come close to explaining what happened on that inauspicious Father's Day.

Because the authorities had not been able to solve the bloody massacre, they had chosen King as a sacrificial victim. "Do not let the enormity of this crime sway your deliberations." Decide the case on the evidence, based on the seasoning of reasonable doubt. The prosecution asks you to dilute reasonable doubt and focus on innocent acts which, linked together, might later seem to be suspicious. But do not follow this opaque path. Do not be swayed by sympathy, by the bloody shirt, or by commendations. Remain on the firm ground of reasonable doubt.

And reasonable doubt abounds. There is the question of the unidentified shoeprints in the subbasement, in the unidentified fingerprints and palmprints in the control room. There is the evidence of the ferocious kick to the Plexiglas, the ferocious kick to the drywall. But nobody saw Jim King walking around with a limp in the wake of the murders. Had he so kicked the wall, he would have surely injured his leg.

"Everything in this case is built on speculation, not hard fact. The fingerprints are hard facts—none are of Jim King. Palmprints are hard facts—none are of Jim King. Shoeprints are hard facts—none are of Jim King." Nor was any of the loot found despite the police's repeated searches of King's house, safe-deposit box, and every other bank in the region. No clothing fitting the description of the robber was found at King's house. Indeed, witnesses swore that they had never seen King dressed comparably to the robber.

Scott further asked more of the unanswered questions about the crime. Did the intruder accidentally set off the alarm to staircase C when he used it to access the concourse level? Or did the murderer or murderers deliberately open it to isolate a guard, knowing that more than two guards were on duty? Why was one videotape left in the monitor room? Earlier that morning, Bill McCullom was reported to have been by the motor bank which it surveyed. Was it left to implicate McCullom? Or had the killer simply missed it?

Continuing his rhetorical questions, Scott asked why did Phillip Mankoff take Scott McCarthy into the cash vault at a time when guards were ordered to stay out? Why did the alarm to staircase C sound at 8:15 and 8:17, an hour before the murders? Indeed, it seemed that these two veteran guards, Phillip Mankoff and William McCullom, did a number of "inexplicable things" on Father's Day. Why? Once more the prosecution had no explanations.

These unanswered questions show that the crime was not committed by one man, but by two men or even more. It was surely not committed by someone who simply commuted to and from Golden in record time. The criminal was assisted by inside information and cooperation.

Nor was the eyewitness testimony conclusive. At the most, we have a consensus of what the tellers believed they saw during a "few short seconds." That was the whole purpose of the composite drawing, a drawing which Tom Tatalaski, the pompous director of bank security, had positively identified as Mike McKown.

Scott reviewed the testimony of Dr. Greene and the problematic nature of the identifications. "What changed between June 20 and July 3 and 5? King's face? The photos? The witnesses? The perceptions?" Why did none of the eyewitnesses see any moles on the robber since anyone looking at King would immediately see his moles?

To be sure, they are "not glaring moles, angry moles," but they are very noticeable moles. Given the six eyewitnesses who had seen the robber, one would have surely remembered the moles. They did not see the moles because Jim King was not the robber.

But what about the claim that the eyewitnesses could have identified King as the robber by his voice? Some of the witnesses swore that the gunman had a deep voice. "You've heard Jim King's voice for four hours—it's a higher, musical kind of voice," not the lower, deeper voice described by the eyewitnesses.

Turning his attention to the evidence about the alternative suspects, Scott reviewed Paul Yocum's role in the case. No, Yocum did not commit the crime. The police and FBI spent weeks trying to prove Yocum's involvement. Eventually, they dropped this probe. A small law firm with limited resources obviously cannot do better than the law enforcement authorities in solving the case. Still, look at the evidence against Yocum. It showed that anybody who had ever worked at the bank "could have been ensnared in a web of suspicion." While Yocum is innocent, the incriminating evidence against him is far greater than anything which has been produced against Jim King.

Yocum was justifiably bitter against the United Bank. In a letter to his father, the alternate suspect bemoaned how the false accusation of theft against him had ruined his life. Think about the horrors he suffered as an unjustly accused man. But, Scott continued, do not let this lead you into amateur psychology.

It would be very easy, my co-counsel noted, to try to link Yocum's problems with his father to the death of the four guards on

Father's Day. That, however, is only a diversion, a dead end. Specifically turning to the prosecution's efforts to inflame the jury and have it convict King based on such pop psychology and character assassination, Scott continued: "I ask you to reject as slanderous nonsense any claim by anybody that Jim King committed these crimes to prove something. Whoever did commit the crimes, committed them for greed!" It was most ludicrous of all to say that King as a chess player committed the crimes as if being a chess player automatically made one a maniacal killer.

Please put any such amateur psychology out of your minds. Two legitimate psychologists testified in the case: Drs. Nicoletti and Greene. Dr. Nicoletti told you about the general behavioral traits of a "typical" police officer. Even the prosecution admitted that King was not such a typical officer. Dr. Greene informed you of the problematic nature of eyewitness identifications.

Scott then reviewed the overlays. They were not a trick as the prosecution asserts, but a demonstration of how difficult it is to identify a well-known person under a disguise. Add to this the fright and surprise of being the victim of an armed robber, and it is hard for a victim to make an unquestioned identification. Anybody could be behind the disguise. There was nothing to connect it or the composite drawing to Jim King. The composite is only a sketch of the composite.

"Jim King is not the phantom of the opera, majestic in the labyrinths." He was a good police officer and a "quiet, diligent bank guard." If the bank had listened to his complaints about the poor security system, the out-of-focus cameras, and the easy access to secured areas, this crime would never have been committed. It is ironic that because King had noted the flaws of the bank's security system, the prosecution has accused him of these crimes.

It was also ironic that the prosecution sought to use King's unpublished writings, especially his police manual, against him. But do not go off on any of the prosecution's tangents. Judge the evidence for what it is—innuendo and character assassination. Opposed to this, "you were able to judge Jim King for yourself while he was under the greatest possible stress. You saw, not an angry, disappointed, bitter man capable of murder, but a quiet, gentle man waiting for this horrible time to end."

Four innocent men were killed on Father's Day. The crime was a terrible tragedy. But an "even greater tragedy is to let the police close the case and throw the book at Jim King." Guilty parties are lurking out there. They hope this will happen, "knowing their secrets will be safe if Jim King is convicted. Don't let this happen."

Bill Buckley's Rebuttal

Mr. Buckley made the rebuttal argument for the prosecution. It began around 6:00 PM. He had wanted to postpone his argument until the next morning so that the jury would start its deliberations with his words ringing in its ears. Judge Spriggs, however, insisted that the final arguments be completed that day.

With recesses, the lead prosecutor's closing argument lasted until about 8:30. It was extremely forceful and well arranged as he reviewed excerpts of the testimony. Most of the time he stood two feet from the jury. This was rare in Colorado courts. Usually, the lawyer is expected to stand behind the lectern, approximately 20 feet from the jury. By standing in the jurors' faces, holding a hand microphone to further accentuate his voice, Mr. Buckley sought to gain power and intimacy for a guilty verdict. (Had I known that Judge Spriggs would permit the lawyers to stand so close to the jury box, I would have likewise positioned myself next to the jurors during my final argument.)

Mr. Buckley's rebuttal argument was as powerful and as hard-hitting as Mr. Sims' summation. Together, they were the strongest part of the state's case. Once more, the lead prosecutor emphasized all the coincidences. To make sure the jury fully understood his case, the district attorney placed some large charts right in front of the jury. Nearly one hundred reasons were listed of why and how King must have been the murderer.

The charts were filled with the same old syllogisms. For example, an insider committed the robbery, King was an insider, therefore King was guilty. The charts similarly noted how King had shaved off his mustache, did not have a good alibi for where he was during the robbery, and could not produce his service revolver. This was not coincidence, but proof of King's guilt. The fact that most of the eyewitnesses had placed the gun in the robber's right hand while one claimed it in the left hand was ominous: police officers were taught to shoot with both hands; the robber must have used both hands; hence, King is guilty.

I objected to the placement of the charts which were virtually shoved in the jury's face. To accentuate that King was literally in the center of things, the prosecutor included a graphic consisting of concentric circles of all the people who might have been involved in the crime. Naturally, Jim King was the bull's eye.

Mr. Buckley scoffed at our alternate suspects. It must have been some getaway artist for a man to wait more than three hours after the murders to go wandering around the airport, seeking to rent a car. Paul Yocum did not have the brains to commit the crime. Nor was there any mystery about the coffee cup and cigarette butts which were found in the tunnel where the 5:04 alarm had sounded. The storage clerk who accessed the tunnel left stuff like that there all the time. The fan or a light could easily have caused the alarm. But, Mr. Buckley concluded, we can't know what happened at 5:04 because the killer took the log book which would have explained the guards' response. Besides, if the killer had been lurking in the tunnel, how to explain the 9:14 call from the man identifying himself as Bob Bardwell. What happened? After holing up in the storage area for hours, did the murderer go outside where he had to be readmitted to the bank?

Most ludicrous of all was the introduction of evidence about some guy who was "looking for a hooker." It had no connection with anything else. We had raised these issues, Mr. Buckley proclaimed, as smoke screens to cloak the guilt of Jim King. Ignore them. "The killer is sitting in this courtroom, as cold, and as cool, and as collected as he was that day."

Mr. Buckley again reviewed the evidence. To be sure, nothing directly connected the gloves with King, but they couldn't be disproved either. It was true that King's shoes did not match the shoeprints at the murder scenes, but it was suspicious that a pair somewhat comparable to the killer's shoes was found in his house. Similarly, it was indicative of King's guilt that he had the bank plans at his house.

The bank plans showed that King was a pack rat, that he never threw anything away. So why did his gun disappear? Even if his beloved, valuable, heavy-duty Colt Trooper had a cracked cylinder, why didn't he seek to fix it and preserve it as a memento of his career and gift to his son? What kind of father wouldn't do that for his son? And why did he dispose of his good leather gun belt and holster? Why didn't he save his speed loaders? Obviously, he had destroyed this crucial evidence which he knew would convict him of these awful crimes.

It was "incredible" that King, who knew that the gun had a cracked cylinder, would have carried it for two months as a bank guard. Here was a man who was insistent that the guards be armed, a man who was supposedly a conservative, cautious individual, and he's carrying a dangerous weapon that can blow up on him? Why didn't he at least inquire about the costs of repairs? Why didn't he ask for the free use of one of the bank's Smith & Wesson revolvers? It "defies common sense. It is just totally outrageous."

The prosecutor also reviewed the ballistic evidence. The murderer "could pick up the shells, he could take the videotapes, he could shave his mustache, and he could change his appearance. But he didn't have the time to take the 17 bullets out of the four lifeless bodies." These bullets matched those which had once been issued to police officers. Therefore, King must be the murderer.

Typical of Mr. Buckley's closing was his dramatic account of precisely what happened to the killer's 18 bullets. The fact that he only had these 18 bullets explained why King had killed the guards, but not the tellers. He only had 18 bullets with him, and never imagined he would encounter four guards and have to use all of his ammunition on them.

Mr. Buckley took us to the incinerator room where he had the intruder fire off the six bullets that killed Bill McCullom. The murderer used his first speed loader to put six more bullets into the gun. The criminal then spent five more shots killing Phillip Mankoff and Scott McCarthy. Suddenly, he was shocked to see Todd Wilson enter the control room. He immediately shot him. But he observed that his first shot had not killed the guard. The crazed assassin, consequently, used his second speed loader to fill the revolver with his last six bullets. He was not sparing of them as he pumped five more bullets into Wilson. Finally, with only one bullet left, and yet to commit the robbery, the killer fired his last shot into the doorknob of the supervisor's office. Hence the robber could only rely on the intimidation of the pistol when he burst into the vault. If he had had more bullets, he would have surely killed the tellers as well.

Make no mistake about it, Mr. Buckley reminded the jury, King is an icy, vicious killer. The only reason he stole but $200,000 rather than $1 million was because he was running out of time and knew he had to flee. He had spent far more time than he had expected in the control room, trying to break into the supervisor's office. Tellers from another section of the bank were scheduled to pick up checks from the armored vault at ten o'clock. Hence King had to leave by 9:56 so he would not be caught.

As he neared the end of his argument, over my strong objection and motion for a mistrial, the prosecutor fabricated evidence! Suddenly, opposed to all the previous testimony, including the fact that none of the eyewitnesses had seen the robber wearing gloves, Mr. Buckley insisted that King had left no fingerprints because he had been wearing the latex gloves the police had discovered in the trash on the seventh floor of the parking garage.

Mr. Buckley similarly repeated all of the other police charges, innuendoes, and suspicions as he insisted that the evidence is conclusive. The charts simply confirm the obvious. A former guard, a man who carried a .38 Colt revolver, a man with a bad attitude and a vendetta against the bank and the world, must have committed these bloody crimes. On point after point, Jim King matches the unusual circumstances. You will surely agree as you return a verdict of guilty on all counts against James William King.

14

Awaiting the Verdict: The Nine-Day Agony

Upon the conclusion of the final arguments on the evening of Monday, June 8, the jury was sequestered. Judge Spriggs had advised its members to pack seven days worth of clothing. The court placed the jury in a hotel that was directly east of the United Bank. The jury started deliberating the next morning. Nobody expected an immediate verdict since the jury first had to sort out and view all of the exhibits, some of which it had only seen from afar during the trial.

A most agonizing part of life as a trial lawyer is waiting for the jury to return. While it obviously needs to take its time to discuss the case and evaluate all the evidence, you never know when it is going to reach a verdict. In one high-profile case I tried in November 1973, when I defended a Chicano activist, Ernesto Vigil, against charges that he had shot at a police officer, the jury acquitted him in 30 seconds. Hung juries, moreover, are relatively rare. One report during the deliberations was that in 95 percent of all cases the jury reaches a verdict.

Since my office is only a block away from the courthouse, I usually go there and try to do other work awaiting the verdict.

Sometimes, I find it impossible to concentrate since I am so anxious to learn what the jury has decided, especially here where the death penalty loomed. As the jury pondered King's fate, I had trouble sleeping. I had no appetite. My mind wandered from other subjects as I mentally kept retrying the case.

While awaiting the verdict, Judge Spriggs called the lawyers into court and told us to prepare to argue the question of the death penalty should the jury rule King guilty. Consequently, in my file of the case are drafts of arguments I assembled of why death was not the appropriate sentence for King. I had lined up 33 witnesses to testify in King's behalf should the jury rule him guilty. The prosecution, in its efforts to execute King in the wake of a guilty verdict, announced it wanted to call numerous relatives of the slain guards who would only be appeased by King's death. But I was confident that we would never need to proceed that far.

While the jury deliberated, we got another communication from Dewey Baker, the California bank robber. Once more he confessed to the crime. "Does that job out there sound like an amateur did it?" he asked. "That guy, Jim King, he wouldn't know how to rob a bank. They could have tracked him by the puddles he . . . left on the floor. I don't want to die. But I know it's got to happen sooner or later. And when it does, I don't want that poor guy's life on my mind."

To preserve our appeal record, we moved that Judge Spriggs declare a mistrial and reopen the case based on Baker's revelations. He ruled against us, noting that there is "not a scintilla of evidence" of Baker's involvement other than "jailhouse chatter. . . . We've all been around long enough to recognize this for what it is."

Baker, in turn, retracted his confession. Observing that King was a former police officer, he noted that the world is divided between "us and them. He's a them. I hope he fries." With this, he disappeared from the case. Meanwhile, other developments threatened a mistrial.

Despite my previous motions, I did not want a mistrial. Following the closing arguments, the media had polled individuals who had been watching the trial on national Court TV. The overwhelming verdict was not guilty, that the prosecution had failed to provide evidence beyond a reasonable doubt that King had committed the

Photo by Phil Goodstein

The jury was placed in the Warwick Hotel, a building literally in the shadow of the United Bank.

crimes. The jury, though, did not seem as sure as we waited, and waited, and waited.

Day after day the jury deliberated. Some eavesdroppers claimed to have heard angry voices from the jury room. During the third day of deliberations on Thursday, June 11, the jury asked: "Is it permissible to view the videotaped statements of the vault tellers which they had made to the police immediately after the robbery?" Since these had not been shown during the trial, Judge Spriggs refused the request. He answered the jury that afternoon: "No, you must rely on your recollections of the testimony." I took this as a positive sign, believing it indicated that the jury had doubts about the veracity of the eyewitness identifications.

During the jury's deliberations, the bench on which members of the King family sat outside the courtroom disappeared. Shortly after noon on June 11, I received a call from Mr. Buckley. He claimed that the family sat in such a place whereby the jurors had to walk past it whenever they left the courtroom on breaks. This might bias the jury. Therefore, the district attorney had the bench removed!

Often the jury took long recesses during its deliberations. It was sometimes taken to lunch at restaurants in the far Denver suburbs. At these times, the 12 jurors were joined by the two alternates, two bailiffs, and a deputy sheriff. Eventually, the court paid an $8,143.73 bill for lodging the jury during the deliberations.

Shortly after the bench disappeared, we received a call from the district attorney's office telling us it had heard rumors that the jury was tainted. Late on June 11, investigators for the district attorney's office confirmed that one juror, Dorothy Stevenson, who worked in the flight kitchen of United Airlines, had told co-workers, both after she had been summoned for jury duty and during the jury selection process itself, that she thought King was guilty.

Stevenson was the juror whom I had heard might be biased during jury selection. Two phone calls to my office said that Stevenson had informed co-workers that she believed that King was guilty. I mentioned them to the court. Investigators from the district attorney's office had checked out these allegations and reported back to the court that there was no substance to them. Judge Spriggs therefore did not to do anything about Stevenson's presence on the jury.

On May 27, I got another report that the wife of a police sergeant worked at the United Airlines flight kitchen with the 54-year-old Stevenson. I raised this point during the trial outside of the presence of the jury. We questioned Stevenson in chambers. She claimed that as a supervisor, she had a lot of enemies at her workplace. I quickly established that she was not a supervisor and her explanation was a lie. In view of Stevenson's deceit, she should be dismissed for an alternate. Judge Spriggs, however, did not believe that this was sufficient cause to dismiss the juror. I objected, asking for a mistrial which he similarly rejected.

Ironically, Judge Spriggs had already pondered dismissing Stevenson during the first week of testimony when she was coughing incessantly. Viewers on Court TV were bothered by the coughing and had called to complain that the noise was so bad that it drowned out the answers of the witnesses. Stevenson explained that her coughing was due to her asthma and allergies caused by the courtroom's air conditioning system. Judge Spriggs noted that the coughing was causing such a disruption that if it did not cease by the end of the week, he would remove her from the panel for the peace of all. Shortly thereafter, upon taking medication prescribed by her physician, Stevenson ceased coughing.

It had appeared from the beginning that Stevenson very much wanted to be on the jury. During voir dire, she noted she had previously served on three or four juries—court rules do not allow me to ask what the decisions were in those cases. She also made it known that she was a strong believer in photo identifications. Her daughter had once identified a man involved in a crime through a photo lineup. While this gave me reason to pause, she had a good profile concerning the death penalty. That, along with her statement that she would fairly judge the evidence, and the fact that I had even more qualms about the person who would replace her, convinced me to let her remain on the jury.

While the closing arguments were underway, the district attorney's office received a call from a police officer, further reporting Stevenson's possible bias. An investigator sought to check this out, but he was unable to verify it. Another hearing was held on this matter. Once more, Judge Spriggs ruled that the evidence did not warrant dismissing Stevenson from the panel. Once more, I objected.

Only when the jury had completed its third day of deliberations did the district attorney's office claim it had finally been able to confirm Stevenson's pretrial statements that she thought King was guilty. Mr. Buckley immediately informed Judge Spriggs. He likewise called Scott at 10:00 PM on June 11, telling him the news.

The prosecution insisted that it had only been able to discover this development after the jury had begun its deliberations on account of United Airlines. It conceded that it had uncovered evidence of Stevenson's deceit on Monday while the final arguments were under way. However, United Airlines refused to allow the district attorney's investigators to question Stevenson's co-workers. Rather than immediately informing Judge Spriggs of this development and having the court issue subpoenas forcing United Airlines to have its workers talk to the court, the district attorney's office sat on its hands until Thursday evening.

In the wake of this development, Judge Spriggs ordered the jury to suspend its deliberations on Friday morning, June 12, while the court probed the matter. Deputies were sent to the airport to bring five witnesses who had knowledge of Stevenson's bias to a hearing in Judge Spriggs' chambers. Four of her co-workers reported having heard Stevenson discuss the case, noting that she had stated that she believed that King was guilty shortly after his arrest. Stevenson similarly continued to discuss the case during the jury selection process after Judge Spriggs had specifically ordered her not to discuss the case with anyone. One other witness, however, claimed that she had only heard Stevenson judge King guilty prior to the beginning of jury selection. During the hearing, it was brought out that Stevenson was not liked by her co-workers.

We reviewed the court records on Stevenson, specifically her vow on May 13 that she had an open mind, "I don't believe everything I read in the paper or see on TV. With all the things I've read and heard, I haven't heard enough to make a decision." Judge Spriggs did not think the evidence was conclusive against Stevenson. He therefore declined to remove her from the jury and replace her with an alternate.

The possibly prejudiced nature of this juror is one of the reasons there are alternates. Should anything happen to a juror during the course of a trial whereby he or she has to be dismissed from the panel, an alternate takes over. Once the jury had begun its deliberations in this case, the two alternates were sequestered separate from the rest of the jury. They were not allowed to listen in on the deliberations. Should a juror be disqualified, the jury would have to begin its deliberations all over again with the alternate.

Until 1991, the law was that the alternates would be dismissed prior to the beginning of the jury's deliberations. The law was amended to hold the alternates during the deliberations in a capital case. If the jury found the defendant guilty, the alternates were to sit again as alternates on the jury during the death penalty phase of the trial. The rules are so specific about how the jury must act as a unit during deliberations that the jurors are instructed to cease their discussions should any of their fellows need to go to the restroom or take any other break. It was unclear whether one of the alternates could take over from a dismissed juror in the middle of the deliberations.

I objected to the suspension of the jury's deliberations. All that did was raise questions in the jurors' minds that something else was going on. I did not move for a mistrial—obviously the prosecution wanted me to do so. I thought the trial had gone well for us. I did not want to try the case again. The prosecution had learned our strategy and heard our witnesses. In case of a mistrial, it would take measures in a second trial to overcome its weaknesses. I feared that if I moved for the dismissal of Stevenson and her replacement by an alternate, Judge Spriggs might declare a mistrial.

The prosecution pushed me, claiming that I was waiving my right to mistrial by failing to move for Stevenson's discharge from the jury. But I thought I had covered my client. If the jury ruled against King, I could use Stevenson's presence on the jury in a motion for a new trial. If it were rejected, I could cite my previous motion for a mistrial on Stevenson's account on appeal. Indeed, her possible prejudice was precisely the product of the massive, unending, biased media accounts of the case which I had tried to contain in my early requests for a gag order.

I was also suspicious that the prosecution did not move for a mistrial or demand that Stevenson be replaced by an alternate. It was worried. The jury had already been out for three days, an encouraging sign for the defense.

As I reflected on the matter, I thought that the prosecution had said nothing when it first learned of Stevenson's deceit on Monday in the hope that the jury would quickly find King guilty. Otherwise, why had it delayed informing the court of this matter? I concluded that it had not moved for her dismissal or a mistrial because, if a mistrial was granted at the prosecution's behest, the district attorney would be skating on the thin ice of double jeopardy.

In the wake of such a mistrial, the district attorney's office knew that I would be able to establish that the prosecution had already known and lied about Stevenson's prejudice during voir dire when I first raised the issue. Under such circumstances, it was very likely that King could not be retried. I would argue that the prosecution had acted unethically and had hidden this vital evidence from the court and defense. A jury that is discharged without the consent of the accused and for a legally insufficient reason—including deceit by the prosecution—results in a wrongly granted mistrial. Under such circumstances, any attempt to try the defendant again is equivalent to double jeopardy. The result, on account of the prosecution's actions concerning Stevenson, would be that King could not again stand trial. Meanwhile, the jury resumed its deliberations as we waited, and waited, and waited.

On Sunday, June 14, the jury sent another note to Judge Spriggs. "We feel we are at an impasse (which could be firm or a result of personalities)." Therefore, the jurors specifically wanted to know how and when the judge decided that the jury was hung. They also asked "is it possible to get a better definition of 'reasonable doubt' (i.e., for lay people?)." Judge Spriggs simply told them to reread the instructions and continue their deliberations.

I was hopeful that this was the last logjam before the jury saw that there was enough reasonable doubt about the prosecution's case to rule King not guilty. "After one or two more days, these people are going to want to get back to their own lives," I told the media. The papers reported that, for once, Mr. Buckley agreed with me.

The jury sent another note to the court on Tuesday, June 16:

> Twice one of the jurors has said she's not sure she understands the difference between proving the defendant guilty beyond a reasonable doubt and proving him innocent. She doesn't understand that the prosecution must prove he's guilty beyond a reasonable doubt and that the defense *doesn't have to prove anything*. She continually says she's confused about that.

Judge Spriggs again told the jury to read his instructions, notably numbers one and six, and continue its deliberations. He had given the jury a standard legal definition of reasonable doubt in his written instructions which he had read to it before the start of the closing arguments:

> A doubt based upon reason and common sense which arises from a fair and rational consideration of all the evidence, or the lack of evidence, in the case. It is a doubt which is not a vague, speculative, or imaginary doubt, but such a doubt as would cause reasonable people to hesitate to act in matters of importance to themselves.

"If someone is incapable of understanding these instructions, there isn't much I can do about it," he observed.

After reviewing the note, I told the press I was sure we were one vote away from an acquittal. "This is a person who said, 'I don't care what the evidence is, I think he's guilty.'" When I was asked how I knew that, I smiled and replied, "circumstantial evidence—just what this case is based on."

Finally, at 10:30 AM on Wednesday, June 17, one year and one day after the Father's Day Massacre, the jury took its final vote. It informed Judge Spriggs at 11:05 that it had reached a verdict. Waiting for the press, it took the court nearly two hours to gather everyone for the announcement of the verdict. I spent part of this time with King in his holding cell near the courtroom.

The Verdict

As I approached Courtroom 16, TV crews, cameras, family members, and spectators were everyplace. So many people were clamoring for admission to the space that Judge Spriggs issued special seating rules. Benches were reserved for both King's family and the families of the victims. Other seats were set aside for representatives of the media. The courtroom was thereupon cleared and the guards conducted a lottery to let the public in. Two of the city's network television stations were broadcasting live from the courtroom. Before asking for the verdict, Judge Spriggs sternly warned spectators that they were to sit silently while the verdict was announced. There were to be no demonstrations. "You are not in a ball park." With that, he called for another recess while the jury was assembled.

Feeling confident, but still nervous, I sat next to King as the jury walked in. I tried to read the faces of its members. They had non-committal expressions. King reported that only two jurors looked directly at him, slightly smiling, giving him a clue as to his fate. Finally, after another fateful pause that seemed to last forever, the verdict was handed to Judge Spriggs shortly before 1:00 PM.

Not guilty, he announced as to the charge of first-degree murder of Bill McCullom. I held my breath. There was always the possibility that the jury might have ruled him guilty of felony murder. After another seemingly lengthy pause, Judge Spriggs

I speak to the media upon King's acquittal.

continued, not guilty of felony murder of Bill McCullom. Not guilty of first-degree murder of Phillip Mankoff. Not guilty of felony murder of Phillip Mankoff. Not guilty, not guilty, not guilty, not guilty, he repeated to each of the counts of first-degree and felony murder.

I was still nervous as the verdict was read. Only after Judge Spriggs had announced not guilty to the charge of aggravated robbery was I able to sigh with relief. Jim tried to remain stoic during the announcement, but it was obvious that he was holding back his tears. I was holding back mine. Finally, my client politely nodded to the jury, telling them "thank you!"

The jury had spent 53 hours over the course of nine days discussing the case in the longest deliberation ever by a Denver jury. Before dismissing the jury and allowing the celebrations to begin, Judge Spriggs had one last instruction to the jury: its members had the right to talk to the media if they wished or avoid them altogether. It was to caucus on this issue in the jury room. Those who wanted anonymity were to be escorted from the courthouse back to the hotel where they were to have their final lunch together. Others were to go to the city council chambers which had been set up for interviews with those involved in the case. It took the jury quite sometime to decide this question.

By then Myra King Church was openly in tears. A sobbing Carol King embraced her sons in court. "Now the whole world knows what I know," she told one and all. It took the authorities about two hours to process King's release. I had asked Judge Spriggs that he be immediately freed. He refused my request whereby King had to make one more trip to jail before finally gaining his freedom.

"I knew I was innocent," King told the press. "But until today, I wasn't sure the system worked. Now, I know one part of it works because the jury found me innocent."

Discussing his feelings, King continued, "I feel good, at least as good as you can feel when you've been abused by the system. I'd have felt a lot better today if they'd gotten the right man in the first place."

After Jim had spent some time privately with Carol, he joined me at my office where we celebrated his acquittal. I gave him a Denver Chess Club T-shirt, wearing a comparable T-shirt to note his vindication. The media quoted me as hailing the jury for its integrity in finding King not guilty. Friends noted that I had grown gray during the case.

King headed home with Carol in the back seat of a beat-up station wagon, driven by Carol's cousin. She reported that Jim and Carol made out like teenagers along the way. Neighbors hung out a "Welcome Home" banner on a hedge in the Kings' front yard as Jim triumphantly returned from court. To mark his homecoming, he and Carol ordered a pizza.

15

Aftermath

Most of the jurors requested anonymity after the verdict. A few spoke out, giving us an idea of what happened during their deliberations. They agreed that the prosecution's case was weak. Time and again, rather than forthrightly identifying King, the eyewitnesses had hedged their bets and had failed to make the initial identification of King. The jurors also thought that vault manager David Barranco was unbelievable when he suddenly declared he knew that King was the robber all along when he could not cite any previous statements to support his testimony.

Shortly after the jury had begun its deliberations it had divided eight to two for an acquittal. Two jurors were undecided. They had problems with King's explanation of how and why he had disposed of his service revolver. Realizing that there was an abundance of reasonable doubt about his guilt, after three days they joined the majority in voting to find King not guilty.

From the beginning of the deliberations, the majority agreed that the prosecution had failed to present convincing evidence that King was guilty beyond a reasonable doubt. One juror—the unemployed actor who was the baseball buff—though, was insistent that King was guilty. The other, Stevenson, pointed out that we had failed to prove King innocent. This division lasted for days. Only on June 17 did Stevenson capitulate, agreeing that the prosecution had failed to prove King guilty beyond a reasonable doubt. About this

Jim and Carol King hug in my office shortly after he was found not guilty of all counts.

time, the baseball buff also changed his mind, leading to King's acquittal.

All the jurors admitted that the deliberations had been a grueling experience; it was the hardest thing they had ever done. In the process of listening to the evidence and reaching their verdict, the jurors further observed that their experiences convinced them there was a lot to the coincidence factor. While jurors are repeatedly instructed during a trial that they are not to discuss the case with anyone else, including their fellow jurors, this does not keep the jurors from becoming acquainted. One down side of jury duty is that jurors are often told to sit and wait while the court turns its attention to motions and hearings requested by the lawyers. During this time, jurors frequently talk about themselves and their families. The jurors found they had a lot in common.

One was their employment. Four had some link with the city's airport. Two jurors, who were from the Midwest, discovered that they had grown up ten miles apart from one another. Members of the jury also learned that they had mutual friends and acquaintances. This was a positive and rewarding illustration of the coincidence factor.

There were a lot of tensions during the deliberations. The panel, however, was able to lighten things up with occasional bursts of laughter. Judge Spriggs' emphasis on having them read and reread his instruction on reasonable doubt, one of the jurors explained, finally helped break the logjam at the end.

The verdict, however, had little impact on the massive prejudicial publicity against King. Reporters subjected jurors to insulting questions about whether they were sure that King was innocent. The implication was that despite the not guilty verdict, King might have done it anyway—there was just too much reasonable doubt for a guilty verdict.

One person who would not go along with this effort to second-guess the meaning of the verdict was Mr. Buckley. The media also pressed him, attempting to get him to express the opinion that not guilty did not mean innocent. To his credit, he refused to agree with such a shallow insinuation. At the most, he lamented that sometimes jurors expressed the sentiment that, deep down, they believed that the defendant was guilty, but had too much reasonable doubt to vote for that verdict. If, in their hearts, Mr. Buckley explained, jurors thought the defendant was guilty, there was no reasonable doubt and they should find the defendant guilty.

Some police officers were quite bitter about the verdict. They were sure that King had gotten away with murder. The victim advocates similarly howled that the victims had been cheated by the verdict. In the process, rather than assisting the families of the victims and helping them understand that a defendant is innocent until proven guilty, these fronts for the prosecution only filled the victims with bitterness against the jury and hatred of due process. By doing so, they only made the families of the dead guards suffer more. The further implication was that the entire presumption of innocence should be junked, avenging the victims through the conviction of innocent defendants.

Nor was the prosecution ready to quit. District Attorney Norm Early publicly proclaimed that "King is guilty as sin in my book." Bluster filled the air about charging King with federal bank robbery or even accusing him of depriving the murdered guards of their civil rights. Fortunately, nothing came of this. In the wake of the acquittal, the authorities announced that the case was on hold and that they had no other suspects.

Photo by Phil Goodstein

The plaque commemorating the
slain guards at the United Bank.

For quite a while after the verdict, King felt that someone was spying on him and intercepting his mail. Nor would the prosecution release King's property, including his computer, a gun cleaning kit, tax records, and his retired police identification card, which the police had seized during the searches of his house and safe-deposit box. The United States Attorney's office demanded the right to inspect them. But it did not do anything with them. I had to file for a court order on December 9, ordering the return of his property. The prosecution made no objection to it and it was granted on December 14.

Not long after the trial, Mr. Buckley left the district attorney's office. In partnership with another former deputy district attorney, Leonard M. Chesler, he has emerged as a defense attorney. Ironically, for someone who was in the lead of prosecuting Jim King, in his new incarnation Mr. Buckley has sometimes defended police officers accused of committing crimes. On occasion, I have referred clients to him through Mr. Chesler.

Scott Robinson left my law office four years after the trial. He has emerged as a prominent media lawyer. Scott frequently appears on camera, commenting about high-profile cases.

A few days after King's acquittal, vault manager David Barranco was picked up for shoplifting. By the time of the trial, he had substance abuse problems and had taken a leave of absence from the bank to enter a treatment program. It had failed and, shortly after the trial, suffering from the post-traumatic stress syndrome, he was arrested as part of a ring of shoplifters which was hitting a suburban department store with the assistance of one of the shop's cashiers.

About four months after the verdict, in late October 1992, Paul Yocum died at age 52 from a massive heart attack. Acquaintances noted that he had been extremely bitter since his arrest for the automated teller theft and had never been the same since his acquittal. Many were sure that there was a close link between the theft from the automated teller and the Father's Day Massacre. If the authorities had not been so insistent to blame Yocum for the former job, they might have solved it. In the process, the latter crime would never have occurred.

With Yocum's death, one more clue to the bank heist disappeared. The Father's Day Massacre is still unsolved. Rumors float that more like $2 million rather than $200,000 was actually taken in the robbery. Since the authorities spent virtually all their efforts in trying unjustly to convict Jim King of it, they let other leads slip whereby it is questionable that the culprits will ever face trial.

The families of the slain guards successfully sued Norwest Banks for its negligent and poor security procedures. (The United Bank was dismissed from the suit when the court ruled it was exempt from liability based on worker compensation laws.) Meanwhile, Jim King regularly plays at the Denver Chess Club, though he otherwise remains reclusive. Illness has disabled Carol. Jim cares for her while he lives with her and two of his sons. There is nothing to compensate him for the year he lost in jail while the media unfairly tainted him as Denver's nefarious Father's Day murderer.

かかか

Arthur Conan Doyle, the creator of Sherlock Holmes, observed: "There is not the mystery in ten murders that there is in one game of chess." As a chess player, I agree with Doyle, but the Jim King case combined the intrigue of a chess game and a murder. Now, a Holmes is needed to find the true perpetrator of the Father's Day Massacre, a crime that can still be solved.

Acknowledgments

I had just completed conducting a walking tour when a participant came up and asked me if I knew anything about the Curry-Chucovich House. A Denver landmark and the only surviving 19th-century single-family house in the central business district, it is the law office of Walter Gerash. Coincidentally, I happened to have a tour planned by it in a couple of weeks. After I shared my knowledge about the structure, my questioner asked me if I would like to know more about the house and see the interior. That was when I met Douglass Gerash, the older son of Walter Gerash.

I was well aware of Walter Gerash as a colorful trial attorney whose cases frequently received media attention. I discovered that he had long thought about writing his memoirs. His goal was to show how his court battles have reflected the social, political, and economic struggles of the Rocky Mountain West.

After two years of vigorous research into Mr. Gerash's career during which I went through approximately 1,000 boxes of his records, we decided to focus on one case to exemplify how he defends his clients. The Father's Day Massacre was selected since it illustrates the dynamics of a heavily publicized trial. Through looking at this case, we wanted to show the problems media sensationalism poses in getting an unbiased jury. It also illustrates Mr. Gerash's views on gag orders, the need to challenge the prosecution at all stages of the case, the use of the preliminary hearing, why and how the jury serves as the conscience of the community, the nature and technique of voir dire, the importance of opening statements, and much more.

I wrote a draft of this volume by intently going through Mr. Gerash's file of the King case. I then watched the videotapes of the trial as they were broadcast on Court TV. I followed this by reading all the newspaper reports I could uncover in addition to watching tapes of news broadcasts about the trial. In the process of my research, I talked to people knowledgeable about the case. Mr. Gerash reviewed drafts of the text. In the process, I owe thanks to many individuals.

325

From the beginning of this project, Mr. Gerash's former partner, Scott Robinson, was always helpful. He shared his memories of the trial and other cases in which he assisted Mr. Gerash. Scott's secretary, Mary Lou Grayvell, was forever ready with a joke and information.

The people around Mr. Gerash's office kindly tolerated me. His former secretaries, Mary Nation, Annette Calvert, and Lenia J. Alston assisted in whatever ways they could. So did his current secretary, Melia Danielson. Madaly Finstad oversaw the office during the beginning of the project. She arranged for me to get the needed archival materials. Susan Decker recalled her role in serving subpoenas in the case and visiting King in jail. Angie Genella, Liz DiazSantiago, Patsy Laflin, and Oscar Lee likewise made me feel welcome at the office.

Mr. Gerash's younger son, Daniel, and his brother-in-law, Wally Prugh—both attorneys who work with him in his law firm of Gerash, Miranda, and Gerash—shared their knowledge of the case and Walter Gerash's career. Douglass Gerash pushed his father to complete this project, read drafts of the text, and wrote a draft of the prologue. Douglass's wife, Kathy, assisted him. Mr. Gerash's lifelong friend, Jack Rabinowitz, suggested the title of the book.

Judges Larry Bohning and Brian Campbell discussed their involvements in the case, presiding, respectively, at the advisement of King and the preliminary hearing. Judge Bohning also talked about the gag order. While Judge Richard Spriggs refused to talk about the case, noting that there still is a potential federal jeopardy against King for felony murder on the bank robbery charges, he made available copies of the tapes of the Court TV broadcast of the trial. The judge also reflected on his many encounters with Mr. Gerash during the days when he was a deputy district attorney.

In view of the possible federal jeopardy, Mr. Gerash did not believe it wise for me to meet directly with Jim King. Rather, Mr. Gerash served as an intermediary. King read a draft of the book and made valuable comments on it.

Lamar Sims refused to talk about the trial. Bill Buckley reflected a little about himself, his views of Mr. Gerash, and his memories of the case. Citing the possible federal jeopardy, he declined to discuss specifics of the Father's Day Massacre. Sergeant Detective Jon Priest did not reply to a letter asking for his comments about the case.

Allen L. Jones recalled his days on the Denver Police Department, serving in the police detail at Stapleton Airport, and the nature of police weaponry. City Councilman Ed Thomas, a former police detective, likewise shared his knowledge of the department. Art Winstanley reflected on the police burglary scandal and the police culture of the early

1960s. Captain Miriam Reed discussed speed loaders and why many police officers believed King to be guilty. Chief Dave Michaud also talked about the department and its views on the case. Sergeant Mike E. Mueller briefly shared his attitudes about King and Walter Gerash.

As always, Jan McConnell did her excellent job of designing the cover. She also helped draw into presentable art some of the fuzzy images from the court file. John Schoenwalter advised about photographs and took my picture for the back cover. Lucas Boyd assisted in helping digitize images, making photos from videotapes, and other artwork. All graphics which are not specifically acknowledged in the text have been taken from police files or Walter Gerash's file of the case. Some of the latter include pictures provided to Mr. Gerash by members of the photo pool who covered the trial.

Walt Young remembered cutting Paul Yocum's hair and the character of the alternate suspect. He and his partner, Angel Garcia, also answered my questions on barbering as it related to the trial. Tony DiVirgilio reflected on his work as an investigator in the case. Mary Dell Simmons talked about the David Twist family. Bob Heiserman shared his knowledge about Walter Gerash's central role in the modern Denver bar. Bob Oblock talked about handguns, speed loaders, and how private investigators view Walter Gerash.

Barbara Eastin provided firm moral support, helping proofread the text. So did Dinah Land and Gayle Novak. Marilyn Megenity of the Mercury Cafe inspired me in this effort. Valarie Abney, Joan Gould, and the staff at Capitol Hill Books likewise offered encouragement. Maxine Lankford assisted in countless ways. Clark Secrest and the people around the publications division of the Colorado Historical Society also reviewed parts of the manuscript. John Ensslin looked at a draft as did Arnold Drake. Dr. George Archuleta critically evaluated the text, commenting on its structure and problems, while noting Mr. Gerash's important role as an attorney in the movement for Chicano liberation. Many others who have had come into contact with Walter Gerash talked about him and encouraged me in this effort.

Phil Goodstein
December 1997

Index